CHAPTER 1: INTRODUCTION TO CLOJURESCRIPT

ClojureScript emerges as a notable language in the landscape of modern web development, built upon the robust foundation of its parent language, Clojure. At its core, ClojureScript maintains the essential principles of functional programming, which are vital in crafting applications that are not only robust but also adaptable and maintainable. This discussion aims to delve into the essence of ClojureScript, examining its philosophical underpinnings, practical applications, and the ways in which it integrates with existing web technologies.

To fully appreciate the value of ClojureScript, one must first understand its lineage. Clojure, the language from which ClojureScript is derived, is a dialect of Lisp that emphasizes immutability and functional programming. These principles are not merely academic concepts but practical tools that influence how developers approach problem-solving in software design. Immutability, for instance, implies that once a data structure is created, it cannot be modified. Instead, any changes result in the creation of a new data structure. This approach eliminates issues related to mutable state and concurrent modifications, which are prevalent in many other programming paradigms.

In translating these principles to the realm of

JavaScript, ClojureScript leverages its functional programming capabilities to offer a more predictable and concise means of developing web applications. JavaScript, being the dominant language of the web, brings with it a set of challenges, including mutable state and diverse coding styles. ClojureScript, however, introduces a functional paradigm that helps mitigate these issues, fostering a development environment that is both powerful and expressive.

A critical aspect of ClojureScript is its interaction with JavaScript through a process known as "transpiling." The ClojureScript compiler translates ClojureScript code into JavaScript, which then runs in the browser or on Node.js. This process is seamless, allowing developers to write in ClojureScript while still deploying code that integrates with the vast ecosystem of JavaScript libraries and frameworks. This interoperability is a key advantage, as it combines the strengths of ClojureScript's functional programming model with the extensive resources available in the JavaScript world.

To illustrate the practical applications of ClojureScript, consider its use in managing state within a web application. Traditional JavaScript applications often handle state management through various means, such as mutable variables or external libraries. In contrast, ClojureScript promotes a functional approach where state is managed immutably. By using immutable data structures, developers can avoid common pitfalls associated with state management, such as unintended side effects and concurrency issues. This immutable approach aligns with the functional programming ethos, where functions operate on immutable data, producing predictable outcomes.

Moreover, ClojureScript's approach to concurrency is particularly noteworthy. In traditional JavaScript, managing concurrent operations can be complex and error-prone, especially with asynchronous code. ClojureScript simplifies this by offering constructs like core.async, which provides a framework for asynchronous programming that is both powerful and easy to use. Core.async facilitates the creation of channels and the coordination of asynchronous tasks, allowing developers to write more manageable and maintainable concurrent code.

Another significant advantage of ClojureScript is its emphasis on code clarity and succinctness. The language's syntax, derived from Lisp, supports a minimalistic and expressive coding style. ClojureScript encourages the use of higher-order functions and immutable data structures, leading to code that is often more concise and easier to reason about compared to its JavaScript counterparts. This syntactical simplicity, combined with its powerful functional capabilities, makes ClojureScript an attractive option for developers seeking to produce high-quality code in a manageable manner.

Additionally, ClojureScript fosters a strong focus on testing and quality assurance. The language's immutable nature simplifies the testing process, as functions operate on consistent data without side effects. This consistency facilitates writing reliable unit tests and ensures that functions behave predictably under various conditions. The emphasis on functional programming principles also supports test-driven development practices, as the clarity and predictability of functions align well with testable code structures.

In exploring the role of ClojureScript within the broader web technologies ecosystem, one must recognize its position as a tool that enhances the capabilities of JavaScript rather than replacing it. ClojureScript's integration with JavaScript libraries and frameworks means that developers can harness the full power of the JavaScript ecosystem while benefiting from ClojureScript's functional programming advantages. This duality allows for the creation of scalable and maintainable web applications that leverage the strengths of both languages.

As we proceed further, it is essential to examine how ClojureScript interacts with other technologies and practices in web development. This exploration will include a closer look at ClojureScript's ecosystem, including libraries, tools, and frameworks that complement its functional programming model. Understanding these interactions will provide a more comprehensive view of how ClojureScript can be effectively utilized in various web development scenarios.

In summary, ClojureScript stands out as a compelling choice for modern web development due to its functional programming roots, emphasis on immutability, and seamless integration with JavaScript. By leveraging these attributes, developers can build web applications that are both scalable and maintainable, benefiting from a development model that prioritizes clarity and predictability. The subsequent discussions will delve deeper into specific aspects of ClojureScript, including its ecosystem, practical applications, and advanced features that further enhance its utility in the web development landscape.

The advantages of ClojureScript extend beyond its functional programming principles and its compatibility with JavaScript. One key aspect that enhances its appeal in modern web development is its approach to code modularity and reusability. The language's design encourages developers to write small, composable functions that can be easily combined to build complex systems. This compositionality is supported by ClojureScript's robust macro system, which allows developers to create new syntactic constructs and domain-specific languages tailored to their specific needs. Macros provide a way to extend the language's syntax and functionality, enabling developers to write more expressive and reusable code. This ability to define custom macros aligns with the functional programming ethos of abstraction and code reuse, facilitating the development of sophisticated web applications with minimal boilerplate.

Another critical feature of ClojureScript is its emphasis on immutability in state management, which plays a crucial role in building reliable and predictable web applications. In ClojureScript, data structures are immutable by default, meaning that once a data structure is created, it cannot be altered. Instead of modifying existing data structures, developers create new ones, reflecting changes in a way that preserves the original state. This approach eliminates issues related to mutable state, such as unintended side effects and race conditions, which are common in traditional imperative programming. By adhering to immutability, ClojureScript helps developers write code that is easier to reason about and less prone to bugs, particularly in concurrent and asynchronous scenarios.

Furthermore, ClojureScript's use of persistent data structures enhances performance and efficiency. Persistent data structures are immutable and designed to efficiently handle modifications, ensuring that changes do not involve copying the entire structure. This efficient handling of data structures allows for optimal performance in applications that require frequent updates or modifications. For instance, persistent lists, maps, and sets in ClojureScript offer performance characteristics that are well-suited for applications with high data manipulation needs. The language's approach to data structure persistence supports the development of scalable and responsive web applications, where performance considerations are critical.

The integration of ClojureScript with existing JavaScript ecosystems further amplifies its practicality in web development. The language's interoperability with JavaScript libraries and frameworks is facilitated through a process known as "interop." ClojureScript's interop capabilities enable developers to call JavaScript functions and access JavaScript objects from within ClojureScript code. This seamless integration allows developers to leverage the extensive libraries and tools available in the JavaScript ecosystem while benefiting from ClojureScript's functional programming features. For example, ClojureScript can be used alongside popular JavaScript libraries such as React or D3.js, enabling developers to incorporate advanced UI components or data visualizations into their applications while maintaining the advantages of ClojureScript's functional approach.

In addition to interop, ClojureScript's development environment is designed to support an efficient and productive workflow. The language benefits from a rich set of tools and libraries that streamline the development process. Tools like Leiningen, a build automation tool for Clojure and ClojureScript, provide a comprehensive solution for managing project dependencies, building artifacts, and running tests. Leiningen's integration with ClojureScript simplifies the setup and configuration of projects, allowing developers to focus on writing code rather than managing build processes. Furthermore, ClojureScript's REPL (Read-Eval-Print Loop) provides an interactive environment for experimenting with code and testing ideas in real-time. The REPL facilitates a rapid development cycle, enabling developers to iterate on their code quickly and gain immediate feedback.

Another noteworthy aspect of ClojureScript is its support for advanced functional programming techniques. The language encourages the use of higher-order functions, which are functions that take other functions as arguments or return functions as results. Higher-order functions enable developers to abstract common patterns and create more reusable and modular code. ClojureScript's support for function composition, currying, and partial application further enhances its capability to handle complex programming tasks with elegance and efficiency. These advanced functional techniques align with the language's philosophy of writing concise and expressive code that can be easily understood and maintained.

As ClojureScript continues to evolve, its community and ecosystem play a significant role in shaping its development and adoption. The ClojureScript community is known for its collaborative and supportive nature, contributing to a vibrant ecosystem of libraries, tools, and resources. Community-driven projects and open-source contributions provide valuable extensions and enhancements to the language, ensuring that ClojureScript remains relevant and up-to-date with emerging trends in web development. Engaging with the community and leveraging community resources can provide developers with additional insights and best practices for using ClojureScript effectively.

In conclusion, ClojureScript offers a compelling choice for modern web development by combining the principles of functional programming with the flexibility and power of JavaScript. Its focus on immutability, efficient state management, and seamless integration with JavaScript ecosystems makes it a valuable tool for building scalable and maintainable web applications. The language's support for advanced functional techniques and its rich development environment further contribute to its effectiveness as a development tool. As we delve deeper into ClojureScript, exploring its ecosystem, libraries, and practical applications, we will uncover additional insights into how this language can be harnessed to create sophisticated and high-quality web solutions.

Exploring the practical aspects of ClojureScript further reveals how its design choices translate into real-world benefits for web development. The language's inherent characteristics facilitate the development of applications that are not only scalable but also resilient and maintainable. To fully grasp these advantages, it is crucial to examine specific features and practices within the ClojureScript ecosystem that enhance its utility in modern web development.

One of the standout features of ClojureScript is its emphasis on immutability, which significantly impacts how data is handled and manipulated. In traditional JavaScript development, mutable data structures often lead to complex and error-prone code, especially when dealing with concurrent operations or large-scale applications. ClojureScript's immutable data structures, such as vectors, maps, and sets, offer a way to avoid these issues by ensuring that data cannot be modified once created. This immutability not only simplifies reasoning about the code but also enhances performance by enabling structural sharing, which allows new versions of data structures to reuse existing memory efficiently. This approach is particularly beneficial in scenarios involving frequent state changes or complex data transformations, as it reduces the likelihood of bugs and performance bottlenecks.

The concept of functional programming in ClojureScript further complements its immutable data structures. Functions in ClojureScript are first-class citizens, meaning they can be passed as arguments, returned from other functions, and assigned to variables. This functional approach promotes a declarative style of programming, where developers describe what the program should do rather than how to do it. Higher-order functions, such as `map`, `filter`, and `reduce`, are commonly used to operate on collections in a concise and expressive manner. These functions facilitate operations like data transformation and aggregation in a way that is both readable and maintainable.

Another critical aspect of ClojureScript is its support for persistent data structures. These data structures are designed to handle modifications efficiently by sharing structure between versions, rather than copying entire data structures. This characteristic is particularly advantageous in functional programming, where data immutability is a core principle. Persistent data structures allow developers to perform updates and transformations without incurring the overhead typically associated with copying large data structures. For instance, when using a persistent map to add or remove key-value pairs, the operation creates a new map while reusing the existing structure as much as possible. This efficient approach to data manipulation contributes to the overall performance and scalability of applications built with ClojureScript.

ClojureScript's seamless integration with JavaScript is another pivotal feature that enhances its practicality. By transpiling ClojureScript code to JavaScript, developers can leverage the extensive ecosystem of JavaScript libraries and frameworks. This interoperation is facilitated through the use of JavaScript interop capabilities, which allow ClojureScript code to call JavaScript functions, access JavaScript objects, and interact with JavaScript libraries. This ability to integrate with existing JavaScript tools and libraries enables developers to build upon a foundation of established technologies while incorporating ClojureScript's functional programming advantages.

A particularly useful tool within the ClojureScript ecosystem is the ClojureScript REPL (Read-Eval-Print Loop). The REPL provides an interactive environment where developers can experiment with code, test functions, and evaluate expressions in real-time. This immediate feedback loop is invaluable for rapid prototyping and debugging, as it allows developers to iteratively refine their code and explore different approaches without the need for lengthy compile and run cycles. The REPL enhances the development experience by facilitating exploratory programming and providing a dynamic way to interact with code.

Moreover, the use of ClojureScript in conjunction with various frameworks and libraries further demonstrates its versatility. For instance, ClojureScript's integration with React through libraries like Reagent allows developers to build user interfaces using a functional approach. Reagent provides a set of abstractions for creating React components and managing state, while adhering to ClojureScript's functional programming principles. This combination enables developers to construct complex and interactive UIs while maintaining a consistent and predictable codebase.

Similarly, the use of ClojureScript with libraries like D3.js for data visualization showcases its ability to handle advanced tasks with ease. D3.js, a popular JavaScript library for creating dynamic and interactive data visualizations, can be effectively utilized within a ClojureScript application. By leveraging ClojureScript's functional programming capabilities, developers can create complex visualizations and data-driven interfaces in a manner that is both elegant and efficient.

In conclusion, ClojureScript's design and features make it a compelling choice for modern web development. Its emphasis on immutability, functional programming, and efficient state management contributes to the development of scalable and maintainable applications. The language's seamless integration with JavaScript ecosystems, along with its support for advanced functional programming techniques, enhances its versatility and effectiveness in various web development scenarios. By leveraging these strengths, developers can harness the full potential of ClojureScript to build sophisticated and high-quality web applications that stand the test of time.

CHAPTER 2: SETTING UP THE DEVELOPMENT ENVIRONMENT

Setting up an efficient development environment is fundamental for working with ClojureScript, as it ensures that you can effectively write, test, and manage your code. To establish a robust environment, several key components need to be configured, including essential tools, project structures, and development environments.

The first step in setting up your ClojureScript development environment involves choosing and installing a build automation tool. Two popular choices are Leiningen and Boot, each offering distinct features that cater to different development needs. Leiningen is the more traditional choice, widely used within the Clojure community for managing dependencies, building projects, and running tests. It utilizes a `project.clj` file where you specify project dependencies, build configurations, and other settings. Leiningen provides a straightforward and well-documented approach to project management, making it an ideal choice for beginners and those seeking stability.

On the other hand, Boot offers a more flexible and composable approach to build automation. It uses a `build.boot` file, which allows for a more modular configuration of build tasks. Boot's pipeline-based approach lets you compose build tasks in a way that can be more powerful and customizable, albeit with a steeper learning curve. The choice between Leiningen and Boot often depends on personal preference and specific project requirements. Both tools are effective, and you can select the one that best fits your workflow.

Once you have chosen a build tool, the next step is to install it and set up your project. For Leiningen, the installation process is straightforward. You can download and install Leiningen from its official website or use package managers like Homebrew for macOS. After installation, you can create a new ClojureScript project using the `lein new` command, which sets up a basic project structure with necessary configuration files.

For Boot, the installation involves downloading the Boot executable and setting it up in your system's PATH. Boot projects are initialized using the `boot new` command, which generates a project structure and configuration file for you. Regardless of the tool you choose, the result is a well-organized project directory that contains source code, build configurations, and other essential files.

With the build tool installed and the project initialized, configuring ClojureScript within your project is the next crucial step. This involves setting up the ClojureScript compiler and integrating it with your chosen build tool. In Leiningen, you need to add the ClojureScript plugin to your `project.clj` file under the `:plugins` section. You will also need to configure the ClojureScript compiler options, such as specifying the source path and output directory for compiled JavaScript code. The `:cljsbuild` section in `project.clj` allows you to define different build configurations, such as development and production builds.

In Boot, configuring ClojureScript involves setting up tasks in your `build.boot` file. You will use the `cljs.build.api` namespace to configure compiler options and build tasks. Boot's modular approach allows you to compose build tasks in a flexible manner, defining how ClojureScript code is compiled and where the output is directed.

An integrated development environment (IDE) with the right plugins can significantly enhance your productivity when working with ClojureScript. Popular IDEs for ClojureScript development include IntelliJ IDEA with the Cursive plugin, Emacs with CIDER, and Visual Studio Code with the Calva extension. Each IDE offers unique features and support for ClojureScript development.

IntelliJ IDEA, when paired with the Cursive plugin, provides a comprehensive development environment with features such as syntax highlighting, code completion, and integrated REPL support. Cursive enhances IntelliJ IDEA's capabilities, offering robust tools for navigating and managing ClojureScript code.

Emacs, with CIDER (Clojure Interactive Development Environment Repl), offers a powerful and customizable environment for ClojureScript development. CIDER provides features like interactive evaluation, debugging, and REPL integration, making it a preferred choice for many Clojure developers.

Visual Studio Code, with the Calva extension, brings a modern and lightweight approach to ClojureScript development. Calva offers features such as live coding, inline evaluation, and integrated REPL support, catering to developers who prefer a more streamlined and efficient development experience.

After setting up your IDE, it's important to configure it to work seamlessly with your ClojureScript project. This involves ensuring that the IDE recognizes the project's structure, dependencies, and build configurations. For example, configuring the REPL within your IDE allows you to interactively test and debug your ClojureScript code, which is invaluable for rapid development and troubleshooting.

With your development tools and IDE configured, you are now ready to create your first ClojureScript project. This initial project will serve as a foundation for exploring ClojureScript's features and capabilities. Start by defining a simple ClojureScript file, such as `core.cljs`, and include basic code to test the setup. This code might include simple functions, data structures, or interactions with the browser's JavaScript environment. Running and testing this initial code will help verify that your environment is correctly set up and that you can compile and execute ClojureScript code successfully.

In conclusion, setting up a ClojureScript development environment involves selecting and installing a build automation tool, configuring the ClojureScript compiler, and integrating an IDE with appropriate plugins. By following these steps, you establish a solid foundation for developing ClojureScript applications, enabling you to effectively manage your code, run tests, and build projects. With a well-configured environment in place, you are well-equipped to delve into more advanced aspects of ClojureScript development and leverage its full potential.

Configuring a development environment for ClojureScript involves more than just installing tools and setting up files; it also encompasses understanding how to leverage these tools to streamline the development process. After initializing your project with Leiningen or Boot, the next step is to delve into the specifics of setting up the development environment to optimize productivity and facilitate effective coding practices.

One of the crucial aspects to address is the integration of build and dependency management systems. For instance, with Leiningen, managing dependencies involves editing the `project.clj` file. This file not only specifies project metadata but also lists all required libraries and their versions. Dependencies are essential for extending the functionality of your project, whether incorporating external libraries or leveraging ClojureScript-specific tools. The `:dependencies` section in `project.clj` should include entries for both ClojureScript itself and any additional libraries you plan to use, such as those for UI components, data manipulation, or integration with JavaScript libraries. Each dependency is specified with a vector containing the library name and version, ensuring that the correct versions are fetched and used during the build process.

Similarly, when using Boot, dependency management is handled through the `build.boot` file. In this configuration file, dependencies are specified using a different syntax but with the same fundamental purpose. By defining dependencies within `build.boot`, you ensure that all required libraries are included in the build process and available for your project. Boot's flexible task management system allows for granular control over the build pipeline, making it possible to customize how dependencies are resolved and managed.

Once dependencies are set up, configuring the ClojureScript compiler is the next essential step. The ClojureScript compiler is responsible for translating ClojureScript code into JavaScript, which can be executed in the browser or on the server. In a Leiningen-based project, this configuration is specified in the `:cljsbuild` section of `project.clj`. Here, you can define various build targets, such as development or production, each with its own set of compiler options. For instance, in a development build, you might enable source maps and watch mode to facilitate easier debugging and hot reloading. In contrast, for a production build, you might configure advanced optimizations to minimize the output size and enhance performance.

Boot, on the other hand, uses a more modular approach for configuring the compiler. The `cljs.build.api` namespace provides functions for setting compiler options, defining build configurations, and managing build tasks. With Boot, you can compose various build tasks into a pipeline, allowing you to fine-tune how your code is compiled and processed. This flexibility is advantageous for complex projects that require custom build processes or integration with other tools.

Another key component in setting up the development environment is integrating with version control systems, such as Git. Version control is crucial for managing changes to your codebase, collaborating with other developers, and maintaining a history of modifications. Setting up a `.gitignore` file specific to your ClojureScript project helps ensure that generated files, such as compiled JavaScript or build artifacts, are not included in version control. This practice keeps the repository clean and focused on source code and configuration files.

Configuring your development environment also involves setting up continuous integration (CI) and continuous deployment (CD) pipelines, if applicable. CI/CD pipelines automate the process of building, testing, and deploying code, which enhances development efficiency and ensures code quality. Tools like Travis CI, CircleCI, or GitHub Actions can be integrated with your ClojureScript project to automate these processes. The configuration typically involves specifying build commands, testing procedures, and deployment scripts, all of which are tailored to the specifics of your project and its dependencies.

Additionally, debugging and testing tools play a vital role in a well-configured development environment. ClojureScript projects benefit from various testing frameworks, such as `cljs.test` for unit testing and libraries like `doo` for running tests in different environments. Configuring these tools to work with your build system ensures that tests are run automatically during development and build processes. Integration with debugging tools and browser developer tools is also essential for identifying and resolving issues efficiently. Leveraging features such as source maps allows you to trace errors and debug your ClojureScript code as if you were working directly with JavaScript.

As you move forward with your project, it is also beneficial to familiarize yourself with best practices for project organization and code management. Structuring your project files logically, adhering to naming conventions, and documenting your code are practices that contribute to maintainable and scalable development. For instance, organizing source files into directories based on functionality or module boundaries helps keep the project manageable and facilitates easier navigation.

In conclusion, setting up a ClojureScript development environment requires more than just installing tools. It involves configuring build and dependency management systems, integrating version control, setting up CI/CD pipelines, and utilizing debugging and testing tools. By carefully addressing these aspects, you ensure a well-structured and efficient environment that supports productive development practices and enhances the overall quality of your ClojureScript projects.

Having established a robust foundation with the initial setup and configuration of your development environment, it is now crucial to focus on the finer aspects of managing and optimizing your ClojureScript project. This phase involves enhancing the development workflow, integrating with various tools and services, and ensuring that your environment is conducive to both productivity and scalability.

A key aspect of optimizing your development environment is integrating build automation tools effectively. Beyond the basic configurations, it is important to leverage advanced features offered by Leiningen and Boot to streamline and enhance the build process. For Leiningen users, utilizing the `lein figwheel` plugin is instrumental in setting up a development environment that supports live reloading. This plugin enables you to make changes to your ClojureScript code and see the results in real time without needing to refresh the browser manually. Configuring Figwheel involves specifying its settings in the `project.clj` file under the `:figwheel` key, where you can define options such as auto-compilation and watch directories.

For those employing Boot, the `boot-reload` task serves a similar purpose, allowing for live reloading during development. The `boot-reload` task can be configured to monitor changes in specified directories and automatically rebuild the project when changes are detected. Integrating this task into your Boot build pipeline can significantly improve development efficiency by reducing the time spent on manual build and reload processes.

In addition to build automation, integrating a comprehensive testing strategy is essential. Effective testing not only ensures the correctness of your code but also aids in maintaining code quality as the project evolves. For ClojureScript projects, testing can be approached using various frameworks and libraries. The `cljs.test` library provides a straightforward approach for unit testing, allowing you to write and execute tests directly within the ClojureScript environment. Configuring `cljs.test` involves setting up test namespaces and ensuring that your test files are correctly included in the build process.

Furthermore, integrating with tools like `doo` facilitates

running tests in different environments, such as browsers or Node.js. `doo` allows for running ClojureScript tests in a headless browser environment, which is particularly useful for projects that require end-to-end testing or have browser-specific dependencies. Setting up `doo` involves configuring it within your build tool, either Leiningen or Boot, and specifying the test runner and test environments.

Version control and code management are also critical aspects to address as your project progresses. Utilizing Git effectively involves more than just committing code; it encompasses managing branches, handling merge conflicts, and maintaining a clean commit history. Establishing a branching strategy, such as Git Flow, helps in organizing the development process and managing features, releases, and hotfixes systematically. Configuring hooks and continuous integration (CI) pipelines to automate tests and code quality checks ensures that code changes are validated before merging them into the main branch.

Continuous integration and deployment (CI/CD) are vital for automating the build, test, and deployment processes. Setting up CI/CD pipelines involves configuring tools like Jenkins, GitHub Actions, or GitLab CI to automate various stages of the development lifecycle. This includes defining build steps, running tests, and deploying code to staging or production environments. Properly configuring these pipelines ensures that your ClojureScript application is tested and deployed consistently, reducing the risk of introducing errors and improving overall deployment reliability.

As your project grows, managing dependencies and project configurations becomes increasingly important. Regularly reviewing and updating dependencies is crucial to ensure that your project remains secure and up-to-date with the latest library versions. Tools such as `lein ancient` for Leiningen or similar plugins for Boot can help in identifying outdated dependencies and providing recommendations for updates. It is also important to review and optimize project configurations to ensure that build times and resource usage are kept to a minimum.

Integrating additional tools and services into your development environment can further enhance productivity. For example, setting up monitoring and logging services can help in tracking application performance and identifying issues in real time. Tools like Sentry or Loggly can be integrated to capture and analyze runtime errors and logs, providing valuable insights into application behavior and facilitating faster issue resolution.

Ensuring a consistent development environment across different team members is another important consideration. Using containerization technologies such as Docker can help in creating reproducible development environments that are consistent across different machines and platforms. By defining your development environment in a Dockerfile, you can ensure that all team members are working with the same configuration, reducing the risk of environment-specific issues and improving collaboration.

In summary, optimizing your ClojureScript development environment involves a multifaceted approach that includes leveraging build automation tools, integrating comprehensive testing strategies, and employing effective version control and CI/CD practices. By focusing on these aspects, you create a development environment that not only supports productive coding practices but also ensures the scalability and maintainability of your ClojureScript projects.

CHAPTER 3: CORE CONCEPTS OF CLOJURESCRIPT

Embarking on a journey into ClojureScript requires a firm grasp of its foundational concepts to navigate its distinct paradigms and leverage its capabilities effectively. At the heart of ClojureScript lies a syntax and set of constructs that embody the principles of functional programming. Understanding these elements will equip you to harness the language's unique features and create robust applications.

The syntax of ClojureScript, much like its parent language Clojure, revolves around the use of expressions rather than statements. This distinction signifies a shift from imperative programming paradigms, where commands are executed sequentially, to a more declarative style where the focus is on the evaluation of expressions. Each expression in ClojureScript returns a value, and these values can be nested within other expressions. This approach fosters a highly expressive and concise codebase, where the relationship between different components of the code is directly tied to their evaluation.

Central to ClojureScript's syntax is its treatment of data. The language features a rich set of data types designed to support immutable data structures. Understanding these data types is crucial as immutability is a core tenet of ClojureScript, influencing how data is managed and manipulated. The basic data types include numbers, strings, characters, and booleans, each of which serves as a fundamental building block in the language. ClojureScript also introduces more complex data types such as lists, vectors, maps, and sets.

Lists in ClojureScript are ordered collections of elements, denoted by parentheses. They are particularly useful for representing sequences where the order of elements is significant. Vectors, on the other hand, are similar to lists but are represented with square brackets and offer efficient random access to elements. Maps, indicated by curly braces and key-value pairs, are used to associate values with keys, enabling associative access and manipulation of data. Sets, which are collections of unique elements, are denoted by a hash followed by curly braces. These data types are all immutable; once created, they cannot be changed. Instead, operations on these data structures return new versions with the desired modifications, preserving the original data.

Functions are another cornerstone of ClojureScript and are fundamental to its functional programming paradigm. In ClojureScript, functions are first-class citizens, meaning they can be passed as arguments to other functions, returned as values, and assigned to variables. Defining a function in ClojureScript is achieved using the `defn` macro, which allows you to specify the function name, parameters, and body. The syntax is designed to be straightforward yet powerful, enabling the creation of complex behavior with concise declarations.

For example, a simple function to add two numbers might be defined as follows:

```clojure
(defn add [x y]
  (+ x y))
```

In this function, `defn` is used to create a new function

named `add` that takes two parameters, `x` and `y`, and returns their sum. The `+` operator within the function body is an example of an expression that evaluates to a value, in this case, the result of the addition.

Beyond basic functions, ClojureScript supports more advanced constructs such as higher-order functions, which are functions that accept other functions as arguments or return functions as results. Higher-order functions are essential for functional programming, enabling the creation of abstract and reusable code patterns. Common higher-order functions include `map`, `filter`, and `reduce`, each of which operates on sequences and demonstrates the power of functional abstraction.

Another fundamental concept in ClojureScript is macros. Macros allow you to extend the language by defining new syntactic constructs. Unlike functions, which operate on values, macros operate on code itself. They enable you to generate and transform code during compilation, providing a powerful mechanism for metaprogramming. Defining a macro is similar to defining a function, but with the `defmacro` keyword. Macros are particularly useful for creating domain-specific languages or embedding custom syntactic sugar into your code.

For instance, consider a macro that simplifies error handling by defining a custom `try-catch` construct. The macro would transform the `try-catch` syntax into the corresponding code that implements the desired error-handling logic. This capability allows developers to create expressive and maintainable code while adhering to the principles of functional programming.

Understanding these core concepts—data types, functions, and macros—provides a solid foundation for working with ClojureScript. By grasping the immutable nature of its data structures, the role of functions as first-class citizens, and the transformative power of macros, you can begin to appreciate the language's unique approach to programming. Each of these elements contributes to the overall philosophy of ClojureScript, emphasizing simplicity, expressiveness, and the power of functional abstraction.

The immutability of data structures in ClojureScript is a distinguishing feature that aligns with the functional programming paradigm. This immutable nature means that once a data structure is created, it cannot be altered. Instead of modifying existing structures, operations produce new structures that reflect the changes. This principle helps prevent many common bugs associated with mutable state, such as unintended side effects and concurrent modification issues. By adhering to immutability, ClojureScript ensures that data transformations are predictable and consistent, which is particularly valuable in complex systems where data integrity is paramount.

Understanding how to work with immutable data structures involves grasping the concept of persistent data structures. ClojureScript utilizes persistent data structures to efficiently handle modifications while preserving the original data. For instance, when a vector is updated, a new vector is created with the updated value, while the old vector remains unchanged. Despite this seemingly costly operation, persistent data structures are designed to share unchanged parts between versions, which optimizes both time and space complexity. This sharing mechanism ensures that operations on data structures are both fast and memory-efficient.

Functions in ClojureScript are not only first-class but also highly composable. Function composition allows developers to build complex operations by combining simpler functions. This compositional approach is facilitated by the use of higher-order functions such as `comp`, which takes a sequence of functions and returns a new function that is the composition of those functions. For example, you might use `comp` to create a function that applies a series of transformations to a given input. This ability to compose functions enhances modularity and reusability, as you can build complex behavior from simple, well-defined components.

Moreover, ClojureScript provides support for anonymous functions, also known as lambda expressions. These functions are defined inline and are often used as arguments to higher-order functions. Anonymous functions are particularly useful for short-lived operations that do not warrant a named definition. They are defined using the `fn` macro and can capture variables from their surrounding lexical scope. This capability allows for flexible and expressive coding patterns, such as passing a custom sorting function to a `sort` operation or defining an ad-hoc transformation for data processing.

Macros in ClojureScript offer a powerful means of extending the language by manipulating code itself. While functions operate on values, macros operate on the code's structure, enabling the creation of new syntactic constructs and domain-specific languages. Macros are defined using the `defmacro` keyword, and they return code that is evaluated in place of the macro call. This code generation capability allows for sophisticated metaprogramming techniques, such as creating custom control flow constructs or embedding new syntactic forms.

For example, a macro might be used to create a custom `loop` construct that enhances the language's standard looping capabilities. The macro could transform a `loop` expression into the corresponding code that performs the desired iteration, allowing for more expressive and readable code. This transformation is performed at compile-time, ensuring that the generated code is optimized and efficient.

Another critical aspect of ClojureScript is its integration with JavaScript. ClojureScript compiles to JavaScript, enabling seamless interaction with existing JavaScript libraries and frameworks. This interoperation is facilitated by the language's ability to interface with JavaScript through a set of foreign function interface (FFI) constructs. Using these constructs, ClojureScript code can call JavaScript functions, access JavaScript objects, and even work with JavaScript libraries directly. This capability makes it possible to leverage the vast ecosystem of JavaScript while benefiting from the functional programming features of ClojureScript.

In practical terms, integrating ClojureScript with JavaScript involves understanding how to work with JavaScript interop features. This includes using `js/` prefix to access JavaScript global objects and methods, and leveraging the `aget`, `aset`, and `js->clj` functions for array and object manipulation. These interop features bridge the gap between ClojureScript and JavaScript, enabling developers to utilize existing libraries and tools within a ClojureScript project. For instance, you might use ClojureScript to build the core logic of an application while incorporating JavaScript libraries for user interface components or data visualization.

Additionally, ClojureScript's REPL (Read-Eval-Print Loop) offers an interactive development experience, allowing developers to test code snippets, explore data structures, and experiment with functions in real-time. The REPL is a powerful tool for iterative development and debugging, providing immediate feedback and facilitating rapid prototyping. By leveraging the REPL, you can interactively explore the language's features, refine your code, and gain a deeper understanding of ClojureScript's behavior.

Mastering these core concepts—immutability, data structures, functions, macros, JavaScript interop, and the REPL—lays a solid foundation for effective ClojureScript programming. By embracing the language's principles and harnessing its unique features, you can develop scalable and maintainable applications that leverage the full potential of functional programming. Each of these concepts contributes to a coherent and expressive language, empowering developers to build robust software solutions while adhering to the functional paradigm.

The concept of functional programming in ClojureScript is deeply intertwined with its approach to handling state and side effects. Unlike imperative languages, where state changes are frequently and explicitly managed, functional programming emphasizes pure functions. A pure function is one that, given the same inputs, will always produce the same output and does not cause any side effects. This predictability makes pure functions easier to reason about, test, and debug. In ClojureScript, embracing pure functions often involves leveraging higher-order functions and avoiding direct mutation of data.

The language's standard library includes a rich set of functions designed to support functional programming patterns. Functions such as `map`, `filter`, and `reduce` are pivotal in processing collections in a declarative manner. For instance, the `map` function applies a given function to each element of a collection, returning a new collection with the results. This approach to handling collections allows for concise and expressive data transformations. Using `filter`, one can create a subset of a collection based on a predicate function, while `reduce` enables the accumulation of a single result from a collection by iteratively applying a function.

In addition to these core functions, ClojureScript provides sequence abstraction that allows for a more flexible and powerful manipulation of collections. Sequences in

ClojureScript are lazy, meaning that their computation is deferred until needed. This laziness optimizes performance by avoiding unnecessary processing and enables operations on large data sets without requiring all data to be held in memory simultaneously. The sequence abstraction supports various operations, including transformation, filtering, and aggregation, which are seamlessly integrated into the language.

Another key aspect of functional programming in ClojureScript is the concept of immutability. Immutability is a cornerstone of functional programming and is enforced by the language's design. Data structures in ClojureScript, such as lists, vectors, maps, and sets, are immutable by default. This immutability guarantees that once a data structure is created, it cannot be modified. Instead, operations that alter data structures return new versions of the structures with the modifications applied. This immutability simplifies reasoning about code and prevents common issues associated with mutable state, such as race conditions in concurrent programming.

The handling of state in ClojureScript is further facilitated by its use of atoms, refs, agents, and vars. These concurrency primitives provide mechanisms for managing state changes while maintaining the principles of immutability. Atoms offer a way to manage shared, mutable state in a controlled manner, using a compare-and-swap mechanism to ensure atomic updates. Refs provide coordinated, transactional updates to multiple pieces of state, ensuring consistency across changes. Agents allow for asynchronous updates to state, providing a way to handle tasks that can be performed concurrently. Vars, on the other hand, are used for dynamic variable binding, allowing for state to be managed in a more flexible manner within a specific scope.

Macros in ClojureScript extend the language by allowing

developers to define new syntactic constructs. Macros operate on the code itself, generating new code during compilation. This ability to manipulate code at compile-time enables the creation of custom control structures and domain-specific languages. For example, a macro might be used to implement a custom looping construct or to create a domain-specific language for a specific problem domain. Macros are a powerful tool for metaprogramming, but they require careful consideration to avoid introducing complexity or obscuring code readability.

ClojureScript's integration with JavaScript allows for seamless interaction between the two languages. This interop capability is crucial for leveraging existing JavaScript libraries and frameworks while building applications with ClojureScript. The language provides several constructs for interacting with JavaScript, including the `js/` prefix for accessing JavaScript global objects and functions, and the `js->clj` function for converting JavaScript objects to ClojureScript data structures. This interoperability facilitates the integration of ClojureScript with various web technologies and enables the use of existing JavaScript resources within ClojureScript projects.

The REPL (Read-Eval-Print Loop) in ClojureScript enhances the development experience by providing an interactive environment for experimenting with code. The REPL allows developers to evaluate expressions, inspect results, and iteratively develop code. This interactive workflow supports rapid prototyping and debugging, enabling immediate feedback and facilitating a more dynamic coding process. The REPL is an invaluable tool for exploring the language's features and refining code.

Mastering the core concepts of ClojureScript—functional programming, immutability, concurrency primitives, macros, JavaScript interop, and the REPL—lays a strong foundation for effective software development. By leveraging these concepts, developers can harness the full potential of ClojureScript to build robust, maintainable, and scalable applications. Embracing these principles not only enhances code quality but also aligns with the functional programming paradigm, fostering a more disciplined and expressive approach to software development.

CHAPTER 4: DATA STRUCTURES AND IMMUTABILITY

In ClojureScript, immutability is not just a feature but a fundamental principle that influences how data is managed and manipulated throughout the development process. The immutability of data structures simplifies reasoning about code, reduces the risk of unintended side effects, and facilitates concurrent programming. To understand how ClojureScript achieves this, it is essential to explore its primary data structures: vectors, maps, and sets, and how these structures operate within an immutable paradigm.

Vectors in ClojureScript are ordered collections that are particularly well-suited for scenarios where the order of elements is significant. They are implemented as persistent data structures, meaning that every update operation produces a new version of the vector while retaining the old version. This immutability is crucial in functional programming, as it ensures that changes to data do not affect other parts of the system that rely on the original data.

When working with vectors, ClojureScript provides a range of functions to access and manipulate elements. For instance, the `conj` function adds an element to the end of the vector, returning a new vector with the added element. Similarly, the `assoc` function allows for updating an element at a specific index, creating a new vector with the updated value. It is important to note that these operations do not modify the original vector but instead produce a new vector with the desired changes. This approach prevents side effects and ensures the integrity of the data across the application.

Maps, another core data structure in ClojureScript, represent associative collections where data is stored as key-value pairs. Like vectors, maps are persistent and immutable. Operations such as `assoc` and `dissoc` are used to add or remove key-value pairs, respectively. The `assoc` function updates or adds a key-value pair in a new map, while `dissoc` removes a key-value pair, returning a new map without the specified entry. These functions facilitate the manipulation of associative data without altering the original map, thus preserving immutability.

One of the key advantages of using immutable maps is the ability to maintain consistent state across different parts of the application. Since maps are immutable, any transformation or update results in a new map, allowing for safe and predictable state management. This characteristic is particularly beneficial in functional programming, where managing state changes without side effects is crucial.

Sets in ClojureScript are collections that ensure the uniqueness of elements and support operations such as union, intersection, and difference. Like vectors and maps, sets are persistent and immutable. Functions like `conj` and `disj` are used to add or remove elements from a set, respectively. The immutability of sets allows for efficient and reliable data manipulation, as each operation produces a new set with the specified changes while leaving the original set unchanged.

The immutable nature of these data structures simplifies complex data manipulations and avoids common pitfalls associated with mutable state. For example, in a mutable environment, updating a data structure in one part of the system can inadvertently affect other parts that rely on the original state. In contrast, ClojureScript's persistent data structures ensure that each modification results in a new version, preserving the original data and preventing unintended side effects.

To illustrate the advantages of immutability, consider a scenario where an application needs to maintain a list of user records. Using ClojureScript's immutable vectors, you can efficiently manage updates and deletions without affecting the original list. For example, if a user record needs to be updated, you can use the `assoc` function to create a new vector with the updated record. The original vector remains unchanged, allowing other parts of the application to continue working with the unmodified data.

Similarly, when working with maps, immutability ensures that changes to user information, such as adding or removing entries, do not impact the original map. By using functions like `assoc` and `dissoc`, you can create new maps with the required modifications while maintaining the integrity of the original data. This approach simplifies the management of state and ensures that data transformations are predictable and controlled.

In practice, the use of immutable data structures in ClojureScript promotes a functional programming style that emphasizes pure functions and minimizes side effects. By leveraging these data structures, developers can write code that is more maintainable, testable, and reliable. The immutability of vectors, maps, and sets not only simplifies data manipulations but also aligns with the principles of functional programming, providing a solid foundation for building robust and scalable applications.

The persistent nature of ClojureScript's data structures

ensures that each modification results in a new version, preserving the original data and avoiding unintended consequences. This approach enhances the predictability and safety of data management, allowing developers to focus on building functional and expressive applications without the complexity of mutable state. Through practical examples and a deeper understanding of immutability, it becomes evident that ClojureScript's data structures offer powerful tools for managing and manipulating data in a functional programming paradigm.

In exploring the core data structures of ClojureScript, it becomes clear that their design reflects a deep commitment to immutability and functional programming principles. As we delve deeper into how these structures function, it is essential to understand not just their use but also the mechanisms that enable their persistent, immutable nature.

Vectors, maps, and sets in ClojureScript are implemented as persistent data structures. This persistence is achieved through a combination of structural sharing and efficient updates. Structural sharing means that when a data structure is modified, the new version shares parts of its structure with the old version, minimizing the overhead of creating new data structures. This efficiency is crucial in functional programming, where immutability can lead to frequent data transformations.

Let's first consider vectors in more detail. A vector in ClojureScript is a sequence where elements are stored in a contiguous block of memory. Despite their apparent similarity to arrays in other languages, vectors in ClojureScript are immutable. When you update an element in a vector, a new vector is created, sharing the underlying structure with the original. This means that the new vector includes the modification but retains a reference to the unchanged portions of the original vector.

This approach is supported by a sophisticated underlying data structure called a "tree" in which the vector is divided into smaller chunks. When an element is updated, only the relevant parts of the tree are modified. This tree-based approach allows for efficient indexing and updating operations, with the complexity of these operations typically logarithmic in relation to the size of the vector. For example, appending an element to a vector or updating an element at a specific index involves a new version of the vector being created with minimal computational overhead, thanks to structural sharing.

Maps, on the other hand, are associative data structures that store key-value pairs. In ClojureScript, maps are implemented as hash maps or as trees, depending on the size and use case. Hash maps are used for small to moderately sized maps, offering efficient average-case performance for lookups, insertions, and deletions. For larger maps, ClojureScript uses tree-based implementations that offer better performance characteristics for large datasets.

The immutability of maps is particularly useful when dealing with stateful operations. When you modify a map using functions like `assoc` or `dissoc`, you create a new map that reflects the changes while keeping the original map intact. This approach is advantageous in scenarios where state history is important, such as undo functionality in applications. By preserving the original state, developers can implement features like undo and redo with relative ease, as each state change results in a new map rather than altering the existing one.

Sets in ClojureScript are collections of unique elements. They are implemented in a manner similar to maps, where each element is treated as a key with a dummy value. The immutability of sets ensures that operations like adding or removing elements result in new sets rather than altering the existing ones. This immutability is crucial for tasks that involve set operations such as union, intersection, and difference. By using immutable sets, operations can be performed safely and predictably without risking unintended modifications to the original set.

An important aspect of working with these immutable data structures is understanding how they interact with the broader application state. Because these structures are persistent, they allow for functional programming practices that emphasize immutability and statelessness. This paradigm shift reduces the complexity of managing application state and enhances the ability to reason about code. For instance, in a web application, using immutable data structures can simplify the process of handling state changes in response to user interactions, as each state change produces a new immutable version of the data.

In practice, leveraging ClojureScript's immutable data structures can lead to more predictable and maintainable code. For example, when dealing with a form submission in a web application, you might use a vector to maintain a list of form inputs. Each input change creates a new vector, reflecting the updated state without altering the previous state. This approach aligns well with reactive programming models, where state changes trigger updates in the user interface, ensuring that the application state remains consistent and easy to manage.

Moreover, immutability helps prevent common bugs associated with mutable state, such as unexpected side effects and race conditions in concurrent environments. By ensuring that data structures do not change once created, ClojureScript reduces the potential for bugs related to shared mutable state, making it easier to reason about the behavior of the application.

In summary, ClojureScript's vectors, maps, and sets offer powerful tools for managing data in an immutable and functional style. By understanding how these data structures are implemented and how they interact with application state, developers can harness their full potential to create robust and maintainable applications. The persistence and efficiency of these structures enable a programming style that promotes immutability and functional principles, simplifying complex data manipulations and enhancing the overall reliability of the codebase.

The immutable nature of ClojureScript's data structures offers a powerful paradigm shift in how data is managed and manipulated. By emphasizing immutability, ClojureScript enables more predictable and robust application behavior, which is critical for developing complex systems. In this discussion, I'll explore additional facets of working with these data structures, including their interaction with concurrency, performance considerations, and practical use cases in application development.

One of the key advantages of immutable data structures is their inherent safety in concurrent environments. When multiple threads or processes need to access or modify data, mutable data structures can lead to race conditions and inconsistencies. This issue arises because mutable data can be changed by one thread while another thread is reading it, potentially leading to unpredictable behavior. In contrast, immutable data structures, by definition, cannot be altered once created. This characteristic ensures that any concurrent operations do not interfere with each other, as each thread or process works with its own version of the data.

For instance, in a multi-threaded web server scenario, each request might need to access shared data structures. If these structures are immutable, each request operates on a separate instance, avoiding conflicts and inconsistencies.

This approach greatly simplifies the design of concurrent applications, reducing the need for complex synchronization mechanisms and minimizing the potential for bugs associated with mutable state.

Performance considerations also play a significant role when dealing with immutable data structures. While it might seem that creating new versions of data structures for each modification could lead to inefficiencies, ClojureScript employs sophisticated techniques to ensure performance remains optimal. The use of structural sharing, as mentioned previously, allows new data structures to reuse parts of the old structures. This technique ensures that updates are efficient both in terms of time and memory.

Moreover, ClojureScript's data structures are designed to be persistent and have performance characteristics that are generally well-suited for functional programming. For example, vectors provide constant-time access and update operations, which is essential for performance in many applications. Maps and sets, implemented as hash maps and trees, offer efficient average-case performance for various operations, making them suitable for a wide range of tasks. Understanding these performance characteristics helps in making informed decisions about which data structure to use based on the specific requirements of the application.

In practical application development, immutable data structures can simplify complex data manipulations. Consider a scenario where an application needs to handle user input and perform a series of transformations on the data. With immutable vectors, each transformation creates a new vector, reflecting the updated state while preserving the original. This approach allows for a clear and predictable sequence of operations, where each step can be independently verified and tested. The resulting code is easier to reason about and debug, as the immutable nature of the data ensures that state changes do not have unintended side effects.

A common pattern in functional programming, and thus in ClojureScript, is to use immutable data structures in combination with functional transformations. Functions such as `map`, `filter`, and `reduce` operate on immutable collections, producing new collections as results. These functions are inherently composable, meaning that they can be combined to build complex data processing pipelines. For example, applying a sequence of transformations to a vector of data can be achieved in a concise and readable manner, with each transformation step being a clear and isolated operation.

Another practical aspect of immutability is its role in state management in modern applications, especially those built using frameworks that emphasize a unidirectional data flow. In such frameworks, application state is often represented using immutable data structures, with state changes being managed through actions and reducers. This pattern promotes a clear separation between state and behavior, enhancing the maintainability and scalability of the application. By leveraging immutable data structures, developers can ensure that state transitions are predictable and traceable, which is crucial for debugging and testing.

In conclusion, the immutable data structures provided by ClojureScript offer numerous benefits, including enhanced safety in concurrent environments, optimal performance through structural sharing, and simplified data manipulation through functional transformations. By embracing these structures, developers can build more reliable and maintainable applications, leveraging the power of immutability to manage state and data effectively. The ability to reason about data transformations and state changes without worrying about mutable state simplifies complex programming tasks, leading to more robust and predictable software systems.

CHAPTER 5: FUNCTIONAL PROGRAMMING PRINCIPLES

Functional programming represents one of the foundational paradigms of ClojureScript, profoundly influencing how code is structured and executed. This section delves into core principles of functional programming, including first-class functions, higher-order functions, and function composition. These principles not only define the essence of functional programming but also guide the development of clean, efficient, and maintainable code.

To begin with, the concept of first-class functions is central to functional programming. In ClojureScript, functions are first-class citizens, meaning they can be treated as values and manipulated like any other data type. This allows for functions to be passed as arguments to other functions, returned as values from functions, and assigned to variables. This capability enables a high degree of abstraction and reusability in code. For example, when defining a function that performs a specific operation, I can pass this function as an argument to another function that applies it to a sequence of values. This technique facilitates the creation of generic, reusable components that can be adapted to different contexts without modification.

Higher-order functions, a natural extension of first-class functions, take this flexibility a step further. These functions either accept other functions as parameters or return functions as results. In ClojureScript, higher-order functions are instrumental in creating concise and expressive code. For instance, the `map` function is a higher-order function that applies a given function to each element of a collection, returning a new collection of results. This approach allows for operations on collections to be expressed in a declarative manner, making the code more readable and expressive. Similarly, `filter` and `reduce` are higher-order functions that enable filtering and aggregation of data, respectively, providing powerful tools for data manipulation in a functional style.

Function composition is another fundamental principle that leverages the power of first-class and higher-order functions. Function composition involves creating new functions by combining existing ones. This technique promotes code modularity and clarity by enabling complex operations to be expressed as a series of simple, composable functions. In ClojureScript, function composition is often achieved using the `comp` function, which takes a sequence of functions and returns a new function that applies them in sequence. For example, if I have two functions, `f` and `g`, composing them with `comp` results in a new function that first applies `g` and then `f`. This composition of functions allows for the creation of complex transformations from simpler building blocks, enhancing both code maintainability and readability.

An essential aspect of functional programming is immutability, which works hand-in-hand with the principles discussed above. By ensuring that data structures cannot be altered after their creation, ClojureScript encourages a programming style where functions operate on data without side effects. This immutability aligns with the principles of functional programming by simplifying reasoning about code and preventing unintended interactions between different parts of a program. For example, when using higher-order functions like `map`, the original collection remains unchanged, and a new collection with the transformed elements is returned. This approach eliminates issues related to mutable state and ensures that functions have predictable behavior.

In practice, these functional programming principles can be applied to various scenarios. Consider a situation where I need to process a list of numbers, applying a series of transformations such as doubling each number, filtering out the odd results, and then summing the remaining numbers. By leveraging first-class functions, higher-order functions, and function composition, I can implement this series of operations in a clean and expressive manner. I might start by defining a function to double a number, then use `map` to apply this function to each element of the list. Next, I can use `filter` to remove odd numbers and finally apply `reduce` to compute the sum of the remaining numbers. This approach not only results in concise and readable code but also aligns with the functional programming principles of modularity and immutability.

To summarize, functional programming principles such as first-class functions, higher-order functions, and function composition are integral to ClojureScript and offer powerful tools for writing clean, maintainable code. By understanding and applying these principles, I can harness the full potential of ClojureScript's functional programming capabilities, leading to more efficient and expressive solutions to programming challenges.

In functional programming, one of the foundational principles is the notion of first-class functions. This concept is pivotal as it treats functions as first-class citizens, akin to any other data type such as integers or strings. In practice, this means functions can be assigned to variables, passed as arguments to other functions, and returned as values from other functions. This capability introduces a profound level of flexibility in programming, allowing for higher abstraction and more modular code.

First-class functions facilitate the creation of more abstract and reusable code. For example, if we have a function that performs a common transformation, we can encapsulate this transformation within a function and pass it around as needed. Consider a scenario where we have several pieces of data that require a similar transformation. Instead of duplicating code, we can define a function once and apply it wherever necessary. This not only reduces redundancy but also centralizes logic, making it easier to maintain and update.

A crucial extension of first-class functions is the concept of higher-order functions. These functions either take one or more functions as arguments or return a function as a result. Higher-order functions enable powerful programming patterns such as function chaining, currying, and composing functions. They promote code that is more modular and expressive. For instance, consider a higher-order function that takes a list of numbers and a function that performs an operation on each number. We can use this higher-order function to apply various operations, such as doubling each number or calculating the square root, without modifying the core logic of the function.

In ClojureScript, the `map` function is an exemplary higher-order function. It applies a given function to each element of a collection, returning a new collection with the results. This function embodies the power of higher-order functions by abstracting the iteration process, allowing us to focus on the operation to be performed rather than the mechanics of looping. For example, if we need to apply a function `f` to every element in a list, we can achieve this succinctly with `map`:

```clojure
(map f [1 2 3 4])
```

The result is a new list with `f` applied to each element, showcasing how higher-order functions simplify operations on collections.

Function composition, another key principle, involves combining multiple functions into a single function, which produces a new function that represents the composition of these functions. This principle is particularly useful for creating complex operations from simpler functions. In functional programming, composition is often represented using function composition operators or combinators. For instance, in ClojureScript, the `comp` function can be used to compose multiple functions:

```clojure
(def my-composed-function (comp f g h))
```

In this example, `my-composed-function` represents the composition of `f`, `g`, and `h`, where `h` is applied first, followed by `g`, and finally `f`. This pattern facilitates a declarative approach to building complex functions and enhances readability by focusing on the "what" rather than the "how" of computations.

A practical application of function composition is in creating pipelines of data transformations. Suppose we need to process a list of numbers by first filtering out the even numbers, then doubling each of the remaining numbers, and finally summing the results. Using composition, we can define separate functions for filtering, doubling, and summing, and compose them into a single pipeline:

```clojure
(defn process-data [data]
  (->> data
    (filter even?)
    (map ( 2 %))
    (reduce +)))
```

In this pipeline, `->>` is a threading macro that passes the data through each function in sequence, illustrating how function composition can streamline and organize data processing tasks.

Another important aspect of functional programming is immutability. In functional programming, data is treated as immutable, meaning that once created, it cannot be changed. Instead of modifying existing data, new data structures are created. This principle is crucial for writing predictable and reliable code, as it eliminates side effects and ensures that data remains consistent throughout the program's execution.

Immutability enhances code safety and simplifies reasoning about program behavior. For instance, when working with immutable data structures, we can be confident that no unexpected changes will occur, which reduces the likelihood of bugs and makes debugging more straightforward. In ClojureScript, immutable data structures such as lists, vectors, and maps are inherently designed to support this principle. Operations that appear to modify these structures actually return new versions with the changes applied, preserving the original data.

In conclusion, the principles of first-class functions, higher-order functions, function composition, and immutability are central to functional programming and ClojureScript. These principles contribute to writing more modular, reusable, and maintainable code. By leveraging these concepts, developers can craft elegant solutions to complex problems, embracing a functional approach that fosters clarity and efficiency in programming.

A deeper dive into functional programming reveals additional concepts that enhance the power and utility of functional programming principles. One such concept is currying, which involves transforming a function that takes multiple arguments into a series of functions, each taking a single argument. Currying facilitates partial application, where a function can be applied with some arguments, producing a new function that requires the remaining arguments. This is particularly useful for creating specialized functions from more general ones and for building highly reusable code.

In ClojureScript, currying is implicitly supported through functions that return other functions. For example, consider a function that adds two numbers:

```clojure
(defn add [x y]
  (+ x y))
```

We can use this function with partial application to create a new function that adds a fixed number to any given number. By leveraging `partial`, we can achieve this:

```clojure
(def add-5 (partial add 5))
(add-5 10) ; returns 15
```

Here, `add-5` is a curried version of `add` with the first argument fixed at 5. This technique simplifies function composition and allows for greater flexibility in function usage.

Another significant principle is referential transparency, which means that an expression can be replaced with its value without changing the program's behavior. Referential transparency is closely linked to immutability and contributes to the predictability of functional programs. In functional programming, functions are expected to be pure, meaning they do not produce side effects or depend on external state. This purity ensures that given the same inputs, a function always produces the same output, which simplifies reasoning about code and testing.

For instance, consider a function that calculates the square of a number:

```clojure
(defn square [x]
  (x x))
```

This function is referentially transparent because it always returns the same result for the same input and does not alter any external state. Such purity enables various optimizations and reasoning techniques, including memoization, which caches function results to improve performance. Memoization is particularly effective in scenarios where the function is called repeatedly with the same arguments, reducing redundant computations.

Closely related to referential transparency is the concept of lazy evaluation. Lazy evaluation defers the computation of values until they are actually needed, which can improve efficiency and support the construction of infinite data structures. In ClojureScript, lazy sequences are a key feature, allowing for the creation of sequences that are computed on-demand rather than in advance. This can be especially advantageous when working with large datasets or complex transformations.

For example, a lazy sequence can be generated using `lazy-seq`:

```clojure
(defn infinite-numbers [n]
  (lazy-seq (cons n (infinite-numbers (inc n)))))
```

Here, `infinite-numbers` generates an infinite sequence starting from `n`. Since it is a lazy sequence, elements are computed only when needed, allowing for efficient processing of potentially unbounded data.

Moreover, functional programming emphasizes the use of functional data structures, which are designed to work seamlessly with immutable data. Functional data structures such as persistent lists, vectors, and maps offer efficient ways to work with immutable data while preserving performance. For instance, ClojureScript provides persistent data structures that support structural sharing, meaning that modifications to a data structure create new versions without copying the entire structure. This allows for efficient and safe data manipulation.

Consider the example of using persistent vectors:

```clojure
(def v [1 2 3])
(def v2 (conj v 4)) ; v2 is [1 2 3 4]
```

In this case, `v2` is a new vector that includes the additional element, while `v` remains unchanged. This approach to data manipulation aligns with functional programming principles by ensuring immutability and leveraging efficient data structures.

Lastly, the concept of monads often emerges in discussions of functional programming, particularly in languages with strong functional capabilities. Monads are abstract data types used to represent computations instead of values. They provide a way to handle side effects, manage state, and sequence operations in a controlled manner. While ClojureScript does not have built-in monads, similar concepts can be applied using constructs such as `core.async` for managing asynchronous operations and stateful computations.

In summary, advanced functional programming concepts such as currying, referential transparency, lazy evaluation, functional data structures, and monads enhance the capabilities of functional programming and contribute to writing efficient, modular, and maintainable code. By integrating these principles into your programming practice, you can leverage the full power of functional programming to address complex challenges and build robust, reliable software solutions.

CHAPTER 6: BUILDING USER INTERFACES WITH REAGENT

Reagent, a prominent library in the ClojureScript ecosystem, offers an elegant and efficient approach to building user interfaces by leveraging React's capabilities. This section will delve into the core aspects of Reagent, including component creation, state management, and event handling, demonstrating how it simplifies the development of interactive web applications.

To begin, understanding Reagent's relationship with React is crucial. Reagent provides a ClojureScript interface to React, allowing developers to use familiar React concepts through a ClojureScript-centric API. The fundamental unit of Reagent is the component, which can be defined using a simple and expressive syntax. Components in Reagent are defined as functions that return a Reagent element, which is analogous to a React element. These components are composable and can be nested, facilitating the construction of complex user interfaces from simple building blocks.

For example, creating a basic component in Reagent involves defining a function that returns a Reagent element. The syntax is concise and integrates seamlessly with ClojureScript's data structures. Consider a simple component that renders a greeting message:

```clojure
(ns my-app.core
 (:require [reagent.core :as r]))

(defn greeting-component []
 [:div "Hello, welcome to Reagent!"])
```

In this snippet, `greeting-component` is a Reagent component that renders a `div` element with a welcome message. The `[:div "Hello, welcome to Reagent!"]` notation is a ClojureScript vector representing a Reagent element. This vector syntax, known as hiccup, is used to describe the structure of the user interface declaratively.

Managing state in Reagent is another fundamental aspect of building interactive user interfaces. Reagent introduces a concept called atoms, which are references to stateful data. Atoms provide a way to create mutable state that can be updated and reacted to within components. The `reagent.core/atom` function creates an atom, and its value can be modified using `reset!` or `swap!`. Components can be reactive to changes in atoms, automatically updating the UI when the underlying state changes.

To illustrate, let's create a component that includes a counter with buttons to increment and decrement its value. Here's how we might implement this:

```clojure
(ns my-app.core
 (:require [reagent.core :as r]))

(def counter-state (r/atom 0))

(defn counter-component []
```

```
[:div
 [:p "Counter value: " @counter-state]
 [:button {:on-click (swap! counter-state inc)} "Increment"]
 [:button {:on-click (swap! counter-state dec)} "Decrement"]])
```

In this example, `counter-state` is an atom that holds the current counter value. The `@counter-state` dereferences the atom to access its value. The `:on-click` handlers for the buttons use `swap!` to update the atom, triggering a re-render of the `counter-component` whenever the state changes.

Handling events is integral to interactive web applications, and Reagent provides a straightforward approach to event management. Events in Reagent are managed through standard ClojureScript functions that are attached to UI elements. These functions can interact with atoms or other stateful constructs to update the user interface in response to user actions.

For example, consider a form component that allows users to enter text and submit it. We can manage the form's input state and handle submission as follows:

```clojure
(ns my-app.core
  (:require [reagent.core :as r]))

(def input-state (r/atom ""))

(defn form-component []
  (fn []
    [:div
     [:input {:type "text"
              :value @input-state
              :on-change (reset! input-state (-> % .-target .-value))}]
     [:button {:on-click (js/alert (str "Submitted: " @input-state))}
```

"Submit"]]))
```

In this form component, `input-state` is an atom that holds the current input value. The `:on-change` event handler updates the atom with the new value whenever the user types in the input field. The `:on-click` event handler triggers an alert displaying the submitted value.

Reagent's integration with React ensures that components are efficiently updated and rendered. It leverages React's virtual DOM to optimize the rendering process, minimizing direct manipulation of the actual DOM and improving performance. This integration allows developers to benefit from React's robust ecosystem while writing in a ClojureScript-friendly manner.

Overall, Reagent simplifies the development of interactive user interfaces by providing a ClojureScript-friendly API that abstracts away much of the complexity of React. Its component-based architecture, reactive state management with atoms, and straightforward event handling make it an effective tool for building modern web applications. By utilizing these features, developers can create dynamic and responsive user interfaces with ease, harnessing the power of both ClojureScript and React.

Expanding on the practical aspects of Reagent, we encounter the concept of component lifecycle management, a crucial area for creating complex user interfaces. While Reagent abstracts many of React's lifecycle methods, understanding how Reagent manages component lifecycle events enhances the ability to build robust applications. Lifecycle methods such as `componentDidMount`, `componentDidUpdate`, and `componentWillUnmount` are essential for managing side effects and performing setup and teardown operations.

In Reagent, lifecycle management is handled through
```

the use of Reagent's `r/with-let` and `r/with-reagent` functions. These functions allow for initialization and cleanup operations in a way that integrates seamlessly with Reagent's reactivity model. For instance, if you need to set up an external library or subscribe to a data source when a component mounts, you can use `r/with-let` to manage such side effects.

Consider a component that integrates with an external library for chart rendering. To ensure that the chart is properly initialized and cleaned up, you might use `r/with-let` as follows:

```clojure
(ns my-app.core
  (:require [reagent.core :as r]))

(defn chart-component []
  (r/with-let [chart (js/Chart. (js/document.getElementById "chart-container")
                       js {:type "line"
                           :data js {:labels ["January" "February"]
                                     :datasets js [{:label "My Dataset"
                                                    :data [10 20]}]}})]
    (fn []
      [:div chart-container])))
```

In this example, `chart` is initialized when the component mounts, and the `r/with-let` ensures that the chart is properly set up. The `fn []` inner function returns the UI elements, ensuring that the chart is rendered in the `chart-container` div.

Reagent's Reagent Subscriptions are another advanced feature that simplifies state management in more complex applications. Subscriptions provide a way to derive and manage state across multiple components, allowing for a more centralized approach to state management. Subscriptions are particularly useful for situations where components need to react to changes in shared state or when the state needs to be computed based on other state values.

To define a subscription, you use `r/ratom` to create a reactive atom that can be shared across components. For instance, suppose you want to create a subscription that provides the total number of items in a shopping cart. You might define a subscription as follows:

```clojure
(ns my-app.core
 (:require [reagent.core :as r]))

(defonce cart-state (r/atom {:items [{:name "Item 1" :quantity 2}
                                     {:name "Item 2" :quantity 3}]}))

(defn total-items []
 (r/ratom (reduce + (map :quantity (:items @cart-state)))))
```

In this example, `cart-state` is a reactive atom containing the cart items, and `total-items` is a subscription that calculates the total quantity of items in the cart. The `r/ratom` function ensures that any component relying on `total-items` will be updated whenever the cart state changes.

Handling routing within a Reagent application is another important aspect. While Reagent itself does not include routing capabilities, it integrates well with routing libraries such as `reitit`. Routing allows for the creation of single-page applications (SPAs) with navigation and state management across different views.

To use `reitit` for routing in a Reagent application, you first need to set up routes and then create components that respond to these routes. Here's a basic example of how routing can be set up:

```clojure
(ns my-app.core
 (:require [reitit.core :as r]
    [reitit.ring :as ring]
    [reagent.core :as r]
    [reagent.ratom :refer [reaction]]))

(def router (r/atom (r/router [["/" home-page]
       ["/about" about-page]])))

(defn home-page []
 [:div "Welcome to the home page"])

(defn about-page []
 [:div "This is the about page"])

(defn app []
   (let [current-route (reaction (r/match-route @router (.-pathname js/location)))]
    (fn []
    [:div
    [:header "My App"]
    [:main [(:handler @current-route)]]])))
```

In this example, `router` is an atom holding the route configuration, and `app` dynamically renders components based on the current route. This setup allows for a single-page application with different views handled by Reagent components.

Form validation and handling user input effectively are critical aspects of building interactive applications. Reagent facilitates form management through reactive state and event handling, allowing for responsive and user-friendly forms. Implementing validation logic involves defining functions to check the validity of form fields and providing feedback to users.

Consider a form component where users need to input an email address. Validation can be performed as follows:

```clojure
(ns my-app.core
 (:require [reagent.core :as r]))

(defn validate-email [email]
 (re-matches ".+@.+\..+" email))

(defn email-form []
 (let [email (r/atom "")
       error (r/atom nil)]
  (fn []
   [:div
    [:input {:type "text"
             :placeholder "Enter your email"
             :value @email
             :on-change (let [new-email (-> % .-target .-value)]
                         (reset! email new-email)
                         (reset! error (if (validate-email new-email)
                                        nil
                                        "Invalid email address")))}]
    (when @error
     [:p {:style {:color "red"}} @error])
         [:button {:on-click (js/alert (str "Submitted email: " @email))} "Submit"]])))
```

In this form component, the `validate-email` function checks the format of the email address, and the `error` atom holds validation messages. The form updates reactively as users input data, providing immediate feedback on validation results.

Overall, Reagent's flexibility and integration with React provide a powerful toolkit for building user interfaces.

By understanding and applying advanced features such as lifecycle management, subscriptions, routing, and form validation, developers can create sophisticated and responsive web applications that leverage the full potential of both ClojureScript and React.

In extending the discussion on Reagent, a nuanced exploration of performance optimization in Reagent applications is crucial. Optimizing performance involves understanding how Reagent interacts with React's rendering lifecycle and leveraging techniques that reduce unnecessary re-renders and improve application efficiency. This section delves into various strategies for optimizing Reagent-based applications, emphasizing practical implementations and considerations.

One fundamental aspect of performance optimization in Reagent is minimizing re-renders. Reagent's reactivity model can trigger re-renders when reactive atoms change, which might lead to performance issues if not managed correctly. To mitigate this, it's essential to understand how to control and limit reactivity to only the necessary parts of the application. By using Reagent's built-in functions and leveraging React's optimization techniques, we can significantly enhance performance.

A common technique for optimizing rendering is to use reagent's `r/with-let` and `r/atom` wisely. These functions allow you to manage component state and side effects efficiently. For instance, if a component does not need to react to certain state changes, you can isolate its state within a local `r/atom` to prevent unnecessary re-renders. Here's an example illustrating this principle:

```clojure
(ns my-app.core
  (:require [reagent.core :as r]))

(defn expensive-component []
```

```
  (let [local-state (r/atom {:value 0})]
    (fn []
      [:div
       [:button {:on-click (swap! local-state update :value inc)}
        "Increment"]
       [:p "Value: " (:value @local-state)]])))

(defn parent-component []
  (let [global-state (r/atom {:some-data "data"})]
    (fn []
      [:div
       [:h1 "Parent Component"]
       [expensive-component]])))
```

In this example, `expensive-component` manages its own state independently, ensuring that updates to `global-state` in `parent-component` do not trigger re-renders of `expensive-component`.

Memoization is another key strategy for improving performance. Memoization involves caching the results of expensive computations so that they are not recalculated on every render. In Reagent, memoization can be implemented using Reagent's `r/track` and `r/atom`. The `r/track` function tracks dependencies and only recomputes values when necessary. For instance:

```clojure
(ns my-app.core
  (:require [reagent.core :as r]))

(defn expensive-calculation [input]
  ;; Simulate an expensive computation
  (Thread/sleep 1000)
  ( input input))

(defn memoized-component [input]
```

```
  (let [result (r/track (expensive-calculation input))]
    (fn []
      [:div "Result: " @result])))

(defn app []
  (let [input (r/atom 5)]
    (fn []
      [:div
       [memoized-component @input]
       [:button {:on-click (swap! input inc)} "Increase Input"]])))
```

In this setup, `expensive-calculation` is memoized with `r/track`, so it only recalculates when `input` changes. This approach prevents redundant calculations and enhances the responsiveness of the application.

Code splitting and lazy loading are advanced techniques used to improve the initial loading time of web applications. Reagent integrates well with these strategies, which involve breaking the application into smaller chunks and loading them only when needed. This technique is especially useful for large applications where loading all components at once can be inefficient.

To implement code splitting in a Reagent application, you can use dynamic imports combined with React's `Suspense` and `lazy` functions. For example:

```clojure
(ns my-app.core
  (:require [reagent.core :as r]
            [cljs.core.async :as async]
            [react :refer [Suspense lazy]]))

(def lazy-component (lazy (fn [] (r/atom (js/require "path/to/component")))))

(defn app []
```

```
   (fn []
    [:div
     [Suspense {:fallback "Loading..."}
     [lazy-component]]]))
```

In this example, `lazy-component` is loaded only when it is needed, reducing the initial load time and improving user experience.

Finally, profiling and debugging are essential practices for optimizing performance. Using tools such as React DevTools can help identify performance bottlenecks and optimize rendering behavior. These tools provide insights into component rendering times, state changes, and the overall performance of the application.

By incorporating these performance optimization strategies into your Reagent applications, you can build more efficient and responsive user interfaces. Reagent's seamless integration with React, combined with these techniques, ensures that you can handle complex applications with ease while maintaining high performance.

This exploration of Reagent's capabilities illustrates its robustness in building interactive web applications. From managing state and handling events to optimizing performance and integrating advanced features, Reagent offers a powerful toolkit for developing modern web applications with ClojureScript.

CHAPTER 7: STATE MANAGEMENT WITH RE-FRAME

When addressing state management in complex applications, the Re-frame framework provides a compelling approach grounded in ClojureScript. Re-frame stands out due to its emphasis on unidirectional data flow and a clear separation of concerns, which are fundamental for creating scalable and maintainable applications. This exploration into Re-frame will cover its architecture and components, detailing how to structure applications, manage state efficiently, and leverage Re-frame's features to achieve a well-organized codebase.

At the core of Re-frame is its event handling system, which plays a pivotal role in managing application state. Events in Re-frame are akin to messages or commands that trigger changes in the application state. They are processed by event handlers, which are pure functions responsible for updating the application's state in response to these events. This design allows for a clear and predictable state transition model.

For instance, consider a simple Re-frame application with a counter. To handle the increment and decrement operations, we define events like `:increment` and `:decrement`. These events are associated with event handlers that update the state accordingly. Here's a basic implementation:

```clojure
```

```clojure
(ns my-app.events
  (:require [re-frame.core :as re-frame]))

(re-frame/reg-event-db
 :increment
 (fn [db _]
   (update db :count inc)))

(re-frame/reg-event-db
 :decrement
 (fn [db _]
   (update db :count dec)))
```

In this example, `reg-event-db` registers event handlers that modify the application state. The `db` parameter represents the application's current state, and the event's payload is passed as the second argument. Each handler updates the state immutably, preserving the integrity of the application data.

Subscriptions are another critical aspect of Re-frame's architecture. They provide a way to retrieve and react to slices of the application state. Subscriptions are declarative and allow components to access the necessary state without directly interacting with the global state. This approach promotes modularity and reusability of components.

In the case of our counter application, we would define a subscription to access the current count:

```clojure
(ns my-app.subs
  (:require [re-frame.core :as re-frame]))

(re-frame/reg-sub
 :count
 (fn [db _]
   (:count db)))
```

Here, `reg-sub` registers a subscription that extracts the `:count` value from the application state. Components can then use this subscription to render the current count without needing to know the details of state management.

Managing effects is another crucial aspect of Re-frame. Effects represent side-effects or external interactions that occur as a result of events, such as HTTP requests, logging, or navigation. Re-frame provides a mechanism to handle these effects declaratively, separating side-effect management from state management. Effects are managed through effect handlers, which process effectful actions triggered by events.

For example, if an event triggers an HTTP request, you would define an effect handler to handle the request and update the state based on the response:

```clojure
(ns my-app.effects
  (:require [re-frame.core :as re-frame]))

(re-frame/reg-fx
 :http-get
 (fn [url]
   ;; Perform the HTTP GET request
   (js/fetch url
     (.then (fn [response] (.json response)))
        (.then (fn [data] (re-frame/dispatch [:handle-response data]))))))
```

In this example, `reg-fx` registers an effect handler for the `:http-get` effect. This handler performs an HTTP GET request and dispatches another event with the response data. By managing effects separately from state, Re-frame maintains a clear separation of concerns and ensures that state transitions remain predictable and controlled.

Structuring a Re-frame application involves organizing events, subscriptions, and effects in a way that promotes clarity and maintainability. A typical structure includes separate namespaces for events, subscriptions, and effects, each responsible for different aspects of the application. This separation of concerns helps in managing complexity and ensures that each part of the application has a well-defined role.

For a scalable application, it is beneficial to structure events and subscriptions hierarchically. For instance, events related to user authentication might be grouped under a `:user` namespace, while events related to data fetching could be under a `:data` namespace. Similarly, subscriptions can be organized to reflect the different data slices they provide access to. This hierarchical organization aids in maintaining a clear and manageable codebase, especially as the application grows in complexity.

Maintaining a clear separation of concerns is essential for enhancing the scalability and maintainability of Re-frame applications. By following Re-frame's architectural patterns, such as using pure functions for event handlers, declarative subscriptions, and separate effect handlers, developers can create applications that are easier to reason about and extend. This approach not only improves code quality but also facilitates testing and debugging, as each component can be isolated and examined independently.

In summary, Re-frame's architecture—comprising events, subscriptions, and effects—provides a robust framework for managing state in complex applications. By adhering to Re-frame's principles and structuring applications effectively, developers can achieve a scalable and maintainable codebase, ensuring that state management remains clear, predictable, and manageable.

In leveraging Re-frame for state management, understanding the core principles behind its design is crucial. The framework revolves around a few fundamental concepts that ensure a robust and scalable application architecture. These principles not only streamline the development process but also enhance the maintainability of the application over time.

A key element of Re-frame's architecture is the event-handling mechanism. Events in Re-frame are dispatched to signal a change in the application's state, triggering a sequence of operations that ultimately result in state updates. These events are processed by handlers that are defined as pure functions. Pure functions, by their nature, have no side effects and produce consistent outputs given the same inputs. This characteristic is vital in ensuring that the state transitions are predictable and debuggable.

For example, when an event such as `:user-login` is dispatched, it is handled by a corresponding event handler that updates the application's state to reflect the user's login status. The handler might look like this:

```clojure
(ns my-app.events
 (:require [re-frame.core :as re-frame]))

(re-frame/reg-event-db
 :user-login
 (fn [db [_ user-info]]
   (assoc db :user user-info)))
```

In this example, the `:user-login` event updates the database to include the user's information. The `assoc` function is used to immutably add the `:user` key to the database. This immutability ensures that the previous state remains unchanged, thereby preventing unintended side effects.

Subscriptions, another cornerstone of Re-frame, provide a declarative way to retrieve and react to slices of the application's state. Subscriptions are crucial for maintaining a clean separation between state management and UI rendering. They allow components to access the state they need without direct manipulation or dependency on global state, which enhances modularity and reusability.

To illustrate, consider a subscription that provides access to the user's information:

```clojure
(ns my-app.subs
  (:require [re-frame.core :as re-frame]))

(re-frame/reg-sub
 :user
 (fn [db _]
   (:user db)))
```

Here, the `:user` subscription extracts the user information from the application's state. Components can then utilize this subscription to display user-specific data without directly querying or altering the state, thus adhering to the principle of unidirectional data flow.

Managing effects is another vital aspect of Re-frame. Effects represent side-effects or operations that are triggered by events but do not directly modify the state. Examples include making HTTP requests, navigating to different views, or interacting with external APIs. In Re-frame, effects are handled declaratively through effect handlers, which process and manage these operations separately from state management.

Consider an effect that performs an HTTP GET request to fetch user data:

```clojure
(ns my-app.effects
 (:require [re-frame.core :as re-frame]))

(re-frame/reg-fx
 :fetch-user-data
 (fn [user-id]
  (js/fetch (str "/api/users/" user-id)
   (.then (fn [response] (.json response)))
      (.then (fn [data] (re-frame/dispatch [:user-data-received data]))))))
```

In this example, the `:fetch-user-data` effect handler initiates an HTTP request to fetch user data and subsequently dispatches an event `:user-data-received` with the retrieved data. By isolating effects from state management, Re-frame maintains a clear and organized approach to handling external interactions.

Structuring a Re-frame application involves organizing the various components—events, subscriptions, and effects—into a coherent and manageable architecture. Typically, a Re-frame application will have dedicated namespaces for each of these components, reflecting their distinct roles. This organization aids in keeping the codebase modular and ensures that each part of the application adheres to its specific responsibilities.

For instance, event handlers might be grouped under an `events` namespace, subscriptions under a `subs` namespace, and effect handlers under an `effects` namespace. This modular approach not only clarifies the code structure but also simplifies the development and debugging processes.

Additionally, ensuring that state management is efficient and maintainable requires attention to detail in how state is updated and accessed. Immutable data structures are a key practice in this regard, as they help prevent unintended state mutations and ensure consistency across the application. By leveraging Re-frame's immutable state updates and declarative subscriptions, developers can build applications that are both scalable and robust.

Effective state management also involves careful consideration of performance optimization. Since Re-frame operates on immutable data, there can be performance implications related to how data is updated and rendered. Re-frame provides mechanisms to optimize performance, such as batching updates and leveraging subscriptions to minimize unnecessary re-renders.

By following these principles and practices, Re-frame enables the development of complex applications with a clear and manageable state architecture. Its emphasis on immutability, separation of concerns, and declarative state management promotes a scalable and maintainable codebase. As applications grow in complexity, adhering to these practices will ensure that state management remains robust and efficient.

To deepen our understanding of state management with Re-frame, it's crucial to examine how Re-frame integrates with event handling and how it influences application state and user experience. The process begins with the dispatching of events, which serve as triggers for state changes. These events are processed through a system of event handlers and effect handlers that work together to ensure that state updates occur efficiently and predictably.

In a well-architected Re-frame application, events are dispatched to signal changes that need to be reflected in the state. For instance, if a user interacts with a form to submit data, an event such as `:submit-form` is dispatched. This event is then processed by an event handler, which updates the state accordingly. Here's a deeper look at how this interaction works:

```clojure
(ns my-app.events
 (:require [re-frame.core :as re-frame]))

(re-frame/reg-event-db
 :submit-form
 (fn [db [_ form-data]]
   (assoc db :form-data form-data)))
```

In this snippet, the `:submit-form` event updates the application's state with the data from the form. The use of `assoc` ensures that the state is updated immutably, preserving the previous state while applying the changes.

A crucial aspect of handling events is ensuring that the application's state remains consistent and predictable. This is achieved by designing event handlers that are pure functions, meaning they do not produce side effects and always return the same result for the same input. This purity is essential for debugging and maintaining a clear flow of data through the application.

Subscriptions play a pivotal role in Re-frame's architecture by providing components with access to the state. Subscriptions are designed to be reactive, meaning they automatically update the UI when the underlying state changes. This reactive nature is achieved through the subscription function, which extracts the necessary state and returns it to the components.

For example, consider a subscription that retrieves a list of items from the state:

```clojure
(ns my-app.subs
 (:require [re-frame.core :as re-frame]))
```

```
(re-frame/reg-sub
 :items
 (fn [db _]
   (:items db)))
```

In this case, the `:items` subscription allows a component to access the list of items stored in the state. The component will re-render automatically whenever the `:items` data changes, ensuring that the UI reflects the most current state without manual intervention.

Handling effects is another integral part of Re-frame's state management. Effects represent operations that are external to the state itself, such as making network requests or interacting with the browser's local storage. In Re-frame, effects are managed declaratively through effect handlers, which ensure that these operations are executed in response to events but do not directly alter the state.

For instance, if an event requires fetching data from an API, the effect handler would look like this:

```clojure
(ns my-app.effects
  (:require [re-frame.core :as re-frame]))

(re-frame/reg-fx
 :fetch-items
 (fn [url]
   (js/fetch url
     (.then (fn [response] (.json response)))
         (.then (fn [data] (re-frame/dispatch [:items-received data]))))))
```

Here, the `:fetch-items` effect handler performs an HTTP request to fetch data from a given URL and dispatches another event `:items-received` with the fetched data. This separation of effects from state management ensures that the core state remains focused on representing the application's current status while external operations are handled separately.

The integration of events, subscriptions, and effects is designed to be seamless, promoting a clean architecture where state management and side effects are well defined. By adhering to Re-frame's principles, developers can build applications that are both scalable and maintainable. The framework's emphasis on immutability, pure functions, and clear separation of concerns enables the development of complex applications with a high degree of reliability and ease of debugging.

Optimizing performance in a Re-frame application is another important consideration. Although Re-frame's declarative approach generally leads to efficient updates, there are strategies to further enhance performance. For example, minimizing the number of re-renders by leveraging subscription optimizations or batching updates can significantly impact application responsiveness. Re-frame provides tools and techniques for monitoring and improving performance, such as the use of `reagent`'s `reaction` to memoize computations and reduce unnecessary updates.

Testing is also a critical aspect of maintaining a high-quality Re-frame application. Given that Re-frame's state management revolves around pure functions and declarative subscriptions, it is well-suited for testing. Unit tests can focus on verifying that event handlers produce the expected state changes, while integration tests can ensure that components react appropriately to state updates. Tools such as `cljs.test` and `re-frame-testing` facilitate the creation of robust test suites, ensuring that the application behaves as intended and maintaining confidence in its correctness as it evolves.

By understanding and applying these principles, developers can effectively manage state in complex applications using Re-frame. The framework's design promotes a clear separation of concerns, immutability, and a declarative approach to side effects, all of which contribute to a scalable and maintainable codebase. As you continue to develop with Re-frame, these practices will help you create applications that are not only functional but also efficient and resilient.

CHAPTER 8: INTEGRATING JAVASCRIPT AND EXTERNAL LIBRARIES

ClojureScript's seamless interoperability with JavaScript is a powerful feature that enables developers to harness the vast ecosystem of JavaScript libraries and tools while working within a ClojureScript environment. This integration opens up a wide range of possibilities, from using established libraries to creating custom wrappers that fit neatly into the ClojureScript paradigm. Understanding how to effectively bridge these two languages will enhance your ability to build versatile and feature-rich applications.

To begin with, calling JavaScript functions from ClojureScript code involves leveraging the `js/` namespace, which provides access to global JavaScript objects and functions. For example, if you wish to use a JavaScript function such as `alert` in your ClojureScript code, you can do so directly:

```clojure
(js/alert "Hello from ClojureScript!")
```

In this simple example, `js/alert` references the JavaScript global `alert` function, and you can pass arguments to it just as you would in JavaScript. This direct invocation allows you to utilize JavaScript's built-in functions and APIs seamlessly within your ClojureScript code.

More complex interactions involve integrating with external JavaScript libraries. These libraries might not have ClojureScript bindings available, so you'll need to interact with them using JavaScript interop. Suppose you want to use a library like `lodash`, a popular utility library. First, you need to include the library in your project, typically via a package manager like npm. Once installed, you can access it in your ClojureScript code as follows:

```clojure
(ns my-app.core
  (:require [cljsjs.lodash]))

(defn example []
  (let [result (js/_.map [1 2 3] (str "Number: " %))]
    (println result)))
```

Here, `cljsjs.lodash` is a ClojureScript package that provides bindings to the `lodash` library. The `js/_.map` function is used to apply a transformation to an array, demonstrating how you can call JavaScript library functions within ClojureScript code.

Creating ClojureScript wrappers for JavaScript libraries involves encapsulating JavaScript functionality within idiomatic ClojureScript constructs. This practice enhances readability and maintains consistency with ClojureScript's functional programming style. For instance, consider wrapping a JavaScript library that performs complex data manipulations. You might create a namespace that provides a more ClojureScript-friendly API:

```clojure
```

```
(ns my-app.utils
  (:require [cljsjs.lodash]))

(defn map-data [coll f]
  (js/_.map coll (fn [x] (f x))))
```

In this example, `map-data` is a ClojureScript function that wraps the `lodash` `map` function. It provides a more idiomatic way to use the library's functionality, leveraging ClojureScript's higher-order functions.

Handling asynchronous operations from JavaScript libraries requires careful management to ensure that ClojureScript's functional and immutable principles are preserved. JavaScript's promise-based APIs can be integrated into ClojureScript using `js/Promise` or by utilizing libraries such as `cljs-ajax` for HTTP requests. For instance, to work with a promise returned by a JavaScript function, you can use ClojureScript's core.async library to handle asynchronous results:

```clojure
(ns my-app.core
  (:require [cljs.core.async :refer [<! >! chan timeout]]
            [cljsjs.jquery]))

(defn fetch-data [url]
  (let [result-chan (chan)]
    (.get js/$ url
      (fn [data]
        (go (>! result-chan data))))
    result-chan))
```

In this code, `js/$` represents jQuery's `get` function, which performs an HTTP request. The response is captured in a core.async channel, allowing you to work with the result in a non-blocking manner that aligns with ClojureScript's concurrency model.

Interop considerations also include handling JavaScript exceptions and ensuring that errors are managed effectively. JavaScript exceptions can propagate into your ClojureScript code, so it's essential to wrap potentially error-prone JavaScript calls with appropriate error handling constructs:

```clojure
(ns my-app.core)

(defn safe-alert [message]
  (try
    (js/alert message)
    (catch js/Error e
      (println "An error occurred:" (.message e)))))
```

Here, the `try` and `catch` blocks are used to catch and handle exceptions that may occur during the execution of the `js/alert` function. This approach helps maintain robustness and provides feedback when JavaScript interop introduces errors.

Integrating JavaScript and external libraries into ClojureScript projects extends the functionality of your applications while leveraging the strengths of both languages. By understanding and effectively using JavaScript interop, creating ClojureScript wrappers, and managing asynchronous operations and exceptions, you can build applications that are both powerful and idiomatic to ClojureScript's functional programming paradigm.

When integrating JavaScript libraries with ClojureScript, understanding the intricacies of JavaScript's event-driven nature is crucial for smooth interactions between the two languages. JavaScript libraries often rely on event-based mechanisms to handle user interactions, asynchronous operations, and other dynamic changes. To effectively use such libraries within a ClojureScript environment, we need to ensure that these events are managed in a way that aligns with ClojureScript's functional and immutable principles.

Consider a scenario where you are working with a JavaScript library that provides a widget with various events, such as clicks or data updates. To handle these events in ClojureScript, you might need to attach event listeners to the widget and define handlers that process these events. For instance, if you are using a library that emits events for user actions, you can set up event handlers like so:

```clojure
(ns my-app.core
 (:require [cljsjs.jquery]))

(defn setup-widget []
 (let [widget (js/$ ".widget")]
  (.on widget "click" (fn [event]
           (js/console.log "Widget clicked!")))))
```

In this example, the `js/$` function from jQuery is used to select a widget element, and the `.on` method attaches a click event handler. The handler function logs a message to the console when the widget is clicked. This approach demonstrates how you can interact with JavaScript's event system from ClojureScript.

Moreover, integrating JavaScript libraries often involves managing external state and ensuring that it interacts correctly with ClojureScript's immutable state management. For instance, if a JavaScript library maintains its own internal state, such as a UI component's properties, you need to synchronize this state with your ClojureScript application's state. This can be achieved by using ClojureScript's reactive paradigms or by explicitly updating your application's state in response to changes in the JavaScript library.

For example, if you are using a charting library that updates its internal state when data changes, you may need to periodically query this state and reflect it in your ClojureScript application:

```clojure
(ns my-app.core
 (:require [cljsjs.chartjs]))

(defn update-chart []
    (let [chart (js/Chart. (js/document.getElementById "myChart") js {:type "line" :data js {:labels ["January" "February"] :datasets js [{:data [10 20]}]}})]
  (.update chart)))
```

In this case, `js/Chart` is a constructor function from Chart.js, which initializes a chart with some data. To keep the chart updated with the latest data from your application, you would call the `.update` method on the chart instance. This approach ensures that the chart's state remains in sync with your application's data.

Handling asynchronous operations with JavaScript libraries requires careful coordination between ClojureScript's concurrency model and JavaScript's promise-based APIs. ClojureScript's `core.async` library provides a way to manage asynchronous code, and it integrates well with JavaScript promises. When dealing with libraries that return promises, you can convert these promises into channels and handle them asynchronously within your ClojureScript code.

Consider an example where you use a JavaScript library that performs an asynchronous operation and returns a promise. You can work with this promise using core.async to manage the asynchronous result:

```clojure
(ns my-app.core
  (:require [cljs.core.async :refer [<! >! chan]]
            [cljsjs.axios]))

(defn fetch-data [url]
  (let [result-chan (chan)]
    (.get js/axios url
      (fn [response]
        (go (>! result-chan (:data response)))))
    result-chan))
```

In this code, `js/axios` represents the Axios library for making HTTP requests. The `.get` method returns a promise, and once the request is completed, the result is sent to a core.async channel. This approach allows you to handle the result in a non-blocking manner and integrate it seamlessly with your ClojureScript application.

In addition to handling promises, managing errors and exceptions when working with JavaScript libraries is essential to ensure robustness and reliability. JavaScript exceptions can arise from various sources, including network failures, invalid inputs, or library bugs. To handle these exceptions effectively, you should wrap JavaScript function calls with appropriate error handling constructs.

For instance, if a JavaScript library function might throw an error, you can use ClojureScript's `try` and `catch` constructs to manage these exceptions:

```clojure
(ns my-app.core)

(defn safe-call [fn & args]
  (try
    (apply fn args)
```

```
  (catch js/Error e
    (js/console.error "An error occurred:" (.message e)))))
```

In this function, `safe-call` takes a JavaScript function and its arguments, applies the function, and catches any errors that may occur. This approach helps maintain application stability by providing a way to handle errors gracefully.

Finally, when creating ClojureScript wrappers for JavaScript libraries, it is important to design these wrappers in a way that respects ClojureScript's idioms while providing a seamless interface to the underlying JavaScript functionality. This might involve abstracting complex JavaScript APIs into simpler, more idiomatic ClojureScript functions or creating custom abstractions that fit well within the ClojureScript ecosystem.

By following these practices, you can effectively integrate JavaScript libraries into your ClojureScript projects, leveraging the rich set of tools available in the JavaScript ecosystem while maintaining a clean and functional ClojureScript codebase.

To fully harness the power of JavaScript libraries within ClojureScript, creating robust wrappers for these libraries can significantly enhance the integration process. Wrappers act as intermediaries between the JavaScript API and your ClojureScript code, translating JavaScript's imperative style into a more idiomatic functional style. This approach not only makes the libraries more accessible but also aligns them with ClojureScript's functional paradigms, enhancing readability and maintainability.

When constructing a ClojureScript wrapper for a JavaScript library, the first step is to ensure that the wrapper exposes functions in a way that fits naturally with ClojureScript's functional style. This often involves creating higher-level abstractions that encapsulate the complexity of the JavaScript

API, allowing you to work with a more intuitive and cohesive set of functions.

For instance, if you are wrapping a JavaScript library that handles complex data manipulations, such as a charting library, you might provide a set of ClojureScript functions that abstract away the library's configuration details. Consider the following example of creating a wrapper for a charting library:

```clojure
(ns my-app.chart
 (:require [cljsjs.chartjs]))

(defn create-line-chart [element-id data-options]
 (let [ctx (js/document.getElementById element-id)]
  (js/Chart. ctx (clj->js data-options))))
```

In this example, the `create-line-chart` function abstracts the instantiation of a Chart.js chart. The function takes an element ID and data options, converts the data options from ClojureScript data structures to JavaScript objects using `clj->js`, and then creates the chart. This wrapper simplifies the chart creation process, allowing users to focus on specifying the chart's data and options without dealing directly with the JavaScript API's intricacies.

Handling state synchronization between ClojureScript and JavaScript libraries is another critical aspect of integration. JavaScript libraries often manage their own state, which can be challenging to synchronize with the state maintained in your ClojureScript application. To address this, you can implement a mechanism to periodically synchronize or update the library's state based on changes in your application state.

Consider a scenario where you have a JavaScript library managing a UI component with its own state, such as a date picker. To keep this component's state in sync with your application's state, you might set up a function to update the component whenever your application's state changes:

```clojure
(ns my-app.date-picker
 (:require [cljsjs.jquery]
    [cljs.core.async :refer [put! chan]]))

(defn update-date-picker [element-id date]
 (let [picker (js/$ (str "" element-id))]
  (.setDate picker date)))
```

Here, the `update-date-picker` function updates the date picker's state by setting the date directly on the element. This ensures that any changes to your application's date state are reflected in the date picker. Synchronizing state like this helps maintain consistency between your application's data and the UI components managed by JavaScript libraries.

Managing asynchronous interactions between ClojureScript and JavaScript libraries is another area that requires attention. JavaScript libraries frequently use asynchronous methods, such as callbacks or promises, to handle operations like data loading or user interactions. Integrating these asynchronous operations with ClojureScript involves using core.async channels or similar constructs to manage the flow of data.

For example, when dealing with a JavaScript library that fetches data asynchronously, you can wrap the asynchronous function in a core.async channel to handle the data within ClojureScript:

```clojure
(ns my-app.data-fetch
 (:require [cljs.core.async :refer [chan >! <! go]]
    [cljsjs.axios]))

(defn fetch-data [url]
```

```clojure
(let [data-chan (chan)]
  (.get js/axios url
    (fn [response]
      (go (>! data-chan (:data response)))))
  data-chan))
```

In this code, the `fetch-data` function uses the Axios library to perform an HTTP GET request. The response data is sent to a core.async channel, allowing you to work with the data asynchronously in ClojureScript. This integration pattern helps manage the complexity of asynchronous operations and aligns them with ClojureScript's concurrency model.

When integrating error handling between ClojureScript and JavaScript, it is essential to create robust mechanisms to handle errors that may arise from JavaScript operations. This involves wrapping JavaScript function calls with try-catch blocks and providing meaningful error messages or fallback mechanisms to handle issues gracefully.

For example, if you are using a JavaScript library to perform a critical operation, you can handle potential errors as follows:

```clojure
(ns my-app.error-handling
  (:require [cljsjs.some-library]))

(defn perform-operation [params]
  (try
    (js/someLibrary.performOperation (clj->js params))
    (catch js/Error e
      (js/console.error "Operation failed:" (.message e)))))
```

In this example, the `perform-operation` function calls a method from a hypothetical JavaScript library. If the operation fails, the error is caught and logged to the console, providing insight into what went wrong.

Lastly, performance considerations are crucial when integrating JavaScript libraries. Ensuring that library usage does not lead to performance bottlenecks involves careful profiling and optimization. JavaScript libraries can introduce overhead if not used efficiently, so it is important to monitor performance and optimize interactions as needed.

By implementing these strategies for wrapping JavaScript libraries, synchronizing state, managing asynchronous interactions, and handling errors, you can effectively integrate JavaScript libraries into your ClojureScript projects. This approach leverages the strengths of both languages, providing a powerful toolkit for building sophisticated web applications.

CHAPTER 9: ASYNCHRONOUS PROGRAMMING WITH CORE.ASYNC

In the realm of modern web development, managing asynchronous operations efficiently is pivotal for ensuring smooth and responsive user experiences. core.async is a powerful ClojureScript library designed to handle asynchronous programming and concurrency in a functional manner. By leveraging core.async, developers can manage complex workflows involving multiple asynchronous tasks with greater clarity and control.

core.async introduces two primary abstractions for managing concurrency: channels and go blocks. Channels act as communication conduits that facilitate the transfer of data between different parts of an application, while go blocks enable the execution of asynchronous code in a non-blocking manner. Understanding and effectively utilizing these abstractions can significantly streamline the process of handling asynchronous tasks.

At the core of core.async is the concept of channels. A channel is a first-class entity that allows for the safe and efficient exchange of data between different parts of a program. Channels in core.async are analogous to queues, where data can be placed in the channel and subsequently retrieved. Creating a channel is straightforward, and it serves as the fundamental building block for managing asynchronous communication.

For example, to create a channel and use it to pass data, you can utilize the `chan` function:

```clojure
(ns my-app.async
  (:require [cljs.core.async :refer [chan >! <! close! go]]))

(def my-channel (chan))

(go
 (>! my-channel "Hello, core.async!"))
```

In this snippet, `my-channel` is created using the `chan` function, and a value is put into the channel using the `>!` operation within a `go` block. The `go` block is a macro provided by core.async that allows you to write asynchronous code in a way that resembles synchronous code. By wrapping the asynchronous operation in a `go` block, you ensure that it runs asynchronously without blocking the execution of other code.

Retrieving data from a channel is done using the `<!` operation:

```clojure
(go
 (let [message (<! my-channel)]
   (println message)))
```

Here, the `<!` operation is used to take a value from the channel. The `go` block will pause and wait for a value to be available in the channel before continuing. This approach

simplifies the handling of asynchronous data retrieval, allowing you to focus on processing the data once it is available.

Handling multiple asynchronous tasks can be managed efficiently by combining channels with `go` blocks. For instance, if you need to perform several asynchronous operations and synchronize their results, you can use core.async's facilities to coordinate these tasks. Consider the following example where multiple asynchronous operations are run concurrently:

```clojure
(ns my-app.async
 (:require [cljs.core.async :refer [chan <! >! go]]))

(defn async-task [id]
 (let [c (chan)]
  (go
   (<! (js/setTimeout (>! c (str "Result from task " id)) 1000)))
  c))

(defn run-tasks []
 (let [task1 (async-task 1)
    task2 (async-task 2)]
  (go
   (println (<! task1))
   (println (<! task2)))))
```

In this example, `async-task` creates a channel that will eventually receive a result after a delay. The `run-tasks` function starts two such tasks concurrently and prints their results. Using `<!` within a `go` block, the program waits for both tasks to complete and then processes their results. This pattern allows you to handle multiple asynchronous tasks concurrently, coordinating their outcomes in a straightforward manner.

In addition to channels and go blocks, core.async provides constructs for composing and managing complex workflows. For instance, the `alts!` function allows you to wait on multiple channels simultaneously, processing whichever channel becomes ready first. This is useful for scenarios where you need to handle the result of the first available asynchronous operation among several:

```clojure
(ns my-app.async
  (:require [cljs.core.async :refer [chan alts! go]]))

(defn async-task [id]
  (let [c (chan)]
    (go
      (<! (js/setTimeout (>! c (str "Result from task " id)) 1000)))
    c))

(defn run-tasks []
  (let [task1 (async-task 1)
        task2 (async-task 2)]
    (go
      (let [[result _] (alts! [task1 task2])]
        (println result)))))
```

In this code, `alts!` waits for either `task1` or `task2` to provide a result. The function then prints the result of the first task to complete. This pattern is particularly useful for handling scenarios where multiple sources of data or events are involved, and you need to act upon the first available result.

Error handling in asynchronous workflows is another crucial aspect. core.async provides mechanisms for managing errors in asynchronous operations. One approach is to use channels to propagate error information alongside regular data. By including error handling logic within `go` blocks, you can ensure that errors are managed gracefully and do not disrupt the flow of your application.

Consider extending the previous examples to handle errors:

```clojure
(ns my-app.async
 (:require [cljs.core.async :refer [chan <! >! go]]))

(defn async-task [id]
 (let [c (chan)]
  (go
   (try
    (<! (js/setTimeout (>! c (str "Result from task " id)) 1000))
    (catch js/Error e
     (>! c (str "Error: " (.message e))))))
   c))

(defn run-tasks []
 (let [task1 (async-task 1)
    task2 (async-task 2)]
  (go
   (println (<! task1))
   (println (<! task2)))))
```

Here, `async-task` now includes a try-catch block to handle any potential errors that occur during the asynchronous operation. If an error is encountered, it is sent through the channel as an error message. This allows for effective error handling and reporting in your asynchronous workflows.

By mastering core.async, you can manage asynchronous operations in ClojureScript with greater ease, ensuring that your applications remain responsive and capable of handling complex workflows. The library's abstractions for channels and go blocks provide a powerful toolkit for addressing the challenges of asynchronous programming and concurrency in a functional programming environment.

In the realm of asynchronous programming, managing concurrency effectively is crucial for developing responsive and efficient applications. Core.async, a powerful library within the ClojureScript ecosystem, offers robust abstractions for handling asynchronous tasks. At the heart of core.async are channels and go blocks, which enable a clean and expressive approach to managing concurrency.

Channels in core.async act as conduits for communication between different parts of an application. They are akin to queues that facilitate the transfer of values between producers and consumers. Channels can be thought of as containers that hold messages, which are communicated between various threads of execution. The ability to create and manage channels effectively is central to leveraging core.async for asynchronous programming.

To create a channel in core.async, one uses the `chan` function. By default, channels are unbuffered, meaning that a value placed onto a channel by a producer will be immediately received by a consumer. However, channels can also be buffered by specifying a buffer size when creating the channel. Buffered channels allow for a predefined number of messages to be queued, which can help in scenarios where you need to decouple producers and consumers, enabling producers to continue their work without waiting for consumers to process the messages.

Once a channel is established, communication between different parts of the application is handled using the `>!` and `<!` operations. The `>!` operation is used to place a value onto a channel, while `<!` is used to take a value off the channel. These operations are blocking by default, meaning that they will wait until the operation can be completed. For example, if a producer tries to place a value onto an unbuffered channel, it will block until a consumer is ready to take that

value. Conversely, if a consumer tries to take a value from an empty channel, it will block until a producer places a value onto the channel.

To manage these operations without blocking the main thread of execution, core.async provides the `go` block. A `go` block is a lightweight construct that allows for asynchronous code to be written in a sequential style. Inside a `go` block, you can use the `<!` and `>!` operations to communicate with channels as if they were synchronous operations. This abstraction allows you to write asynchronous code that is easier to read and maintain.

Within a `go` block, the `<!` operation is used to take a value from a channel and suspend the execution of the `go` block until the value is available. Similarly, the `>!` operation is used to place a value onto a channel and then yield control until the value has been consumed. This approach to asynchronous programming ensures that the code remains sequential and comprehensible, even though it is inherently asynchronous.

Consider a scenario where you have a web application that needs to fetch data from multiple sources simultaneously. Using core.async, you can create a channel for each data source and use `go` blocks to manage the asynchronous fetching of data. For instance, you might use the `http/get` function from an HTTP library to fetch data from an API endpoint and place the result onto a channel. Simultaneously, another `go` block might fetch data from a different API endpoint and place that result onto a separate channel. Once the data is fetched, you can use another `go` block to process the results, taking values from the channels and combining them as needed.

The real power of core.async becomes apparent when dealing with more complex workflows. For example, consider a situation where you need to perform a series of asynchronous operations that depend on each other. Using `go` blocks and channels, you can chain these operations together in a way that maintains clarity and avoids the pitfalls of callback hell. Each operation can be represented by a separate `go` block, with channels used to pass data between the stages of the workflow. This allows you to compose complex asynchronous operations in a modular and maintainable fashion.

Error handling in core.async is also managed through channels and `go` blocks. If an error occurs during an asynchronous operation, it can be communicated through a channel designed specifically for error reporting. By having dedicated channels for errors, you can separate error handling logic from the main flow of data processing, resulting in cleaner and more manageable code.

Furthermore, core.async provides additional constructs such as `alts!` and `alts!!` for dealing with multiple channels simultaneously. These functions allow you to perform operations on multiple channels and handle whichever channel responds first. For example, you might use `alts!` to wait for a response from multiple API endpoints and process the result from the fastest response. This is particularly useful in scenarios where you need to implement timeouts or handle multiple asynchronous sources efficiently.

The combination of channels and `go` blocks in core.async allows for a high level of abstraction in asynchronous programming. By managing concurrency with these constructs, you can develop applications that are both performant and maintainable. The sequential style of writing asynchronous code within `go` blocks enhances readability and simplifies the handling of complex asynchronous workflows.

In conclusion, core.async provides a sophisticated and expressive framework for managing asynchronous programming in ClojureScript. Channels serve as the primary mechanism for communication between different parts of an application, while `go` blocks offer a way to write asynchronous code in a sequential style. The ability to buffer channels, handle errors, and work with multiple channels simultaneously makes core.async a versatile tool for developing modern web applications. By leveraging these constructs, you can create responsive and efficient applications that handle asynchronous operations with ease.

To further delve into the capabilities of core.async, it is essential to explore how it integrates with existing ClojureScript constructs and external libraries, enhancing its utility in real-world applications. One significant aspect of core.async is its ability to work seamlessly with other asynchronous libraries and frameworks, providing a coherent approach to managing concurrency.

In ClojureScript, core.async is often used alongside promises, another common construct for handling asynchronous operations. Promises represent a value that may be available now, in the future, or never. They provide a way to manage operations that are asynchronous in nature but might not be natively supported by core.async channels. To integrate promises with core.async, one can use the `promise` function to convert a promise into a channel. This conversion allows the promise to be utilized within the core.async ecosystem, enabling a unified approach to asynchronous programming.

The `promise` function creates a channel that will receive the result of the promise when it is fulfilled. By using this function, one can seamlessly interoperate between promise-based and channel-based asynchronous operations. For instance, if you have a promise that resolves with data from a third-party API, you can convert this promise into a channel and use it within a `go` block to process the data alongside other asynchronous operations.

Additionally, core.async supports the concept of "alts"

operations, which are crucial for managing multiple channels and handling scenarios where you need to respond to whichever channel becomes available first. The `alts!` function allows you to wait for a message from multiple channels and provides the flexibility to handle the fastest response. This is particularly useful in situations where you have multiple potential sources of data and need to process whichever one arrives first. For example, you might use `alts!` to implement a timeout mechanism, where you listen on a channel for a response and another channel for a timeout signal. If the response arrives first, it gets processed; if the timeout occurs, you handle the timeout accordingly.

Core.async also provides mechanisms for dealing with complex channel operations such as combining channels and orchestrating complex workflows. The `pipeline` function is one such mechanism that allows for processing data through a series of stages. Each stage in the pipeline can be represented by a channel or a function that transforms the data. This approach enables a functional and declarative style of handling asynchronous data flows. For instance, you could create a pipeline where data is fetched from an API, transformed, and then filtered before being presented to the user. Each stage in this pipeline can be implemented using channels and `go` blocks, ensuring that the entire process remains manageable and understandable.

Error handling and recovery in core.async are also sophisticated. Channels can be used to communicate error messages, which allows for a clean separation of error handling from the main data processing flow. For example, if a `go` block encounters an exception, it can place an error message onto an error channel. This error channel can then be monitored separately, allowing for dedicated error-handling logic to process any issues that arise. This separation ensures that error handling does not interfere with the normal flow of data and helps maintain a clear and robust application architecture.

Another important aspect of core.async is its support for "taking" values from channels with timeouts. The `timeout` function creates a channel that closes after a specified duration, which can be used to implement timeout logic within `go` blocks. For instance, you might use a timeout channel to enforce a maximum wait time for a response from an external service. If the response does not arrive within the allotted time, the `go` block can handle the timeout case appropriately, such as by retrying the operation or notifying the user.

Core.async's support for concurrency extends beyond simple channel communication. The library provides advanced concurrency constructs such as "async" and "thread" functions, which facilitate concurrent execution of code. The `async` function allows for asynchronous execution of a function without blocking the main thread, while the `thread` function creates a new thread of execution. These constructs can be used in conjunction with channels and `go` blocks to build highly concurrent and responsive applications.

In practice, integrating core.async with external libraries and frameworks requires an understanding of how these tools interact and complement each other. For example, when working with external APIs or databases, you might use core.async channels to handle the results of asynchronous queries. By leveraging channels to manage the flow of data between different components of your application, you can create a cohesive and efficient system that handles complex asynchronous operations with ease.

Moreover, core.async's integration with ClojureScript's functional programming paradigm enhances its effectiveness. Functional programming principles, such as immutability and pure functions, align well with the channel-based model of core.async. By applying these principles, you can design asynchronous workflows that are both reliable and easy to reason about. The use of immutable data structures and pure functions ensures that the state remains consistent and that side effects are minimized, leading to more predictable and maintainable code.

In summary, core.async provides a powerful and flexible framework for managing asynchronous programming in ClojureScript. Its integration with promises, support for advanced concurrency constructs, and ability to handle complex workflows through channels and `go` blocks make it an essential tool for developing modern web applications. By leveraging core.async's capabilities, you can create applications that are responsive, efficient, and maintainable, effectively handling asynchronous tasks and concurrency with clarity and precision.

CHAPTER 10: TESTING CLOJURESCRIPT CODE

Testing is a fundamental aspect of software development that ensures the reliability and correctness of applications. In ClojureScript, the approach to testing is influenced by the functional programming paradigm and the language's immutable nature. This chapter delves into the best practices for testing ClojureScript code, encompassing unit tests, integration tests, and end-to-end tests. I will also introduce popular testing frameworks and tools, and demonstrate how to write effective tests to identify bugs and verify functionality.

Unit testing forms the backbone of a robust testing strategy. It involves testing individual components or functions in isolation to ensure they perform as expected. In ClojureScript, unit tests are typically written using frameworks such as `cljs.test`, which provides a comprehensive set of assertions and test utilities. Writing unit tests in ClojureScript is straightforward, thanks to the language's support for functional programming and immutability, which simplifies testing individual functions and their outputs.

To begin with, unit tests are written in ClojureScript files, often located in a `test` directory parallel to the `src` directory. Each test file corresponds to a specific module or feature of the application. The `cljs.test` namespace is imported to facilitate the creation of test cases. Tests are defined using the `deftest` macro, and assertions are made using functions like `is` and `testing`. The `deftest` macro allows you to group related tests together, while the `is` function is used to assert expected outcomes.

For instance, consider a simple function that adds two numbers. To test this function, you would define a test case that checks whether the function correctly computes the sum of various pairs of numbers. Each test case should cover a range of scenarios, including typical inputs, edge cases, and invalid inputs. This comprehensive approach ensures that the function behaves as expected in different situations. By running these unit tests regularly, you can catch regressions and verify that code changes do not introduce new bugs.

Integration testing takes a broader perspective by evaluating the interaction between multiple components or modules within an application. Unlike unit tests, which focus on isolated functions, integration tests ensure that the components work together harmoniously. In ClojureScript, integration tests can be written using the same `cljs.test` framework or other libraries that provide additional features.

When performing integration tests, it's important to set up a test environment that closely mirrors the production environment. This includes configuring dependencies, setting up necessary data, and simulating real-world scenarios. For example, if your application interacts with an external API, an integration test might involve sending requests to the API and verifying that the responses are handled correctly by your application. This type of test helps ensure that different parts of the application function together as intended.

End-to-end testing, also known as functional or acceptance testing, provides a comprehensive evaluation of an application from the user's perspective. This testing type involves testing the entire application flow, from the user interface to the backend services, to ensure that the system as a whole performs as expected. End-to-end tests often require a more extensive setup and may involve tools designed specifically for browser automation and interaction.

In ClojureScript, end-to-end testing can be performed using tools such as Selenium or Cucumber. Selenium is a popular choice for automating web browsers and simulating user interactions, while Cucumber allows you to write tests in a natural language format, which can be particularly useful for collaboration with non-technical stakeholders. By writing end-to-end tests, you can validate that the application meets user requirements and performs correctly under various conditions.

When writing tests, it's essential to adhere to best practices to ensure their effectiveness and maintainability. Tests should be written with clarity and precision, focusing on a single aspect of functionality at a time. It's also crucial to ensure that tests are independent of one another, meaning that the outcome of one test should not affect others. This independence is vital for reliable test results and efficient debugging.

Additionally, tests should be designed to run quickly and provide meaningful feedback. Slow-running tests can hinder the development process and reduce productivity. By structuring tests to be fast and efficient, you can integrate them into your continuous integration and deployment pipelines, allowing for automated testing and early detection of issues.

Another best practice is to use descriptive test names and messages. Clear and informative names make it easier to understand the purpose of each test and quickly identify failing tests. Test messages should provide context and detail about the failure, helping to pinpoint the root cause of issues.

In conclusion, testing is a crucial aspect of ensuring the reliability and correctness of ClojureScript applications. By employing unit tests, integration tests, and end-to-end tests, you can create a comprehensive testing strategy that covers different aspects of your application. Leveraging frameworks such as `cljs.test` and tools for browser automation will enable you to write effective tests that catch bugs and verify functionality. Adhering to best practices in test design and execution will help maintain a robust and reliable codebase, ultimately leading to higher-quality applications.

Testing ClojureScript code involves more than just writing individual test cases; it also requires an understanding of how to structure your tests and integrate them into your development workflow. As we continue exploring testing strategies, it's crucial to delve deeper into the integration of testing frameworks and the practices that enhance the efficiency and effectiveness of your tests.

In ClojureScript, `cljs.test` is a foundational testing framework, but it often works in tandem with other tools to provide a more comprehensive testing environment. For instance, when testing asynchronous code or dealing with side effects, it's helpful to use tools like `cljs.test` alongside mocking libraries. Mocking allows you to simulate the behavior of complex components or external services, which can be crucial when testing parts of your application that interact with APIs, databases, or other systems.

Mocking in ClojureScript can be achieved using libraries such as `cljs-mock`. This library provides a way to create mock objects that simulate the behavior of real components, allowing you to control their responses and verify interactions. By incorporating mocking into your tests, you can isolate the code under test, ensuring that your tests focus on the logic you intend to validate without being affected by external dependencies. For example, if your application relies on a third-party service for data, you can mock this service to test how your application handles various responses, including success, failure, and edge cases.

Moreover, integrating testing frameworks into your development workflow is essential for maintaining code quality. Continuous integration (CI) systems play a significant role in automating the testing process. Tools like Jenkins, CircleCI, or GitHub Actions can be configured to run your tests automatically whenever changes are made to the codebase. This continuous testing approach ensures that issues are detected early, reducing the likelihood of bugs making it into production. By setting up CI pipelines to include running unit, integration, and end-to-end tests, you create a robust safety net that supports a high level of code quality and reliability.

Test-driven development (TDD) is another practice that complements the testing strategy in ClojureScript. TDD involves writing tests before implementing the actual code. This approach helps define the expected behavior of your code upfront and ensures that your implementation meets these requirements. By adopting TDD, you can create a clear specification for each piece of functionality and incrementally build your application while ensuring that it behaves as expected. This iterative process of writing tests, implementing code, and refactoring encourages better design and helps catch issues early in the development cycle.

When dealing with ClojureScript's unique features, such as its use of immutable data structures and functional programming paradigms, testing practices can be adapted to leverage these strengths. For instance, testing functions that operate on immutable data structures often involves verifying that the function returns the expected result without modifying the input data. This approach aligns with the principles of functional programming, where functions are expected to be pure and free of side effects.

In addition to functional testing, performance testing can also be a critical aspect of ensuring your ClojureScript application operates efficiently. Performance tests focus on evaluating how well your application handles various loads and scenarios, such as large datasets or high-frequency requests. Tools like `lein-cljsbuild` can be used to compile ClojureScript code with optimizations that affect performance. By incorporating performance testing into your workflow, you can identify and address bottlenecks or inefficiencies before they impact end users.

Furthermore, testing user interfaces in ClojureScript applications often involves using tools designed for browser automation. Libraries such as `Karma` and `Jest` can be integrated with ClojureScript to facilitate end-to-end testing of UI components. These tools allow you to simulate user interactions and verify that the UI behaves as expected. Testing UI components involves checking elements like buttons, forms, and dynamic content to ensure they render correctly and respond to user input as intended.

To effectively manage the testing process, consider organizing your test suite into logical groups and maintaining clear separation between different types of tests. Unit tests should focus on individual components or functions, integration tests should evaluate interactions between components, and end-to-end tests should validate the complete application flow. By structuring your tests in this manner, you can ensure that each aspect of your application is thoroughly tested and that test results provide meaningful feedback on the application's overall functionality.

Finally, it is important to regularly review and update your tests as your application evolves. As new features are added or existing features are modified, corresponding tests should be updated to reflect these changes. This ongoing maintenance of your test suite helps ensure that your tests remain relevant and continue to provide accurate validation of your application's behavior.

By integrating robust testing practices, utilizing appropriate frameworks and tools, and adopting methodologies like TDD, you can enhance the reliability and quality of your ClojureScript applications. Effective testing not only helps catch bugs early but also supports the development of well-structured and maintainable code, ultimately leading to more successful and resilient applications.

In the realm of ClojureScript testing, the concept of code coverage is pivotal in ensuring that your tests are thorough and that all relevant parts of your codebase are exercised. Code coverage measures how much of your code is executed when your tests run, providing insights into which parts of your code are tested and which remain untested. Achieving high code coverage is not merely a matter of increasing the percentage of covered lines; it involves ensuring that all critical paths and edge cases are tested.

To assess code coverage in ClojureScript, you can use tools such as `lein-cloverage`, which integrates with Leiningen to provide coverage metrics. This tool analyzes your test runs and produces a report indicating which lines of code were executed during testing. By examining these reports, you can identify areas of your code that are not sufficiently tested and make necessary adjustments. For instance, if a particular function or branch in your application remains untested, you can create additional test cases to address these gaps, thereby improving the robustness of your test suite.

When crafting test cases, it is essential to focus not only on the positive paths but also on potential failure scenarios. This practice ensures that your application can handle erroneous inputs or unexpected conditions gracefully. Testing for edge cases involves considering scenarios that may not be common but could potentially expose vulnerabilities or flaws in your code. For example, if your function processes user input, testing should include cases with invalid or malformed data, ensuring that your application can manage such situations without crashing or producing incorrect results.

Another critical aspect of testing in ClojureScript is the use of property-based testing, which involves defining properties that should hold true for a range of inputs rather than specifying individual test cases. Libraries such as `clojure.test.check` support property-based testing and allow you to specify invariants that your code should satisfy. This approach can be particularly effective for verifying the correctness of functions with complex input domains or those involving combinatorial logic. By generating a wide range of input values, property-based testing helps uncover corner cases and unexpected behaviors that might be missed with traditional example-based tests.

Additionally, testing asynchronous code in ClojureScript presents its own set of challenges. Asynchronous operations, such as API calls or timeouts, require careful handling to ensure that tests do not complete before asynchronous tasks have finished. Tools like `cljs.test` provide facilities for working with asynchronous code, including mechanisms to wait for promises to resolve and to handle asynchronous assertions. It's important to structure your tests to account for the asynchronous nature of the code being tested, ensuring that your assertions are executed only after the asynchronous operations have completed.

Mocking and stubbing external dependencies is another technique that can enhance the effectiveness of your tests. By replacing real dependencies with mock implementations, you can isolate the code under test and control its interactions with external systems. This approach is particularly useful for testing components that rely on external services, such as databases or web APIs. Mocking libraries in ClojureScript, such as `cljs-mock`, allow you to define mock responses and verify that your code interacts with these dependencies as expected. This isolation simplifies the testing process and makes it easier to verify the behavior of individual components.

Incorporating best practices for test organization and maintenance is essential for managing a large test suite. Organizing tests into meaningful groups and maintaining a clear structure helps keep the test suite manageable and facilitates easier debugging. Grouping related tests and using descriptive names for test cases provide clarity on what each test is verifying and helps identify issues more efficiently. Additionally, regularly reviewing and updating tests as the codebase evolves ensures that tests remain relevant and continue to provide accurate validation of your application's behavior.

Continuous integration (CI) systems play a vital role in automating the testing process and ensuring that tests are run consistently throughout the development lifecycle. Integrating your testing framework with a CI system allows for automated test execution on code commits and pull requests. This integration helps catch issues early in the development process and ensures that your application remains reliable as changes are made. CI tools can be configured to run unit tests, integration tests, and end-to-end tests, providing a comprehensive validation of your codebase with each change.

Performance testing is another aspect that should not be overlooked. As applications scale, performance considerations become critical to ensure that the application remains responsive and efficient under varying loads. Performance testing involves evaluating how well your application handles different levels of stress and identifying potential bottlenecks or areas for optimization. Tools such as `lein-bench` can be used to benchmark performance and identify areas where improvements are needed. By incorporating performance testing into your overall testing strategy, you can ensure that your application meets performance expectations and provides a smooth user experience.

In conclusion, effective testing in ClojureScript encompasses a range of practices, from writing thorough unit tests and integration tests to utilizing property-based testing and handling asynchronous operations. By employing tools for code coverage, mocking, and performance testing, you can create a comprehensive testing strategy that ensures the reliability and correctness of your application. Integrating these practices into your development workflow, supported by continuous integration systems, contributes to maintaining high-quality code and delivering robust applications.

CHAPTER 11: PERFORMANCE OPTIMIZATION

In the realm of web development, performance optimization is paramount to delivering applications that are not only functional but also efficient and responsive. Optimizing ClojureScript applications involves a multi-faceted approach that addresses various aspects of performance, including code splitting, lazy loading, and minimizing JavaScript bundle sizes. By employing these strategies and continuously profiling and refining your code, you can enhance the speed and responsiveness of your web applications.

The first strategy for optimizing performance is code splitting. This technique involves dividing your application's code into smaller, manageable chunks that can be loaded on demand rather than loading the entire application upfront. Code splitting improves the initial load time by ensuring that only the essential code required for the initial render is loaded first. This approach can significantly reduce the time to first meaningful paint, which is crucial for providing a smooth user experience. In ClojureScript, code splitting can be achieved using tools like the ClojureScript compiler and build systems such as Leiningen or Shadow CLJS. By configuring your build process to generate separate JavaScript bundles for different parts of your application, you can implement lazy loading and load additional code only when needed.

Lazy loading is closely related to code splitting and involves deferring the loading of non-essential resources until they are actually required. This technique is particularly useful for loading components or modules that are not immediately needed, such as those within a user interface that appears only after a specific user action. In ClojureScript, lazy loading can be implemented using dynamic imports and asynchronous module loading. By leveraging these features, you can ensure that your application loads faster and performs better by avoiding the overhead of loading unnecessary code upfront. This approach not only enhances the initial load time but also optimizes runtime performance by reducing the amount of code that needs to be parsed and executed at any given moment.

Minimizing JavaScript bundle sizes is another crucial aspect of performance optimization. Large bundle sizes can lead to longer download times and increased memory usage, which can adversely affect the performance of your application. To address this issue, it is essential to use techniques such as minification and tree shaking. Minification involves removing unnecessary characters from your code, such as whitespace and comments, to reduce the overall size of your JavaScript files. Tree shaking, on the other hand, involves eliminating unused code from your bundles. By analyzing your codebase and identifying portions of code that are not utilized, tree shaking helps reduce the size of your bundles and improve loading times. Tools like `uglify-js` and `terser` can be employed to perform minification, while modern build tools like Webpack and Rollup support tree shaking as part of their optimization processes.

Profiling your application is an essential step in performance optimization. Profiling involves analyzing your application's performance to identify bottlenecks and areas for improvement. ClojureScript provides various tools and techniques for profiling, including built-in browser developer tools and external profiling libraries. Browser developer tools, such as Chrome DevTools, offer features like the Performance panel and Memory panel to analyze your application's runtime behavior and memory usage. By capturing performance snapshots and examining the execution time of different functions, you can pinpoint areas of your code that are causing performance issues. Additionally, tools like `cljs-devtools` can be used to integrate profiling capabilities into your ClojureScript development workflow, providing more granular insights into your application's performance.

Optimizing your application's performance also involves efficient data management and processing. Handling large datasets or performing complex computations can impact your application's responsiveness. Techniques such as data virtualization and memoization can help address these challenges. Data virtualization involves loading and rendering only a subset of data at a time, which reduces the amount of data that needs to be processed and displayed. Memoization, on the other hand, involves caching the results of expensive function calls to avoid redundant computations. By implementing these techniques, you can enhance the efficiency of data processing and improve the overall performance of your application.

Another important consideration for performance optimization is network efficiency. Minimizing network requests and optimizing the use of network resources can significantly impact your application's performance. Techniques such as request batching, caching, and efficient data serialization can help reduce the number of network requests and the size of data transmitted over the network. For instance, request batching involves grouping multiple network requests into a single request to reduce the number of round trips between the client and server. Caching frequently accessed data can further reduce the need for redundant network requests, leading to faster load times and improved performance. Efficient data serialization formats, such as JSON or Protocol Buffers, can also contribute to reducing the size of data transmitted and improving network efficiency.

In conclusion, optimizing ClojureScript applications involves a comprehensive approach that addresses various aspects of performance, including code splitting, lazy loading, minimizing bundle sizes, and profiling. By implementing these strategies and continuously analyzing and refining your code, you can deliver web applications that are both fast and responsive. Employing techniques for efficient data management, network optimization, and utilizing profiling tools will further enhance the performance of your applications, ensuring a seamless user experience and meeting the demands of modern web users.

Optimizing performance in ClojureScript applications requires a detailed understanding of how different optimization strategies impact both the front-end and back-end of your application. This discussion extends into the realm of effective memory management and minimizing rendering times, both of which are critical for maintaining high performance in dynamic web applications.

Effective memory management is crucial for ensuring that applications run efficiently without consuming excessive resources. One of the first steps in managing memory effectively is to understand the lifecycle of data within your application. Objects and data structures that are no longer needed should be explicitly dereferenced to allow the garbage collector to reclaim memory. In ClojureScript, this involves making use of weak references and ensuring that data structures do not unintentionally hold onto references that prevent garbage collection. Regular profiling of memory usage can help identify memory leaks or excessive memory consumption, allowing for targeted optimizations.

Another key aspect of performance optimization is minimizing rendering times. Rendering performance can often become a bottleneck, especially in applications with complex user interfaces or frequent updates. To address this, it is important to minimize unnecessary re-renders and efficiently manage updates to the user interface. One effective technique is to use virtual DOM implementations, which can optimize the rendering process by minimizing direct manipulations of the actual DOM. By leveraging libraries or frameworks that support virtual DOM, such as Reagent or Rum, you can ensure that updates are applied in an efficient manner, reducing the overhead associated with frequent DOM manipulations.

In addition to virtual DOM optimizations, it is important to consider how data is updated and rendered within your application. Efficient use of immutable data structures can help prevent unnecessary re-renders by ensuring that changes to data result in new data structures rather than mutating existing ones. This immutability can be particularly beneficial when working with components that rely on data to determine their rendering. By leveraging ClojureScript's persistent data structures, you can ensure that only the necessary changes are propagated through your application, leading to more efficient rendering and better performance.

Performance optimization also extends to optimizing network interactions. Web applications often rely on data fetched from remote servers, and optimizing these interactions can have a significant impact on overall performance. Techniques such as request debouncing, where multiple rapid requests are consolidated into a single request, can help reduce the load on your server and improve responsiveness. Additionally, optimizing API interactions by minimizing payload sizes and using efficient data formats can reduce the time spent waiting for data to be transferred over the network.

Caching is another important strategy for optimizing network performance. By storing frequently accessed data locally, you can reduce the need for repeated network requests, leading to faster load times and a more responsive application. Caching strategies can include in-memory caching, where data is stored in the client's memory, as well as persistent caching mechanisms, where data is stored on disk or in local storage. Implementing effective cache invalidation policies is also crucial to ensure that cached data remains accurate and up-to-date.

Furthermore, optimizing asynchronous operations is essential for maintaining a responsive user experience. Asynchronous operations, such as fetching data from APIs or performing background computations, should be managed efficiently to avoid blocking the main thread. Techniques such as using Web Workers for background tasks or employing asynchronous programming patterns can help ensure that these operations do not negatively impact the performance of your application's user interface.

Finally, it is important to continuously monitor and refine your application's performance. Performance optimization is not a one-time task but an ongoing process that involves regular profiling, testing, and iteration. By using profiling tools to analyze your application's performance and identify potential bottlenecks, you can make informed decisions about where to focus your optimization efforts. Continuous integration and deployment practices can also help ensure that performance optimizations are consistently applied throughout the development lifecycle, resulting in a more stable and performant application.

In summary, optimizing ClojureScript applications involves a comprehensive approach that addresses various aspects of performance, including memory management, rendering times, network interactions, and asynchronous operations. By implementing effective strategies and continuously monitoring and refining your application, you can achieve a high level of performance and deliver a seamless user experience. Understanding and applying these techniques will enable you to create web applications that are both efficient and responsive, meeting the demands of modern web users and providing a high-quality experience.

To achieve effective performance optimization in ClojureScript applications, it is essential to delve into advanced techniques such as code splitting and lazy loading. These methods play a crucial role in managing large-scale applications, ensuring that only the necessary code is loaded and executed, thereby improving both initial load times and overall performance.

Code splitting is a technique that divides your application's code into smaller, more manageable chunks that can be loaded on demand. This approach is particularly beneficial for applications with a large codebase, as it reduces the amount of code that needs to be parsed and executed during the initial load. By leveraging code splitting, you can ensure that users are only downloading the code they need for the current view or functionality, rather than the entire application.

In ClojureScript, code splitting can be implemented using various tools and techniques. One effective approach is to use the `cljs.loader` library, which allows for dynamic loading of ClojureScript namespaces. By configuring your build process to generate separate JavaScript files for different parts of your application, you can load these files only when they are required. This technique not only reduces the initial payload size but also improves the application's responsiveness by deferring the loading of non-essential code.

Another critical optimization strategy is lazy loading, which involves loading resources only when they are needed. This technique can be applied to both code and data. For instance, instead of loading all components or routes upfront, you can configure your application to load these elements only when the user navigates to a specific part of the application. Lazy loading is particularly effective in reducing the time it takes for an application to become interactive, as it ensures that only the minimal necessary resources are loaded initially.

Implementing lazy loading in a ClojureScript application involves using asynchronous functions to load resources on demand. This can be achieved through mechanisms such as JavaScript's `import()` function, which allows for dynamic imports of modules. By wrapping these imports in asynchronous functions, you can control when and how different parts of your application are loaded, optimizing both performance and user experience.

Minimizing JavaScript bundle sizes is another key aspect of performance optimization. Large bundles can significantly impact loading times and overall application performance. To address this, it is essential to analyze and reduce the size of your JavaScript bundles. This can be accomplished through techniques such as tree shaking, which removes unused code from your bundles, and minification, which reduces the size of your code by removing unnecessary characters and whitespace.

Tree shaking is particularly useful for eliminating dead code from your application. By leveraging tools such as Webpack or Rollup, you can analyze your codebase and identify which parts of the code are not used. These tools then remove the unused code during the build process, resulting in smaller, more efficient bundles. Additionally, minification tools can further reduce bundle sizes by compressing the remaining code, making it faster to download and parse.

Another aspect of optimizing JavaScript bundle sizes involves modularizing your code. By breaking your application into smaller, self-contained modules, you can ensure that only the necessary code is included in each bundle. This modularization not only helps with code splitting but also makes it easier to manage and maintain your application. Each module can be developed, tested, and optimized independently, leading to a more streamlined and efficient codebase.

Profiling is a critical component of performance optimization, as it allows you to identify performance bottlenecks and areas for improvement. Profiling tools help you analyze various aspects of your application's performance, such as CPU usage, memory consumption, and rendering times. By using these tools, you can gain insights into how your application performs under different conditions and make informed decisions about where to focus your optimization efforts.

In ClojureScript, you can use browser-based profiling tools, such as Chrome DevTools, to analyze your application's performance. These tools provide detailed information about your application's execution, including call stacks, memory usage, and network activity. By examining this data, you can identify slow functions, memory leaks, and other performance issues that may impact your application's responsiveness.

Once performance issues have been identified, it is essential to implement targeted optimizations to address them. This may involve refactoring code, optimizing algorithms, or adjusting resource loading strategies. By continuously monitoring and refining your application's performance, you can ensure that it remains responsive and efficient, even as it evolves and grows.

In summary, optimizing ClojureScript applications involves a multifaceted approach that includes code splitting, lazy loading, minimizing JavaScript bundle sizes, and profiling. By applying these techniques and continuously monitoring your application's performance, you can deliver fast and responsive web applications that provide an optimal user experience. Understanding and implementing these strategies will enable you to create high-performance applications that meet the demands of modern web users and maintain a seamless, efficient user experience.

CHAPTER 12: ADVANCED CLOJURESCRIPT FEATURES

In ClojureScript, advanced features such as macros, multimethods, and protocols offer powerful tools for extending the language and achieving high levels of flexibility and code reuse. By understanding and leveraging these features, you can enhance the expressiveness and maintainability of your code, making it possible to create sophisticated abstractions and domain-specific languages tailored to your needs.

Macros are one of the most distinctive and powerful features in ClojureScript. They provide a way to extend the language by allowing you to write code that generates other code. This capability can be harnessed to create domain-specific languages (DSLs) or to simplify complex coding patterns, making your code more concise and expressive. Unlike functions, which operate on values, macros operate on code itself. This allows them to manipulate and transform code before it is evaluated, offering a level of abstraction that functions alone cannot provide.

The fundamental concept behind macros is that they take ClojureScript code as input, transform it, and produce new code as output. This transformation occurs at compile time, allowing you to write more abstract and reusable code. For example, you might use a macro to create a new syntactic construct that simplifies repetitive patterns or to implement new control structures that align with the specific needs of your application.

To illustrate the use of macros, consider a scenario where you frequently need to log function calls with specific formatting. Instead of writing repetitive logging code throughout your application, you can define a macro that automatically inserts the logging statements wherever needed. This macro would take a function definition, wrap it with logging code, and generate the new function with the desired logging behavior.

In addition to macros, ClojureScript provides multi-methods and protocols as mechanisms for achieving polymorphism and flexibility in your code. Multi-methods allow you to define a single function with multiple implementations based on the types of its arguments. This approach enables you to write more modular and extensible code, as you can easily add new implementations without modifying the existing ones.

A multi-method consists of a dispatch function and multiple method implementations. The dispatch function determines which method to invoke based on the types of the arguments passed to the multi-method. Each implementation is defined for a specific set of argument types, allowing for a flexible and extensible approach to handling different scenarios.

For instance, consider a situation where you need to perform different operations based on the type of data being processed. Using multi-methods, you can define a single function that dispatches to different implementations depending on whether the data is a string, number, or collection. This approach simplifies the code by centralizing the dispatch logic and separating the specific operations into individual implementations.

Protocols, on the other hand, provide a way to define a set of methods that can be implemented by various data types. A protocol specifies a collection of method signatures, while individual data types provide implementations for these methods. This mechanism allows you to define behavior that can be shared across different data types, promoting code reuse and flexibility.

Protocols are particularly useful for defining common interfaces that can be implemented by different types, enabling polymorphism and reducing the need for type-specific code. For example, you might define a protocol for serialization with methods for converting data to and from different formats. Various data types, such as strings, numbers, and custom objects, can then implement this protocol to provide their own serialization logic.

The interaction between macros, multi-methods, and protocols can lead to highly flexible and expressive code structures. For example, you might use macros to generate code that leverages multi-methods and protocols, creating sophisticated abstractions that simplify complex logic and enhance code maintainability. By combining these advanced features, you can build powerful domain-specific languages and abstractions that align with the specific requirements of your application.

In summary, the advanced features of ClojureScript—macros, multi-methods, and protocols—offer powerful tools for extending the language and achieving high levels of flexibility and code reuse. By understanding and leveraging these features, you can enhance the expressiveness and maintainability of your code, creating sophisticated abstractions and domain-specific languages tailored to your needs. These features enable you to write more modular, extensible, and maintainable code, making it possible to tackle complex programming challenges with greater ease and efficiency.

To fully appreciate the power of macros in ClojureScript, it is essential to understand the mechanisms behind their design and implementation. Macros operate at the syntax level, which means they work by transforming code before it is evaluated. This ability to manipulate code during the compilation phase provides a unique opportunity to create reusable and expressive abstractions. The process begins when a macro is invoked; it receives ClojureScript code as input, performs transformations, and outputs new code that integrates seamlessly into the program.

When creating a macro, it is crucial to be mindful of the scope and hygiene. Scope refers to the context within which the macro operates, and ensuring that the generated code does not inadvertently conflict with other code is vital. Hygiene involves ensuring that variable names within the macro do not clash with names in the surrounding code. ClojureScript handles this through a mechanism known as "hygienic macros," which automatically manages variable renaming to avoid name conflicts. This feature helps maintain clean and predictable code transformations.

To demonstrate the practical use of macros, consider a scenario where you need to enforce a set of validation rules across multiple functions. Instead of manually adding validation logic to each function, you can define a macro that wraps each function with the necessary validation checks. The macro would take a function definition, insert validation code, and output a new function that includes these checks. This approach not only reduces code duplication but also centralizes validation logic, making it easier to manage and update.

In addition to macros, multi-methods offer a sophisticated mechanism for dispatching function calls based on the types of arguments. Unlike traditional function overloading, where the function signature must match exactly, multi-methods allow for more flexible dispatching by using a dispatch function to determine which method implementation to execute. This dispatch function can be based on the type or value of the arguments, providing a dynamic and extensible approach to method selection.

For instance, suppose you are designing a system that processes different types of messages, such as text, images, and videos. Using multi-methods, you can define a single function, `process-message`, with multiple implementations tailored to each message type. The dispatch function would analyze the message type and route the call to the appropriate implementation. This approach simplifies the code by consolidating message processing into a single function while allowing for easy extension with new message types.

Protocols, on the other hand, provide a way to define a set of methods that various data types can implement. Unlike multi-methods, which use a dispatch function to select methods, protocols define a contract that data types must adhere to. This contract consists of method signatures that specify the expected behavior for each method. Data types that implement the protocol provide concrete implementations for these methods, enabling polymorphism and code reuse.

To illustrate the use of protocols, consider a scenario where you need to define a common interface for geometric shapes. You might define a protocol, `Shape`, with methods such as `area` and `perimeter`. Various shapes, such as circles, rectangles, and triangles, can then implement this protocol by providing their own implementations for `area` and `perimeter`. This design allows you to write functions that operate on any shape without needing to know the specific type of the shape, promoting code flexibility and extensibility.

The combination of macros, multi-methods, and protocols can lead to highly expressive and maintainable code. For example, you might use macros to generate code that leverages multi-methods and protocols, creating powerful abstractions that simplify complex logic. This approach allows you to build domain-specific languages and abstractions tailored to the specific needs of your application, enhancing both readability and maintainability.

When integrating these advanced features into your ClojureScript projects, it is important to balance their power with practicality. Macros should be used judiciously to avoid unnecessary complexity and to ensure that code transformations are clear and predictable. Multi-methods and protocols should be employed to promote modularity and code reuse, enabling you to write more flexible and maintainable code.

In summary, the advanced features of ClojureScript—macros, multi-methods, and protocols—provide powerful tools for extending the language and achieving high levels of flexibility and expressiveness. By understanding and leveraging these features, you can enhance the maintainability and sophistication of your code, creating abstractions and domain-specific languages that address complex programming challenges. These features enable you to write modular, reusable, and extensible code, making it possible to tackle a wide range of programming tasks with greater ease and efficiency.

To further explore the advanced capabilities of ClojureScript, it is important to delve into the practical aspects of using macros, multi-methods, and protocols in real-world scenarios. By understanding how these features can be applied effectively, we can harness their full potential to create sophisticated and maintainable code.

One of the key benefits of macros is their ability to introduce new syntactic constructs into the language. This can be particularly useful when building domain-specific languages (DSLs) or when you need to encapsulate complex patterns of code. For example, consider a scenario where you need to create a DSL for defining mathematical expressions. Using macros, you can define a set of functions that allow for a more natural and expressive way to write these expressions. The macro can transform these expressions into more standard ClojureScript code that performs the necessary computations. This approach not only simplifies the syntax but also enhances code readability and maintainability.

Another practical application of macros is in the generation of boilerplate code. Often, certain patterns of code are repeated across multiple parts of an application, leading to redundancy and potential for errors. Macros can automate the generation of this boilerplate, ensuring consistency and reducing manual effort. For instance, if you have a set of functions that require similar setup and teardown code, a macro can be designed to wrap these functions with the necessary boilerplate, thereby streamlining the development process and minimizing the risk of discrepancies.

In addition to macros, multi-methods offer a powerful mechanism for dispatching function calls based on dynamic criteria. This capability is particularly useful in scenarios where the behavior of a function depends on the runtime type or value of its arguments. For example, suppose you are building a system for processing various types of events, such as user actions, system notifications, and external messages. By using multi-methods, you can define a generic `handle-event` function that delegates the actual handling to different methods based on the type of event. This allows for a clean and extensible design where new event types can be added without modifying existing code.

Multi-methods also provide a way to implement polymorphism in a more flexible manner compared to traditional object-oriented approaches. Unlike method overloading, where the method signature must match exactly, multi-methods use a dispatch function to select the appropriate implementation based on the arguments provided. This approach allows for more dynamic and extensible code, as new dispatch criteria can be introduced without changing the existing method definitions.

Protocols, on the other hand, offer a mechanism for defining shared behavior across different data types. By specifying a set of method signatures, protocols establish a contract that data types must fulfill. This contract ensures that all types implementing the protocol provide consistent behavior, allowing for code that operates on any type that conforms to the protocol. For example, if you define a protocol `Renderable` with methods such as `render` and `update`, any type that implements this protocol can be used in contexts where rendering and updating are required. This approach promotes code reuse and modularity, as functions can operate on any data type that meets the protocol's contract.

When implementing protocols, it is important to ensure that the methods provided by each type adhere to the protocol's contract. This involves careful design and testing to verify that each implementation behaves as expected. In practice, protocols can be used to define common interfaces for diverse data types, facilitating interactions between components that rely on these interfaces.

The combination of macros, multi-methods, and protocols enables the creation of highly expressive and flexible code in ClojureScript. Macros allow for the introduction of new syntactic constructs and the automation of boilerplate code, while multi-methods and protocols provide mechanisms for dynamic dispatch and polymorphism. By leveraging these advanced features, you can write code that is both powerful and maintainable, addressing complex programming challenges with elegance and efficiency.

As you integrate these features into your ClojureScript projects, it is crucial to balance their use with practical considerations. Overuse of macros can lead to code that is difficult to understand and maintain, while multimethods and protocols should be employed judiciously to avoid unnecessary complexity. By applying these features thoughtfully, you can create robust and extensible systems that harness the full power of ClojureScript's advanced capabilities.

CHAPTER 13: BUILDING RESTFUL APIS

Building RESTful APIs is essential for creating modern web applications that need to communicate with server-side resources efficiently. This section delves into the nuances of setting up RESTful APIs with ClojureScript, covering everything from the foundational principles to practical implementation details. The focus will be on establishing endpoints, handling requests and responses, and leveraging ClojureScript libraries and tools to manage API interactions effectively.

To begin with, it's crucial to understand the REST architectural style, which emphasizes stateless interactions and a uniform interface. RESTful APIs operate over HTTP, and each endpoint typically corresponds to a resource or a collection of resources. Resources are identified using URIs, and HTTP methods (GET, POST, PUT, DELETE) are used to perform operations on these resources. This model aligns with the principles of CRUD (Create, Read, Update, Delete) operations, which are fundamental to RESTful design.

When setting up RESTful endpoints in ClojureScript, one must first choose an appropriate server-side framework or library that integrates seamlessly with ClojureScript. For server-side development in the Clojure ecosystem, tools like Compojure and Ring are often used. Compojure provides a declarative way to define routes and their corresponding handlers, while Ring offers middleware support and utilities for handling HTTP requests and responses. Although these tools are primarily used with Clojure, they can be leveraged effectively when working with ClojureScript, particularly in a full-stack Clojure environment.

To create a RESTful API using these tools, start by defining the routes in your application. Each route corresponds to a specific endpoint and is associated with an HTTP method. For instance, a route to handle user creation might look like `(POST "/users" [request] (create-user request))`, where `create-user` is a function that processes the incoming request to create a new user. Similarly, routes for reading, updating, and deleting resources can be defined with their respective HTTP methods. By mapping these routes to handler functions, you enable the API to respond to different types of requests appropriately.

Handling requests and responses is a crucial part of building RESTful APIs. In ClojureScript, you need to ensure that your handler functions can correctly parse incoming data, perform necessary operations, and generate appropriate responses. For example, when processing a POST request to create a new resource, you would extract the data from the request body, validate it, and then perform the necessary operations to create the resource in your database. After completing the operation, your handler function should generate a response that includes the status code and any relevant data, such as a confirmation message or the newly created resource's details.

In ClojureScript, the use of libraries like `cljs-http` can simplify the process of making HTTP requests from the client side. This library provides a simple and intuitive API for sending requests and handling responses. For instance, to send a GET request to retrieve a resource, you might use `(GET

"/api/resource" {:handler handle-response})`, where `handle-response` is a function that processes the response from the server. By using such libraries, you can manage API interactions efficiently, ensuring that your application can communicate seamlessly with the server-side components.

Error handling and validation are also integral to building robust RESTful APIs. It is essential to validate incoming data to ensure it meets the expected format and constraints before processing it. For instance, if your API requires certain fields to be present in a POST request, you should validate these fields and return an appropriate error message if they are missing or incorrect. Similarly, handling errors in your API responses helps clients understand what went wrong and how to address the issue. Providing meaningful error messages and status codes is crucial for maintaining a good user experience and facilitating debugging and troubleshooting.

Security is another important consideration when building RESTful APIs. Ensuring that your API is protected against common vulnerabilities, such as SQL injection and cross-site scripting (XSS), is critical. Implementing authentication and authorization mechanisms helps secure your API and restrict access to authorized users only. Techniques such as token-based authentication (e.g., JWT) and OAuth can be employed to manage user sessions and permissions effectively. By incorporating these security measures, you can safeguard your API and the data it handles.

Finally, documenting your RESTful API is essential for providing clear and comprehensive information to users and developers. Documentation should include details about each endpoint, the expected request and response formats, and any error codes that might be returned. Tools like Swagger or OpenAPI can facilitate the creation and maintenance of API documentation, offering interactive interfaces that help users understand and test your API.

By carefully setting up your endpoints, managing requests and responses, and incorporating proper validation, error handling, and security measures, you can create a robust and efficient RESTful API with ClojureScript. These practices ensure that your API performs well, is secure, and provides a seamless interaction experience for clients.

When delving deeper into building RESTful APIs with ClojureScript, it's essential to consider the aspects of testing, optimization, and versioning. Testing ensures that your API behaves as expected under various scenarios, while optimization enhances performance, and versioning maintains API stability as it evolves.

Testing is a fundamental practice for ensuring the reliability and correctness of your API. With ClojureScript, integrating tests into your development workflow can be streamlined using tools such as `cljs.test` and `doo`. `cljs.test` provides a framework for writing unit tests, allowing you to assert that individual components of your API function correctly. For instance, you can write tests to verify that your endpoint handlers process requests accurately and return the expected responses. It is also advisable to use a library like `clojure.test.check` for property-based testing, which can help identify edge cases and unexpected behaviors by generating a wide range of input data.

In addition to unit testing, integration testing is crucial for validating the interaction between different components of your API. This involves testing your API endpoints in conjunction with your backend services and databases to ensure that the entire stack functions cohesively. Tools like `ring-mock` can be employed to simulate HTTP requests and responses, allowing you to test your API endpoints in isolation or as part of an integrated system. By simulating real-world scenarios, you can detect issues that might not be apparent in unit tests alone, such as problems with data consistency or response formatting.

Optimization is another critical aspect of building efficient APIs. Performance tuning involves minimizing latency and maximizing throughput, which are crucial for delivering a responsive user experience. One effective strategy is to profile your API using tools such as `cljs-devtools` and browser-based performance analysis tools. Profiling helps identify bottlenecks and inefficient code paths that could be affecting your API's performance. For example, you might discover that certain endpoints have high latency due to inefficient data processing or that specific queries are causing unnecessary delays.

Code splitting and lazy loading are techniques that can significantly impact the performance of your API. Code splitting involves breaking down your codebase into smaller chunks that are loaded only when needed, rather than loading the entire application at once. This approach reduces the initial load time and improves the overall responsiveness of your API. Lazy loading, on the other hand, delays the loading of certain components or resources until they are required. By implementing these techniques, you can ensure that your API remains fast and efficient, even as it scales and handles increasing amounts of traffic.

Caching is another optimization technique that can improve API performance. By storing frequently accessed data in memory or a dedicated caching layer, you can reduce the need for repeated database queries and computations. In ClojureScript, libraries such as `cache` provide mechanisms for implementing caching strategies. You can use these libraries to cache responses for specific endpoints or to cache intermediate results of complex computations. Effective caching can significantly reduce response times and decrease the load on your backend services.

Versioning is an essential practice for managing changes to your API over time. As your API evolves, you may introduce new features, modify existing functionality, or deprecate old endpoints. Proper versioning allows you to maintain backward compatibility and ensure that existing clients continue to function correctly. A common approach to versioning is to include the version number in the URL path, such as `/api/v1/resource`. This method clearly indicates which version of the API a client is interacting with and allows you to manage different versions concurrently.

Another approach to versioning involves using request headers to specify the desired API version. This method offers greater flexibility and can be less intrusive than modifying the URL path. However, it requires careful management of versioning information and may be less transparent to clients. Regardless of the approach you choose, it is crucial to provide clear documentation for each API version and to communicate any breaking changes or deprecated features to your users.

Security is an integral aspect of API development, and implementing robust security measures is crucial for protecting your application and its data. Techniques such as rate limiting, authentication, and authorization help safeguard your API from abuse and unauthorized access. Rate limiting restricts the number of requests a client can make within a specified timeframe, preventing abuse and ensuring fair usage. Authentication mechanisms, such as API keys or OAuth tokens, validate the identity of clients and ensure that only authorized users can access your API. Authorization controls further refine access by granting or denying permissions based on user roles and privileges.

Incorporating comprehensive logging and monitoring into your API is also important for maintaining operational visibility and troubleshooting issues. Logging provides valuable insights into API usage patterns, errors, and performance metrics. By integrating logging frameworks such as `timbre` or `log4j`, you can capture detailed information about API requests and responses, which aids in diagnosing problems and optimizing performance. Monitoring tools, on the other hand, track the health and performance of your API in real-time, alerting you to potential issues before they impact users.

By addressing testing, optimization, versioning, and security, you can build a robust and efficient RESTful API with ClojureScript. These practices ensure that your API performs well, remains secure, and provides a seamless experience for clients, while also accommodating future changes and improvements.

Once you have established the core functionality of your RESTful API, focusing on integration and documentation becomes crucial for ensuring that your API can be effectively utilized by other developers and services. Integration involves connecting your API with external systems and ensuring that it operates seamlessly within your broader application ecosystem. Documentation, on the other hand, serves as a comprehensive guide for users and developers interacting with your API, providing clarity on how to make the most of its features.

Integrating your API with external systems can involve several strategies, depending on the nature of the integration and the systems involved. One common approach is to connect your API with third-party services or databases. This can be achieved using various ClojureScript libraries and tools designed for interacting with external systems. For instance, you might use libraries like `clj-http` or `cljs-ajax` for making HTTP requests to other APIs, allowing your API to consume data or services from external sources. Similarly, you can integrate with databases using libraries such as `korma` or `clojure.java.jdbc`, which provide abstractions for interacting with relational databases and performing queries.

When integrating with external systems, it is important to handle authentication and authorization properly. Many third-party services require API keys, OAuth tokens, or other credentials to grant access. You will need to ensure that your API securely manages these credentials, avoiding exposure and ensuring that access is granted only to authorized users. Additionally, handling errors and failures gracefully is crucial for maintaining a robust integration. Implementing retry logic, proper error reporting, and fallback mechanisms can help mitigate issues that arise during integration.

Documentation is a critical component for any API, as it provides users with the information they need to understand and use the API effectively. Comprehensive documentation should include details on available endpoints, request and response formats, authentication requirements, and any other relevant information. Tools such as Swagger (OpenAPI) and Postman can be invaluable in generating interactive API documentation. Swagger allows you to define your API using a standardized format, automatically generating documentation that is easy to navigate and use. Postman, on the other hand, can be used to create and share collections of API requests, providing a practical way to test and explore your API.

Writing clear and concise documentation is essential for ensuring that developers can quickly understand how to interact with your API. Each endpoint should be described with its purpose, required parameters, and possible responses. Including examples of request and response payloads can further aid understanding. For instance, if your API has an endpoint for retrieving user information, provide a sample request with the necessary parameters and a sample response that illustrates the structure of the data returned. This helps developers grasp how to construct their requests and what to expect in return.

Furthermore, maintaining documentation is an ongoing process. As your API evolves, new endpoints may be added, existing ones modified, or deprecated. It is important to keep your documentation up-to-date with these changes to prevent confusion and ensure that users have accurate information. Versioning your API, as previously discussed, can also be reflected in your documentation, allowing users to reference the correct version of the API they are working with.

Testing your API's integration with external systems and documentation is also a crucial step. Ensure that your API's endpoints interact correctly with third-party services and that the documentation accurately reflects the current functionality of your API. This involves verifying that the examples provided in the documentation work as expected and that the API handles all scenarios, including edge cases, gracefully. Automated tests can be used to periodically check the integrity of your integrations, ensuring that they continue to function correctly as your API or external systems change.

In addition to external integrations and documentation, you should also consider the deployment and monitoring aspects of your API. Deployment involves moving your API from a development environment to a production environment, ensuring that it is available and performing well for end-users. Tools such as Docker can help streamline the deployment process by creating consistent, isolated environments for your API to run in. Containerizing your API ensures that it behaves consistently across different environments and simplifies deployment.

Monitoring is vital for maintaining the health and performance of your API in production. Implementing logging and monitoring solutions allows you to track the usage, performance, and errors of your API. This enables you to quickly identify and address issues before they impact users. Services like Prometheus and Grafana can be used to collect and visualize metrics, while logging frameworks such as ELK (Elasticsearch, Logstash, Kibana) or `timbre` provide powerful logging capabilities for tracking and analyzing API activity.

By focusing on integration, documentation, deployment, and monitoring, you can ensure that your RESTful API is not only functional but also robust, user-friendly, and well-maintained. These aspects contribute to a successful API that meets the needs of its users and integrates smoothly with other systems, providing a reliable and effective service.

CHAPTER 14: REAL-TIME DATA WITH WEBSOCKETS

To effectively incorporate real-time data into ClojureScript applications, utilizing WebSockets represents a powerful approach. WebSockets provide a full-duplex communication channel over a single, long-lived connection, facilitating two-way data exchange between the client and server with low latency. This chapter will delve into the practical aspects of setting up WebSocket connections, managing messages, and integrating real-time updates into your application's user interface.

Initiating a WebSocket connection involves establishing a persistent link between the client and server, allowing for continuous data flow. In ClojureScript, this process begins by creating a WebSocket object. The `goog.net.WebSocket` class from the Google Closure Library provides an abstraction for handling WebSocket connections in ClojureScript. You can initialize a WebSocket connection by specifying the server URL and configuring event handlers to manage the connection's lifecycle.

When you create a WebSocket instance, the first step is to configure it to handle the various stages of the connection. The `goog.net.WebSocket` class offers methods for opening, closing, and sending data through the WebSocket. To establish the connection, use the `open` method and provide the URL of the WebSocket server. Once connected, the WebSocket will begin to receive messages from the server and can also send messages to it.

Handling incoming messages is a crucial aspect of working with WebSockets. In ClojureScript, you can define an event handler to process data received from the server. This involves implementing a function that processes the message event, which contains the data sent from the server. Typically, this data will be in the form of a JSON object or a string, which needs to be parsed and utilized within your application. For instance, if your WebSocket server sends real-time updates about stock prices, your event handler should parse the incoming data and update the relevant parts of your application's UI accordingly.

On the server side, it is essential to implement WebSocket support to handle incoming connections and messages. WebSocket servers operate by maintaining an open connection with the client, allowing for continuous data exchange. Depending on your server environment, you might use different libraries or frameworks to facilitate WebSocket communication. For example, in a Clojure-based server setup, you might use libraries like `aleph` or `http-kit`, which provide WebSocket support and allow for easy integration with ClojureScript clients.

Once the connection is established and messages are being exchanged, integrating real-time updates into your UI requires careful management. In ClojureScript, you typically use Reagent or another reactive library to handle state updates in response to real-time data. Reagent provides a reactive interface for managing application state, making it easy to update the UI based on incoming data. By leveraging Reagent's reactive atoms or cursors, you can ensure that your UI components automatically re-render when the underlying data changes.

For instance, suppose you are building a real-time chat application. As new messages arrive through the WebSocket connection, you need to update the message list in your UI. By binding your message list component to a reactive atom, you can ensure that each new message triggers a re-render, displaying the latest messages to the user in real-time. This reactive approach simplifies the management of dynamic data and ensures that your UI remains in sync with the underlying data.

Handling WebSocket disconnections and reconnections is another important consideration. Network issues or server problems can cause the WebSocket connection to drop, requiring you to implement mechanisms for detecting and managing these disconnections. In ClojureScript, you can use event handlers to respond to connection closure events and attempt to reconnect automatically. This typically involves setting up a retry strategy that attempts to re-establish the connection after a certain period. Properly managing reconnections ensures that your application maintains real-time functionality even in the face of temporary network issues.

Security is also a key aspect of working with WebSockets. WebSocket connections are typically established over the `ws://` or `wss://` protocol, with `wss://` providing a secure, encrypted connection. When implementing WebSockets, ensure that you use `wss://` for secure communication, especially when handling sensitive data. Additionally, implement authentication and authorization mechanisms to control access to the WebSocket server and protect against unauthorized access.

In summary, using WebSockets in ClojureScript applications allows for efficient and real-time data communication, enhancing the responsiveness and interactivity of your application. By setting up WebSocket connections, handling incoming messages, and integrating real-time updates into your UI, you can build applications that deliver timely and dynamic user experiences. Managing connection states, handling disconnections, and ensuring security are crucial for maintaining a robust and reliable real-time data system.

Establishing a robust and efficient WebSocket connection requires a nuanced understanding of both the client-side and server-side components involved. On the client side, after setting up the initial connection using `goog.net.WebSocket`, it is essential to manage various aspects of the WebSocket lifecycle, including connection establishment, message handling, and error management.

Upon initiating a connection, the client will need to handle several events to ensure smooth communication. The `onOpen` event handler, for instance, is triggered when the WebSocket connection is successfully established. This is an opportune moment to send an initial message to the server or perform setup tasks such as authenticating the user or initializing application state. The `onMessage` event handler processes incoming data from the server, which could be in various formats such as JSON or plain text. Parsing and handling this data efficiently is critical for maintaining the application's responsiveness.

Equally important is the `onError` event handler, which manages scenarios where network issues or unexpected problems arise. By implementing robust error handling and logging, you can better diagnose and address connection issues. For example, if the WebSocket encounters a transmission error, you might want to alert the user or attempt a reconnection. Similarly, the `onClose` event handler deals with scenarios where the connection is closed either normally or due to an error. Implementing a reconnection strategy in this handler can help maintain continuous data flow and enhance user experience.

The server-side implementation of WebSockets also requires careful consideration. Servers must be equipped to handle incoming WebSocket requests and maintain persistent connections with clients. Depending on your server technology, you might use various libraries or frameworks to facilitate this. For instance, in a Clojure environment, libraries like `aleph` or `http-kit` are often used to provide WebSocket support. These libraries offer functionalities to manage connections, handle messages, and send data back to clients.

When a WebSocket request is received on the server, it is crucial to authenticate and authorize the connection appropriately. This can involve checking session tokens or other credentials to ensure that only authorized clients can establish a connection. Once authenticated, the server must be capable of processing incoming messages and sending responses or updates as needed. The server-side logic typically involves listening for incoming data, processing it (which might include querying databases or performing computations), and then pushing relevant updates to the connected clients.

For applications that require frequent or high-volume updates, such as live data feeds or real-time notifications, optimizing the efficiency of WebSocket communication becomes critical. Techniques for managing message traffic include batching updates, implementing compression, and optimizing data formats. Batching involves grouping multiple updates into a single message to reduce overhead and improve performance. Compression algorithms can help reduce the size of the data transmitted over the WebSocket, which is particularly useful for large payloads or frequent updates. Moreover, using efficient data formats, such as binary protocols or compact JSON structures, can minimize the data transferred and enhance performance.

Incorporating WebSockets into a ClojureScript application also involves integrating real-time updates into the user interface. This can be achieved through reactive programming paradigms, which allow the UI to respond automatically to changes in data. Reagent, a popular ClojureScript library for building UIs, provides a reactive data model that is well-suited for handling real-time updates. By binding your UI components to reactive atoms or cursors, you ensure that any changes in the underlying data are automatically reflected in the user interface.

For example, in a collaborative application where multiple users can edit documents simultaneously, WebSockets can be used to broadcast changes in real-time. Each client maintains a connection to the server, which sends updates whenever a document is modified. The client-side application listens for these updates and applies changes to the document displayed to the user. By using Reagent's reactive model, the UI components that display the document are automatically updated whenever new data arrives, providing a seamless and interactive experience for users.

Handling real-time data also requires consideration of performance and resource management. WebSocket connections are persistent and can consume resources over time, so managing the number of active connections and ensuring efficient data handling are important. Implementing strategies such as throttling, where updates are limited or aggregated to avoid overwhelming the client or server, can help maintain performance. Additionally, monitoring the performance of WebSocket connections and adjusting configurations based on observed usage patterns can further enhance efficiency.

In conclusion, integrating WebSockets into ClojureScript

applications involves a comprehensive approach, addressing both client-side and server-side aspects of real-time communication. By setting up robust connection management, handling messages effectively, and ensuring efficient data updates, you can leverage WebSockets to create dynamic and responsive applications. The seamless integration of real-time data into the user interface, supported by reactive programming techniques, enables the development of applications that deliver a highly interactive and engaging user experience.

When it comes to ensuring robust real-time communication in your ClojureScript application using WebSockets, it's crucial to address several advanced aspects of connection management and data synchronization. One of the more sophisticated tasks involves dealing with the nuances of state synchronization across multiple clients.

In scenarios where your application serves multiple users who interact with shared data, maintaining consistency becomes essential. For instance, consider a real-time collaborative document editor. As multiple users make changes, the server must manage the synchronization of these changes so that each client sees the same state. This involves handling concurrent modifications, resolving conflicts, and ensuring that updates are applied in a consistent manner.

To achieve this, you can employ conflict resolution strategies. One common approach is the operational transformation algorithm, which ensures that operations from different users are applied in a way that maintains consistency. Another approach is using vector clocks or similar techniques to manage versions of the data and resolve conflicts based on timestamps or causal relationships between operations. Implementing these strategies requires careful consideration of how operations are represented, transmitted, and applied, as well as how to handle cases where multiple changes occur simultaneously.

Another critical aspect is optimizing the WebSocket communication to handle large volumes of data or high-frequency updates efficiently. This involves optimizing both the data payload and the frequency of messages. Data payloads can be minimized by using efficient serialization formats or compressing messages before sending them. For example, binary formats like Protocol Buffers or MessagePack can be more compact than JSON, which reduces the amount of data transmitted over the WebSocket connection. Compression algorithms, such as gzip, can also help reduce the size of the data, especially when dealing with large or repetitive payloads.

Regarding the frequency of messages, you should implement strategies to throttle or debounce updates. Throttling involves limiting the rate at which messages are sent, ensuring that the server or client is not overwhelmed by excessive traffic. Debouncing, on the other hand, involves grouping multiple changes into a single message, which can reduce the number of updates sent and improve performance. These strategies help balance the need for real-time updates with the practical constraints of network bandwidth and processing capacity.

When integrating real-time data into your user interface, it is important to handle updates efficiently to maintain a smooth and responsive experience. In ClojureScript applications using Reagent, you can take advantage of the reactive nature of atoms and cursors to automatically propagate changes through your UI components. By binding your UI components to reactive data sources, any changes received via WebSocket can be immediately reflected in the user interface without requiring manual intervention.

For example, consider a real-time chat application where new messages are received through a WebSocket connection. By using reactive atoms to store the message list, you ensure that the chat window is updated automatically whenever a new message arrives. This reactive model simplifies the process of updating the UI and ensures that users receive the latest information without delays.

In addition to managing data updates, you must also handle scenarios where users disconnect or reconnect. WebSocket connections can be unstable, and users may experience intermittent connectivity issues. To handle these cases gracefully, you should implement mechanisms to detect when a connection is lost and attempt to reconnect. This can involve setting up automatic reconnection logic that tries to re-establish the connection after a certain period or when the network becomes available again.

Furthermore, you should consider providing users with feedback about the connection status. For example, displaying a status indicator that shows whether the application is connected or disconnected can help users understand the state of their real-time interactions. This feedback can also include retry mechanisms or notifications when the connection is re-established or when updates are received after a disconnection.

Another important consideration is security. WebSocket connections, like any other network communication, can be vulnerable to attacks. To secure WebSocket communication, use HTTPS to encrypt the connection and ensure that sensitive data is protected from eavesdropping. Implementing authentication and authorization mechanisms is also crucial to prevent unauthorized access to your WebSocket endpoints. This can involve validating tokens or credentials before allowing a WebSocket connection to be established and ensuring that users have the appropriate permissions to access specific data or perform certain actions.

In conclusion, mastering the use of WebSockets for real-time data in ClojureScript applications involves a comprehensive approach to connection management, data synchronization, and user interface integration. By addressing the challenges of state consistency, optimizing message handling, and implementing robust connection and security mechanisms, you can build applications that deliver seamless and interactive experiences for users. The ability to handle real-time updates efficiently and ensure a responsive user interface is key to creating dynamic and engaging web applications that meet the demands of modern users.

CHAPTER 15: WORKING WITH DATABASES

In the realm of web development, the ability to interact with databases is essential for managing and utilizing persistent data. In the context of ClojureScript, the approach to database interaction involves several key components, including choosing the right libraries, establishing connections, and adhering to best practices for efficient data access and management.

To begin, connecting to a database from a ClojureScript application involves using libraries designed to facilitate such interactions. Since ClojureScript primarily runs on the client side, direct database connections are typically handled through an intermediary service, such as a backend server or a RESTful API, which interfaces with the database. For backend services written in Clojure, libraries such as `clojure.java.jdbc` or `next.jdbc` provide robust tools for managing SQL-based databases. These libraries offer functions for establishing connections, executing queries, and processing results.

When working with databases in ClojureScript, the interaction is often mediated by HTTP requests to a backend API that performs database operations. The `cljs-http` library is commonly used for making HTTP requests from

ClojureScript. This library simplifies the process of sending requests and handling responses, enabling ClojureScript applications to communicate with backend services that interact with databases.

Establishing a connection to a backend service requires careful consideration of security and performance. For example, when configuring a backend to handle database connections, it is crucial to manage connection pooling efficiently. Connection pooling helps to reduce the overhead associated with frequently opening and closing database connections by maintaining a pool of reusable connections. This practice improves performance and scalability, especially under high-load conditions.

Once a connection is established, it is important to handle database queries and updates efficiently. In a ClojureScript application, this typically involves sending data to the backend for processing. The backend, using a library such as `clojure.java.jdbc`, executes the necessary queries and returns the results to the client. It is important to structure queries to minimize performance impacts and ensure that they are optimized for the database engine being used. For instance, indexing frequently queried columns can significantly improve query performance.

In addition to executing queries, managing data access in a ClojureScript context involves dealing with asynchronous operations. Data retrieval from a backend service is often asynchronous, requiring the use of promises or callbacks to handle results when they become available. Libraries like `core.async` provide abstractions for handling asynchronous operations and can be integrated into ClojureScript applications to manage the flow of data.

Data management also involves considering how data is represented and transformed between the client and server. JSON is a common format for data interchange in web applications. ClojureScript's `cljs.core` and `clojure.data.json` libraries facilitate the serialization and deserialization of data to and from JSON format. Properly managing data transformation ensures that data is accurately transmitted and interpreted between the client and server.

Moreover, implementing data validation and error handling is crucial for maintaining data integrity and providing a good user experience. On the client side, it is important to validate user input before sending it to the backend. This can involve checking for required fields, validating formats, and ensuring data consistency. On the backend, validation should be performed again to prevent invalid or malicious data from being stored in the database.

Error handling is another critical aspect of database interactions. Both the client and server should be equipped to handle errors gracefully. On the client side, this involves providing informative error messages to users and handling cases where the backend service is unavailable or returns an error. On the server side, proper error handling includes logging errors for diagnostic purposes and returning appropriate error responses to the client.

In addition to handling individual queries and updates, managing complex data interactions requires an understanding of transactions and concurrency control. Transactions ensure that a series of operations are completed successfully before committing changes to the database. This is particularly important in scenarios where multiple related updates need to be performed atomically. Concurrency control mechanisms, such as locking and optimistic concurrency control, help manage concurrent access to data and prevent conflicts or data corruption.

Implementing robust data management practices is essential

for building reliable and maintainable applications. This includes designing a schema that reflects the application's data requirements, optimizing queries for performance, and ensuring that data integrity is maintained through validation and transaction management.

In summary, working with databases in ClojureScript applications involves a combination of selecting appropriate libraries, managing connections, handling asynchronous operations, and ensuring robust data management practices. By carefully considering these aspects, you can build applications that efficiently interact with databases, provide a seamless user experience, and maintain data integrity.

When managing database interactions in ClojureScript applications, a crucial aspect to consider is how data is efficiently queried and manipulated. While the focus of this discussion has so far centered on connection setups and basic interactions, we must now delve into more complex operations such as querying strategies, data consistency, and transactional integrity.

One of the key elements of querying in a ClojureScript application involves constructing and executing efficient queries. Queries are typically executed on the server side where the database resides, with the client sending requests through HTTP or WebSocket connections. On the server side, libraries such as `next.jdbc` offer a functional approach to constructing SQL queries. For instance, rather than manually crafting SQL strings, which can be error-prone and insecure, `next.jdbc` supports a more programmatic approach, reducing the risk of SQL injection attacks and improving readability.

To efficiently retrieve data, it is essential to use proper indexing strategies. Indexes significantly enhance the speed of data retrieval operations by allowing the database to quickly locate the desired records. In a relational database, creating indexes on columns that are frequently used in WHERE clauses or JOIN operations can drastically reduce query execution time. It is also crucial to analyze query performance regularly and adjust indexes as necessary, based on the evolving patterns of data access.

Handling large volumes of data efficiently requires pagination and batching techniques. Pagination allows you to divide query results into manageable chunks, which can be particularly useful for displaying data in a user interface where loading the entire dataset at once would be impractical. Libraries like `clojure.java.jdbc` or `next.jdbc` provide mechanisms to support pagination through LIMIT and OFFSET clauses in SQL queries. Implementing pagination on the server side ensures that only a subset of data is sent to the client at any one time, improving performance and user experience.

Batch processing is another technique that can enhance performance, especially when dealing with multiple records. Instead of sending multiple individual requests, batch processing involves sending a single request containing multiple operations. This approach reduces the overhead associated with each request and can be implemented using database-specific features like bulk inserts or updates.

Data consistency is another critical concern in database interactions. Consistency ensures that data remains accurate and reliable despite concurrent access and modifications. To achieve consistency, it is essential to use transactions effectively. Transactions are used to group multiple operations into a single, atomic unit of work. This means that either all operations within the transaction are successfully completed, or none of them are. By ensuring that related operations are executed together, transactions prevent partial updates and maintain data integrity.

In Clojure, managing transactions involves using functions provided by database libraries to begin, commit, and rollback transactions. For instance, `next.jdbc` allows for explicit transaction management, giving you control over when transactions start and end. Proper use of transactions can help handle scenarios where multiple users or processes are concurrently accessing and modifying the same data, thus preventing issues like lost updates or data anomalies.

Concurrency control is closely related to transaction management and is vital for maintaining data integrity in multi-user environments. Concurrency control mechanisms, such as optimistic concurrency control and pessimistic locking, manage concurrent access to data. Optimistic concurrency control relies on versioning or timestamps to detect conflicts and resolve them, while pessimistic locking involves locking data resources to prevent other transactions from modifying them until the lock is released. Choosing the appropriate concurrency control strategy depends on the specific requirements and characteristics of the application.

Additionally, database normalization is an important aspect of designing efficient and scalable databases. Normalization involves organizing data to reduce redundancy and improve data integrity. By decomposing data into related tables and defining appropriate relationships, normalization helps to avoid anomalies and ensures that data is stored in a consistent and logical manner.

In ClojureScript applications, while direct database access is typically managed server-side, the client-side implementation should focus on efficiently handling and displaying the data received from the server. This involves managing state effectively, handling asynchronous data updates, and ensuring that the user interface remains responsive.

Effective error handling is also crucial for robust database interactions. On the client side, this includes handling cases where the backend service may be unreachable or returns error responses. Providing meaningful feedback to users and implementing retry mechanisms can enhance the resilience of the application. On the server side, logging errors and exceptions, as well as implementing proper error-handling strategies, helps in diagnosing issues and maintaining application stability.

In summary, working with databases in a ClojureScript context involves more than just establishing connections and executing basic queries. It requires careful consideration of querying strategies, data consistency, transactional integrity, and concurrency control. By implementing best practices in these areas, you can build applications that efficiently manage data, maintain integrity, and provide a seamless user experience.

When delving into advanced data management with ClojureScript, it's essential to understand how to integrate with various types of databases beyond just relational databases. This exploration includes working with NoSQL databases, which are designed to handle unstructured data and scale horizontally.

NoSQL databases, such as MongoDB, Cassandra, and Redis, offer flexible data models that differ significantly from traditional relational databases. For example, MongoDB uses a document-oriented model, where data is stored in JSON-like documents. This format is particularly useful for applications that require rapid schema changes or need to store complex hierarchical data. In ClojureScript, integrating with MongoDB involves using libraries such as `monger` or `monger-cljs`, which provide a ClojureScript interface to MongoDB's JavaScript driver.

Handling data in MongoDB starts with defining schemas that align with the document model. Unlike relational databases, where data is strictly organized into tables, MongoDB's schema-less nature allows for more flexibility. However, this flexibility comes with its own challenges. Ensuring data consistency and integrity in a schema-less environment requires careful design and validation of documents before insertion. ClojureScript applications can use libraries like `monger` to interact with MongoDB, providing functions to insert, query, update, and delete documents.

Another critical aspect of working with NoSQL databases is understanding their consistency models. For instance, Cassandra is designed for high availability and scalability but employs an eventual consistency model. This means that while data is eventually consistent across the cluster, it may not be immediately consistent. ClojureScript applications interacting with Cassandra must account for this eventual consistency by designing application logic that can handle temporary inconsistencies.

Redis, on the other hand, is a key-value store known for its high performance and in-memory data structure. It is often used for caching and session management. Integrating Redis with a ClojureScript application involves using libraries like `carmine`, which provides a Clojure interface to Redis. Redis operations, such as setting and getting values, are straightforward but require an understanding of its data structures and how they can be leveraged for performance optimization.

The choice of database and how it is integrated into a ClojureScript application often depends on the specific requirements of the application. For applications with complex querying needs, a relational database or a more feature-rich NoSQL database like MongoDB might be appropriate. For applications requiring high-speed data retrieval and storage with simple key-value lookups, Redis could be the ideal choice.

In addition to the database type, managing connections and ensuring efficient data access are crucial considerations. Connection pooling is one technique to enhance performance and manage resource usage effectively. Connection pools maintain a pool of open connections that can be reused, reducing the overhead of establishing new connections. In ClojureScript, connection pooling can be implemented using libraries or built-in features provided by the database drivers.

Data caching is another technique to improve performance and reduce the load on the database. By storing frequently accessed data in a cache, applications can serve requests more quickly and minimize database hits. Implementing a caching layer involves deciding which data to cache, how to invalidate or refresh cached data, and integrating caching mechanisms with the database access layer.

Security is also a significant concern when interacting with databases. Protecting sensitive data involves implementing appropriate access controls, encryption, and monitoring. For instance, encrypting data at rest and in transit ensures that unauthorized parties cannot access or intercept sensitive information. Access controls should be enforced at both the database and application levels, with roles and permissions defined to limit access to critical operations and data.

In terms of application design, ensuring that the database access layer is decoupled from the rest of the application can facilitate easier maintenance and testing. Using an abstraction layer or repository pattern allows the application to interact with the database through well-defined interfaces, making it easier to switch database implementations or modify the data access logic without affecting other parts of the application.

Additionally, database migrations are an essential part of managing schema changes and evolving data structures. Migration tools help manage changes to the database schema, ensuring that changes are applied consistently across different environments. In ClojureScript applications, migration management might involve using libraries that support schema evolution or integrating with external migration tools.

To summarize, effective database management in ClojureScript applications encompasses a range of practices and considerations. From integrating with various database types, such as relational and NoSQL databases, to implementing performance optimization techniques like connection pooling and caching, each aspect contributes to building robust and efficient applications. Security, maintainability, and the ability to handle schema changes are also crucial factors that must be addressed to ensure that the application remains scalable and resilient. By applying these practices, you can ensure that your ClojureScript applications interact seamlessly with databases, providing reliable and efficient data management capabilities.

CHAPTER 16: BUILDING SINGLE PAGE APPLICATIONS (SPAS)

Creating a Single Page Application (SPA) with ClojureScript involves crafting a seamless and dynamic user experience through efficient client-side routing and state management. To achieve this, I'll explore the key aspects of SPA development, focusing on utilizing ClojureScript libraries and frameworks that facilitate responsive and interactive applications.

The foundation of an SPA is its ability to load content dynamically without requiring full page reloads. This is achieved through client-side routing, where different views or components are rendered based on the current URL, without refreshing the entire page. ClojureScript offers several tools and libraries to handle client-side routing effectively. One such library is `bidi`, which provides a concise and expressive way to define routes and manage navigation within an SPA.

In implementing client-side routing with `bidi`, one starts by defining routes in a data structure that maps URL patterns to handler functions. This approach enables the application to render different views or components depending on the URL. For example, a route definition might specify that a URL pattern like `/home` should render the `home` component, while `/about` should render the `about` component. By integrating `bidi` with ClojureScript's reactive programming model, it becomes possible to dynamically update the view in response to route changes without reloading the entire page.

Another critical aspect of SPA development is state management. In an SPA, managing the application's state efficiently is crucial to ensure a responsive user experience. ClojureScript provides several options for state management, including libraries like `re-frame` and `om`. `re-frame` is a popular choice for managing application state in a reactive and declarative manner. It leverages an event-handler pattern, where events trigger state changes and views are automatically updated in response to those changes.

With `re-frame`, the application state is stored in a centralized database, known as the "app-db." This approach allows for a clear separation between the state management logic and the view logic. Events are dispatched to modify the state, and subscriptions are used to query the state and update the view accordingly. This pattern simplifies the management of complex state interactions and ensures that the UI remains consistent with the underlying state.

When developing SPAs, responsiveness and interactivity are essential for a positive user experience. This requires implementing features such as asynchronous data loading, real-time updates, and smooth animations. ClojureScript supports asynchronous operations through JavaScript interoperability, allowing you to leverage existing JavaScript libraries for tasks such as fetching data from APIs or handling user interactions.

For asynchronous data loading, libraries like `cljs-http` provide a simple way to make HTTP requests and handle responses. By integrating `cljs-http` with `re-frame`, you can dispatch events to trigger data fetching and update the application state based on the results. This approach enables the application to load and display data dynamically, improving the overall user experience by avoiding blocking operations.

Real-time updates in SPAs often involve incorporating WebSockets or other real-time communication technologies. WebSockets enable bidirectional communication between the client and server, allowing for real-time data exchange. In ClojureScript, WebSocket integration can be achieved using libraries like `cljs-websockets`, which provide a straightforward API for managing WebSocket connections and handling messages.

In addition to managing state and data, implementing smooth animations and transitions is crucial for enhancing the user experience in SPAs. Libraries like `reagent` and `rum` offer tools for creating interactive and animated components in ClojureScript. By leveraging these libraries, you can build responsive user interfaces that provide a fluid and engaging experience.

Handling user input and interactions is another important aspect of SPA development. ClojureScript's integration with JavaScript allows for seamless handling of events and user actions. For example, you can use event listeners to capture user interactions such as clicks, form submissions, and keyboard inputs. By responding to these events and updating the application state accordingly, you can create a dynamic and interactive user interface.

Furthermore, SPA development involves considerations for performance optimization and resource management. Efficient rendering and minimizing unnecessary re-renders are crucial for maintaining a responsive application. Techniques such as virtual DOM diffing, lazy loading, and code splitting can help improve performance and reduce the initial load time of the application.

In summary, building Single Page Applications with ClojureScript requires careful consideration of client-side routing, state management, and interactivity. By leveraging libraries and frameworks such as `bidi`, `re-frame`, and `cljs-http`, you can create SPAs that provide a smooth and dynamic user experience. Implementing asynchronous data loading, real-time updates, and responsive animations further enhances the application's performance and usability. Through effective state management and optimization techniques, you can ensure that your SPA remains responsive and engaging, offering users a seamless and enjoyable experience.

To effectively build Single Page Applications (SPAs) using ClojureScript, one must deeply understand client-side routing and state management. Following the initial setup of routing and state management systems, the next crucial step is to delve into how these components interact and integrate to create a seamless user experience.

In the realm of client-side routing, once the routes are defined using `bidi`, the next challenge is managing route changes and rendering the appropriate views. A robust approach involves creating a routing mechanism that listens for URL changes and dynamically updates the application state and UI accordingly. For instance, leveraging ClojureScript's interoperability with JavaScript enables the use of hash-based routing or the HTML5 History API. The choice between these methods depends on the desired user experience and the application's requirements. Hash-based routing is simpler and more universally supported but can lead to less clean URLs. The History API, on the other hand, offers cleaner URLs and better integration with browser history but requires additional handling for browser compatibility.

Managing application state efficiently is pivotal to ensuring that the SPA remains responsive and interactive. After setting up a state management system with libraries like `re-frame`, the next task is to handle state transitions and interactions smoothly. For example, state changes triggered by user interactions or route updates need to be reflected immediately in the UI. This requires a well-designed event system where events are dispatched to modify the application state, and subscriptions are used to reactively update the UI based on state changes. The separation of concerns provided by `re-frame`—where events, handlers, and views are distinctly managed—helps in maintaining a clean and scalable architecture.

In the context of SPAs, asynchronous operations such as data fetching from remote servers are common. Integrating asynchronous data operations involves dispatching events to initiate data fetching and updating the state with the fetched data. Libraries like `cljs-http` facilitate making HTTP requests and handling responses within a ClojureScript application. By wrapping asynchronous requests in re-frame events, you ensure that data fetching is managed in a predictable manner and that the UI updates seamlessly when new data is available.

Real-time updates are another aspect that significantly enhances the interactivity of SPAs. Implementing WebSocket support within your ClojureScript application allows for bidirectional communication between the client and server. This enables real-time features such as live notifications or chat functionalities. Libraries like `cljs-websockets` provide the necessary abstractions to manage WebSocket connections and handle incoming and outgoing messages. Ensuring efficient handling of WebSocket events and updating the application state accordingly is crucial for maintaining a responsive user interface.

The responsiveness of an SPA also heavily relies on how

effectively animations and transitions are implemented. Utilizing libraries like `reagent` or `rum`, which offer tools for creating interactive components, can help in building a fluid and engaging user experience. Animations can be implemented using CSS transitions or JavaScript-based animation libraries. Ensuring that animations do not negatively impact performance is crucial, as poorly optimized animations can lead to a sluggish user experience. Techniques such as using requestAnimationFrame for animations and minimizing layout thrashing can help maintain smooth performance.

Handling user input efficiently is essential for an interactive SPA. This involves capturing user events such as clicks, form submissions, and keyboard inputs, and updating the application state in response. ClojureScript's integration with JavaScript allows for seamless event handling. For example, you might use event listeners to capture input and dispatch corresponding events to update the state. By processing user inputs in this manner, you ensure that the application responds promptly to user actions, contributing to a dynamic and engaging interface.

Performance optimization is a critical consideration when building SPAs. Techniques such as code splitting, lazy loading, and virtual DOM diffing are essential for improving the performance and reducing the initial load time of the application. Code splitting involves breaking down the application into smaller chunks that can be loaded on demand, rather than loading the entire application upfront. Lazy loading allows for deferring the loading of non-essential resources until they are needed. Virtual DOM diffing, a technique employed by libraries like `reagent`, helps in efficiently updating only the parts of the DOM that have changed, minimizing the performance overhead associated with frequent DOM manipulations.

Effective state management and routing strategies in combination with asynchronous operations, real-time updates, and performance optimizations culminate in the development of a responsive and interactive Single Page Application. By leveraging the capabilities of ClojureScript and its ecosystem of libraries and tools, you can build SPAs that provide a seamless and engaging user experience. As you continue to develop and refine SPAs, maintaining a focus on these aspects will ensure that your application remains performant, responsive, and user-friendly.

The next essential aspect of building Single Page Applications (SPAs) involves ensuring that the application's state is managed effectively and the user interface remains responsive under various conditions. This can be particularly challenging given the complexity and the dynamic nature of SPAs.

Effective state management is crucial for maintaining consistency across the application and ensuring that user interactions are handled smoothly. In the context of ClojureScript, leveraging libraries like `re-frame` provides a robust solution for managing application state in a predictable and organized manner. `re-frame` uses a unidirectional data flow model, which means that all changes to the application state are handled through a central event dispatcher. This approach simplifies debugging and enhances the maintainability of the application, as it ensures that state changes are tracked and managed systematically.

In practical terms, this involves defining a series of events that represent various actions or interactions within the application. Each event is associated with a handler function that processes the event and updates the application state accordingly. For instance, an event might be triggered when a user submits a form, which would then update the state with the new data and potentially trigger a UI update. Subscriptions are used to listen for changes in the state and update the user interface dynamically. This reactive approach ensures that the UI is always in sync with the application state, providing a seamless user experience.

As the complexity of the application grows, managing state transitions and ensuring consistency can become increasingly challenging. Implementing proper state management strategies, such as normalization and encapsulation of state, can help address these challenges. Normalizing the state involves organizing it in a way that avoids duplication and ensures that related data is stored together. Encapsulation involves isolating different parts of the state to ensure that changes in one part do not inadvertently affect other parts. This helps in maintaining a clear and manageable state structure, which is crucial for complex SPAs.

Another important consideration is handling asynchronous operations effectively. In SPAs, interactions with external services or APIs often involve asynchronous requests. Integrating these asynchronous operations with the state management system requires careful coordination. For example, when a data fetch operation is initiated, it is crucial to update the state to reflect the loading status and handle any errors that may occur. Libraries like `cljs-http` facilitate making HTTP requests and managing responses within a ClojureScript application. By dispatching events to handle these asynchronous operations and updating the state accordingly, you ensure that the application remains responsive and provides feedback to the user during data fetch operations.

In addition to managing state and handling asynchronous operations, ensuring that the SPA provides a smooth and responsive user experience involves optimizing performance and minimizing latency. This includes techniques such as code splitting, lazy loading, and efficient rendering. Code splitting involves breaking down the application into smaller chunks that can be loaded on demand, rather than loading the entire application upfront. This reduces the initial load time and improves the perceived performance of the application. Lazy loading allows for deferring the loading of non-essential resources until they are needed, further optimizing performance.

Efficient rendering is also crucial for maintaining a responsive user interface. This involves minimizing the number of DOM updates and ensuring that only the parts of the UI that have changed are re-rendered. Libraries like `reagent` and `rum` leverage virtual DOM diffing techniques to optimize rendering performance. By updating only the parts of the DOM that have changed, these libraries help in reducing the performance overhead associated with frequent DOM manipulations.

Finally, integrating real-time data updates can significantly enhance the interactivity and responsiveness of the SPA. Using WebSockets to enable bidirectional communication between the client and server allows for real-time features such as live notifications or chat functionalities. By managing WebSocket connections and handling incoming and outgoing messages effectively, you can provide users with real-time updates and maintain a dynamic user interface.

Implementing all these strategies requires a comprehensive understanding of the interplay between state management, performance optimization, and real-time data handling. By combining these techniques and leveraging the capabilities of ClojureScript and its ecosystem, you can build robust and responsive Single Page Applications that deliver a seamless user experience. The process involves continuous refinement and adaptation to address the evolving needs of the application and its users, ensuring that the SPA remains performant, interactive, and user-friendly.

CHAPTER 17: DEPLOYMENT AND CONTINUOUS INTEGRATION

Deploying and maintaining applications is a critical phase in the software development lifecycle, ensuring that code changes are seamlessly transitioned from development to production environments. This process encompasses a range of tasks including configuring build processes, setting up continuous integration (CI), and managing deployments across various environments. In the context of ClojureScript applications, several best practices and tools can streamline these tasks, enhancing the efficiency and reliability of your deployment workflows.

The first crucial step in the deployment process involves configuring the build process. ClojureScript applications are typically compiled to JavaScript before deployment, and this compilation process must be carefully managed to ensure that the final output is optimized and ready for production. Tools like Leiningen and shadow-cljs play a pivotal role in this process. Leiningen is a build automation tool that manages dependencies, builds configurations, and other aspects of the Clojure ecosystem. For ClojureScript projects, Leiningen can be configured to run the ClojureScript compiler, manage project dependencies, and handle different build profiles.

On the other hand, shadow-cljs is a ClojureScript build tool specifically designed to work seamlessly with modern JavaScript tooling and libraries. It offers advanced features like incremental builds, better integration with npm, and improved performance. Configuring shadow-cljs involves setting up a configuration file where you define build targets, including development and production builds. The production build should be optimized for performance, which includes minification of JavaScript, dead code elimination, and other optimizations that reduce the size of the final bundle and improve loading times.

Once the build process is configured, setting up continuous integration (CI) is the next critical step. Continuous integration involves automatically testing and building your application every time changes are made to the codebase. This ensures that any issues are detected early in the development cycle, improving code quality and reducing the likelihood of deployment failures.

CI tools like Jenkins, GitHub Actions, and GitLab CI/CD provide platforms to automate the build and testing process. These tools integrate with version control systems such as Git, allowing you to define CI pipelines that automatically trigger builds and tests whenever changes are pushed to the repository. In the context of ClojureScript applications, the CI pipeline typically includes steps to check out the code, install dependencies, run tests, build the application, and package the output.

For instance, a GitHub Actions workflow for a ClojureScript application might involve creating a `.yml` file in the `.github/workflows` directory of your repository. This file defines the CI pipeline, specifying steps such as setting up the Java environment, installing Leiningen or shadow-cljs, running tests, and building the application. The workflow ensures that every commit or pull request is validated, and any issues are promptly addressed.

Managing deployments is another crucial aspect of maintaining your application. Deployments involve transferring the built application to a production environment where it will be accessible to end-users. This process often involves deploying to cloud platforms like AWS, Heroku, or digital ocean. Each platform has its own set of deployment procedures and tools, but the general approach involves uploading the built assets, configuring environment settings, and ensuring that the application is correctly integrated with other services such as databases and APIs.

For instance, deploying to AWS might involve using services like Amazon S3 for static asset hosting and Amazon CloudFront for content delivery. You can automate these deployments using tools like AWS CodePipeline, which integrates with your CI system to deploy builds automatically. Similarly, Heroku offers a straightforward deployment process through Git, where you can push code directly from your repository, and it handles the build and deployment process for you.

Ensuring that your application is correctly configured for different environments is also vital. This includes setting up environment-specific configurations such as API endpoints, database connections, and feature flags. Environment variables play a key role in managing these configurations, allowing you to adjust settings based on the environment in which the application is running. For example, you might use environment variables to differentiate between development, staging, and production environments, ensuring that sensitive information like API keys is securely managed.

Finally, monitoring and logging are essential for maintaining application health and performance. Once deployed, it is crucial to monitor the application for errors, performance issues, and other metrics. Tools like Sentry or New Relic can be integrated into your application to provide real-time error tracking and performance monitoring. Logs generated by the application should be collected and analyzed to identify and address issues promptly, ensuring that the application remains stable and performant in production.

In summary, deploying and maintaining ClojureScript applications involves configuring build processes, setting up continuous integration pipelines, managing deployments across various environments, and monitoring application performance. By adhering to these practices and leveraging the appropriate tools, you can ensure a smooth and efficient development workflow, providing a reliable and high-quality experience for users.

Building on the fundamentals of deploying ClojureScript applications, I'll now delve into more advanced aspects of deployment and continuous integration that enhance the robustness and efficiency of your development lifecycle. As we progress, the focus will shift towards advanced configuration techniques, scaling deployment strategies, and managing post-deployment processes to ensure the long-term success and reliability of your application.

Once the basic build and CI pipeline are set up, configuring advanced deployment strategies becomes essential for handling more complex application requirements. One significant aspect to consider is deployment automation. Automating the deployment process not only reduces the potential for human error but also streamlines the workflow, enabling frequent and reliable releases. Tools like Terraform and Ansible can be invaluable in automating infrastructure provisioning and deployment tasks. Terraform, for instance, allows you to define infrastructure as code, specifying the desired state of your cloud resources, such as virtual machines, databases, and networking components. Ansible complements this by automating configuration management and application deployment across your infrastructure.

In addition to automation, incorporating blue-green deployment strategies can significantly enhance deployment reliability. Blue-green deployment involves maintaining two identical environments: one (the blue environment) runs the current version of your application, while the other (the green environment) hosts the new version. During deployment, you switch traffic from the blue environment to the green environment once the new version is fully tested and confirmed to be stable. This approach minimizes downtime and reduces the risk of deployment-related issues affecting your users.

Canary releases are another advanced deployment strategy that can be particularly useful in managing risks associated with new releases. A canary release involves gradually rolling out the new version of your application to a small subset of users before making it available to the entire user base. This phased approach allows you to monitor the application's performance and user feedback in real-time, making it easier to identify and address potential issues early on.

Scaling deployment strategies also requires careful consideration, particularly when dealing with high-traffic applications. Load balancing is a key technique in distributing incoming traffic across multiple instances of your application, ensuring optimal performance and availability. Cloud platforms such as AWS provide Elastic Load Balancing (ELB) services that automatically distribute incoming application traffic across multiple targets, such as EC2 instances or containers. Integrating load balancing with auto-scaling capabilities ensures that your application can dynamically adjust to varying levels of traffic, adding or removing instances as needed based on predefined metrics.

Another critical aspect of scaling is managing state in distributed environments. Stateless applications are generally easier to scale since they do not rely on server-side sessions or data. However, when state management is necessary, leveraging distributed databases or caching solutions can help maintain consistency across multiple instances. For instance, using a distributed cache like Redis can provide a shared state accessible to all instances of your application, ensuring that data remains consistent and reducing the load on your primary database.

Effective monitoring and logging are integral to maintaining the health and performance of your application post-deployment. Implementing comprehensive monitoring solutions allows you to track application metrics, such as response times, error rates, and resource utilization. Tools like Prometheus and Grafana provide robust monitoring and visualization capabilities, enabling you to set up custom dashboards and alerts based on specific metrics. These tools help you proactively address performance issues and ensure that your application remains responsive and reliable.

In parallel with monitoring, centralized logging is crucial for troubleshooting and debugging. Aggregating logs from multiple instances into a centralized system allows you to analyze and correlate log data more efficiently. Services like Elasticsearch, Logstash, and Kibana (ELK Stack) or cloud-based solutions like AWS CloudWatch Logs provide powerful capabilities for collecting, indexing, and searching log data. Implementing structured logging, where logs are formatted in a consistent and machine-readable way, can further enhance your ability to diagnose issues and track the application's behavior over time.

Security considerations also play a vital role in the deployment process. Ensuring that your application is secure against potential threats requires implementing best practices such as secure configuration management, encryption, and access control. Regular security audits and vulnerability assessments can help identify and address potential weaknesses in your application and infrastructure. Additionally, integrating security testing into your CI pipeline, such as running static code analysis tools or performing penetration testing, helps identify vulnerabilities before they reach production.

Lastly, maintaining a robust rollback strategy is essential for managing deployment failures. A rollback strategy allows you to revert to a previous stable version of your application in the event that a deployment introduces critical issues. Implementing automated rollback mechanisms as part of your deployment pipeline can further streamline this process, minimizing downtime and ensuring that users are not adversely affected by deployment-related problems.

By integrating these advanced techniques into your deployment and continuous integration processes, you can enhance the reliability, scalability, and security of your ClojureScript applications. A well-configured deployment strategy not only facilitates smoother releases but also ensures that your application remains resilient and performant in the face of evolving demands and challenges.

Ensuring the ongoing success of a ClojureScript application involves meticulous attention to deployment and continuous integration practices. This part of the discussion delves into some critical aspects that support a seamless and effective deployment process. I'll address the nuances of handling database migrations, optimizing build processes, and maintaining deployment environments to ensure both stability and scalability.

Database migrations are a crucial aspect of application deployment that often requires careful management. As your application evolves, so too does the structure of its database. Managing these changes without disrupting your live environment can be complex. One approach to streamline this process is to use migration tools that integrate with your application's build pipeline. Tools like `migratus` or `ragtime` for ClojureScript offer capabilities to handle schema changes and data migrations smoothly. By incorporating these tools, you can version control your database schema alongside your application code, enabling you to apply changes in a controlled and systematic manner.

Each migration script should be designed to be idempotent, meaning that applying the script multiple times will not alter the result beyond the initial application. This approach prevents issues that could arise from applying the same migration more than once. Testing migration scripts in a staging environment before applying them to production is also essential. This ensures that any issues can be addressed in a controlled setting, reducing the risk of introducing problems to the live environment.

Optimizing build processes is another key factor in a successful deployment strategy. The build process for ClojureScript applications typically involves compiling source code, managing dependencies, and bundling assets. To streamline this process, it's beneficial to automate as much as possible. Tools such as Leiningen or Shadow CLJS provide comprehensive solutions for managing builds, handling dependencies, and integrating with other parts of your development workflow.

An essential part of optimizing build processes is managing build artifacts. Build artifacts are the output of your build process, such as compiled JavaScript files or bundled assets. Storing these artifacts in a versioned artifact repository or a storage service like AWS S3 allows you to keep track of different versions and ensures that you can roll back to a previous build if necessary. Automated deployment scripts can pull these artifacts from the repository and deploy them to your environments, ensuring consistency and reducing manual intervention.

Maintaining deployment environments is critical to ensure that your application operates smoothly across different stages of development. Environment management involves configuring and managing settings specific to each environment, such as development, staging, and production. Environment variables play a significant role in this process. They allow you to configure application settings that vary between environments without modifying the application code itself.

Using environment-specific configuration files or secrets management services can help manage sensitive information securely. Tools such as HashiCorp Vault or AWS Secrets Manager can securely store and manage credentials and other sensitive data, ensuring that they are only accessible to authorized applications and users.

Additionally, keeping deployment environments isolated from one another prevents unintended interactions between them. For instance, a staging environment should mirror the production environment as closely as possible, but it should not have access to the same data or external services. This isolation allows you to test new features and configurations thoroughly without affecting live users or data.

Monitoring deployment environments is also essential for identifying and addressing issues early. Implementing health checks and application performance monitoring tools provides real-time insights into the status of your application. Tools such as New Relic, Datadog, or Prometheus can help track application performance metrics, detect anomalies, and alert you to potential issues before they impact users.

Managing deployments to various environments requires a well-defined strategy for handling configuration changes and updates. This involves setting up deployment pipelines that can automatically handle rolling updates, blue-green deployments, or canary releases, as discussed previously. Such strategies ensure that changes are gradually introduced and can be rolled back if necessary, minimizing disruptions and maintaining application stability.

Lastly, a comprehensive backup and recovery plan is essential for ensuring data integrity and availability. Regular backups of both application data and database content provide a safeguard against data loss or corruption. Implementing automated backup solutions and periodically testing recovery procedures ensures that you can quickly restore your application to a stable state in the event of a failure.

In conclusion, the deployment and continuous integration processes for ClojureScript applications involve careful planning and execution. By automating build and deployment processes, managing database migrations effectively, optimizing build artifacts, and maintaining isolated and monitored environments, you can ensure a robust and reliable deployment pipeline. These practices not only facilitate smoother releases but also contribute to the long-term success and stability of your application.

CHAPTER 18: SECURITY BEST PRACTICES

In the realm of web development, ensuring the security of ClojureScript applications is of paramount importance. This section delves into critical security best practices that safeguard your application from common vulnerabilities and attacks. By understanding and implementing robust security measures, you can mitigate risks and enhance the overall safety of your application.

A fundamental aspect of securing any web application is robust input validation. This process involves scrutinizing data received from users to ensure it meets the expected format and constraints before it is processed or stored. In ClojureScript, input validation can be managed using various techniques and libraries. One approach is to use the `schema` library, which allows you to define and enforce data structures in your application. By specifying schemas for your data, you can validate incoming data against these schemas, ensuring it adheres to the expected format and constraints. This practice helps prevent malicious input from causing unintended behavior or security issues.

Input validation should be applied at multiple levels, including client-side and server-side. While client-side validation provides immediate feedback to users, it is not sufficient on its own as it can be bypassed. Therefore, server-side validation is essential to ensure that all data is properly checked before being processed or stored. Implementing a consistent validation strategy across your application helps in maintaining data integrity and prevents common attacks such as SQL injection and cross-site scripting (XSS).

Another critical area of security is authentication. Authentication is the process of verifying the identity of users who access your application. In ClojureScript applications, this typically involves integrating with authentication systems that manage user credentials and sessions. One effective approach is to use JSON Web Tokens (JWT) for authentication. JWTs provide a secure way to transmit user credentials and session information between the client and server. By incorporating JWTs, you can ensure that user identities are authenticated and that sensitive information is protected.

When implementing authentication, it is crucial to follow best practices for securely handling and storing credentials. This includes hashing passwords using secure algorithms such as bcrypt before storing them in your database. Plaintext passwords should never be stored or transmitted. Additionally, employing multi-factor authentication (MFA) can further enhance security by requiring users to provide additional verification beyond just their password. MFA adds an extra layer of protection against unauthorized access and is particularly important for applications dealing with sensitive information.

Authorization is the process of determining what actions authenticated users are permitted to perform. It ensures that users have the appropriate permissions to access specific resources or perform certain operations. In ClojureScript applications, managing authorization involves defining roles and permissions and enforcing these rules throughout your application. Implementing role-based access control (RBAC) allows you to assign different permissions to different user roles, ensuring that users can only access resources and perform actions that are appropriate for their role.

Additionally, it is important to enforce least privilege principles, which means granting users only the permissions they need to perform their tasks and nothing more. This approach minimizes the potential impact of a security breach by limiting the scope of access for each user. Implementing granular authorization checks at both the client and server levels helps prevent unauthorized actions and protects sensitive data.

Beyond input validation, authentication, and authorization, securing your ClojureScript application also involves protecting against common web vulnerabilities. One such vulnerability is cross-site scripting (XSS), where an attacker injects malicious scripts into web pages viewed by other users. To mitigate XSS risks, it is essential to sanitize and escape user-generated content before rendering it on the page. Utilizing libraries and frameworks that provide built-in protections against XSS can help ensure that your application handles user input securely.

Another common vulnerability is cross-site request forgery (CSRF), where an attacker tricks a user into performing actions on behalf of another user. To protect against CSRF attacks, you can implement anti-CSRF tokens that are included in requests and validated by the server. These tokens ensure that requests are originating from legitimate sources and are not the result of unauthorized actions.

Implementing secure communication protocols is also a vital aspect of application security. Ensuring that data transmitted between the client and server is encrypted using HTTPS helps protect against eavesdropping and man-in-the-middle attacks. Configuring your web server to enforce HTTPS and utilizing secure encryption standards are fundamental practices for safeguarding data in transit.

Regular security audits and vulnerability assessments are essential for maintaining the security of your application over time. Conducting these assessments helps identify and address potential weaknesses before they can be exploited by attackers. Keeping your dependencies and libraries up to date with the latest security patches and updates is also crucial for minimizing risks associated with known vulnerabilities.

In summary, securing ClojureScript applications requires a multi-faceted approach that includes robust input validation, secure authentication and authorization practices, protection against common web vulnerabilities, and the use of secure communication protocols. By implementing these best practices, you can significantly enhance the security of your application and protect it from potential threats.

In securing ClojureScript applications, it is crucial to address various aspects of security beyond basic input validation, authentication, and authorization. This section delves into more nuanced areas such as secure coding practices, data protection strategies, and the importance of regular security reviews.

Secure coding practices are foundational to preventing vulnerabilities and ensuring that your application resists various types of attacks. One key practice is to avoid hardcoding sensitive information, such as API keys or credentials, directly into your source code. Instead, utilize environment variables or secure secrets management services to handle such information. This approach minimizes the risk of accidental exposure and helps maintain confidentiality. For instance, you can use libraries like `dotenv` to load environment variables into your application securely, avoiding the need to embed sensitive data within your codebase.

Additionally, ensuring that your application adheres to the principle of separation of concerns is vital for maintaining security. This principle dictates that different components of your application should handle distinct responsibilities, which helps to reduce the risk of introducing security flaws. For example, separating business logic from data access and presentation layers allows you to enforce different security measures at each layer. By doing so, you can implement stricter controls on data access and mitigate potential risks arising from code that combines multiple responsibilities.

Another essential aspect of secure coding involves implementing proper error handling and logging. Error messages and stack traces can inadvertently reveal sensitive information about the internal workings of your application, potentially aiding attackers in crafting exploits. To prevent this, ensure that error messages displayed to users are generic and do not disclose internal details. Instead, log detailed error information internally where it can be reviewed by developers. This approach allows you to diagnose issues without compromising security. Logging should be configured to capture important events and potential security incidents, with logs stored securely to prevent tampering or unauthorized access.

Data protection is another critical area of focus in application security. Protecting data both in transit and at rest is essential to maintaining confidentiality and integrity. For data in transit, using encryption protocols such as TLS (Transport Layer Security) ensures that data exchanged between the client and server remains confidential and tamper-proof. Configuring your web server to enforce HTTPS and ensuring that all communication between clients and servers is encrypted is a fundamental practice.

For data at rest, employing encryption methods to protect

sensitive information stored in databases or files is crucial. Encryption algorithms such as AES (Advanced Encryption Standard) provide strong protection for stored data. It is also important to manage encryption keys securely, rotating them periodically and storing them in secure locations. This practice ensures that even if data is accessed unauthorizedly, it remains unreadable without the proper encryption keys.

Regular security reviews and audits are essential for maintaining the security of your application over time. Security threats and best practices evolve, and periodic assessments help identify new vulnerabilities and ensure that your application adheres to current security standards. Conducting vulnerability scans and penetration testing can reveal potential weaknesses that may not be apparent during regular development. Engaging with external security experts or using automated security testing tools can provide valuable insights into your application's security posture.

Another significant consideration is the management of third-party dependencies and libraries. ClojureScript applications often rely on external libraries for various functionalities. However, these libraries can introduce vulnerabilities if they are not properly vetted or updated. Regularly reviewing and updating dependencies to incorporate security patches and fixes is essential for mitigating risks. Tools such as `leiningen` or `shadow-cljs` can assist in managing dependencies and ensuring that you are using the latest and most secure versions.

Additionally, adhering to security best practices for third-party services and APIs that your application interacts with is essential. Ensure that any external services or APIs you integrate with follow secure practices and provide adequate protection for data. When using third-party APIs, review their security policies and ensure that they offer secure authentication methods, such as OAuth, and provide proper data protection measures.

In conclusion, securing ClojureScript applications involves a comprehensive approach that includes secure coding practices, data protection strategies, regular security reviews, and diligent management of third-party dependencies. By implementing these practices, you can build resilient applications that protect against a wide range of threats and maintain a high level of security throughout their lifecycle.

Building on the foundation of secure coding practices, data protection strategies, and regular security reviews, it's essential to also address advanced security considerations that ensure the robustness of ClojureScript applications. These considerations include secure session management, cross-site security, and protection against various types of attacks, including those targeting JavaScript vulnerabilities.

Secure session management is critical for maintaining the integrity of user interactions with your application. Session management involves handling user sessions securely to prevent unauthorized access and session hijacking. One of the primary measures is to use secure, HTTP-only cookies to store session identifiers. This ensures that cookies are only transmitted over secure channels and are inaccessible to JavaScript running in the browser, thereby mitigating risks of cross-site scripting (XSS) attacks. Additionally, setting appropriate cookie attributes, such as `Secure`, `HttpOnly`, and `SameSite`, can further enhance security. The `SameSite` attribute restricts how cookies are sent with cross-site requests, reducing the risk of cross-site request forgery (CSRF) attacks.

Another important aspect of session management is implementing session expiration and renewal policies. Expiring sessions after a period of inactivity or after a predefined time limit helps limit the window of opportunity for attackers to exploit stale sessions. Implementing mechanisms for secure session renewal, such as using refresh tokens, ensures that sessions can be extended safely while maintaining robust security controls. Refresh tokens should be securely stored and handled, typically involving additional validation steps to prevent misuse.

Cross-site security is a broad area that encompasses protecting against various attacks that exploit the interactions between different sites. Cross-Site Request Forgery (CSRF) attacks, for instance, trick users into making unwanted actions on a site where they are authenticated. To protect against CSRF, implementing anti-CSRF tokens in forms and validating these tokens on the server side ensures that requests are genuine and come from authenticated users. Anti-CSRF tokens should be unique per session and difficult to predict, enhancing their effectiveness.

Cross-Site Scripting (XSS) attacks involve injecting malicious scripts into web pages viewed by other users. These attacks can compromise user data and application integrity. To protect against XSS, employing Content Security Policy (CSP) headers is a powerful technique. CSP allows you to specify trusted sources for content such as scripts, stylesheets, and other resources, thereby preventing the execution of untrusted code. Additionally, always escaping user input before rendering it in the application ensures that potentially malicious content is not executed. For instance, when incorporating user input into HTML, using libraries or functions designed to escape HTML characters prevents code injection.

Another attack vector involves exploiting vulnerabilities within JavaScript itself. Given that ClojureScript compiles to JavaScript, the security of your ClojureScript code is intrinsically linked to JavaScript security practices. It is essential to understand and address common JavaScript vulnerabilities, such as those arising from insecure deserialization or prototype manipulation. By leveraging robust libraries and frameworks, which are frequently updated to address known vulnerabilities, you can mitigate the risks associated with these issues. Additionally, applying principles such as least privilege, where functions and objects are given only the minimal permissions necessary, helps reduce the potential impact of a compromised component.

Furthermore, ensuring secure interactions with external services and APIs is paramount. When integrating with third-party services, it is crucial to use secure authentication methods, such as OAuth 2.0, which provides robust mechanisms for securing API interactions. Always validate and sanitize any data received from external sources, as untrusted inputs can introduce vulnerabilities if not properly handled.

Regularly updating dependencies and libraries to incorporate security patches and fixes is another critical practice. Many security issues arise from vulnerabilities in outdated libraries or frameworks. Using tools that track and alert you to known vulnerabilities in your dependencies helps ensure that your application remains protected. Tools like `lein-ancient` or `clojars` can assist in monitoring and managing dependency updates for ClojureScript projects.

In addition to these practices, educating developers and stakeholders about security best practices plays a vital role in maintaining application security. Continuous training and awareness programs help keep the development team informed about emerging threats and best practices, reinforcing a culture of security within the organization.

In conclusion, addressing advanced security considerations in ClojureScript applications involves a multifaceted approach. Secure session management, cross-site security measures, protection against JavaScript vulnerabilities, and secure interactions with external services are all critical components of a robust security strategy. By implementing these practices diligently and staying informed about evolving security threats, you can build resilient applications that provide a secure and trustworthy experience for users.

CHAPTER 19: WORKING WITH EXTERNAL APIS

When integrating external APIs into ClojureScript applications, a meticulous approach is required to ensure seamless functionality and robust interaction with third-party services. This process encompasses various stages, including authentication, request management, and response handling. Each stage demands careful consideration to uphold security and efficiency, while effectively leveraging the capabilities provided by external APIs.

The initial phase of integrating an external API involves understanding and configuring the authentication mechanisms provided by the API service. Many APIs require authentication to access their resources, which typically involves using API keys, OAuth tokens, or other forms of credentials. For APIs that utilize API keys, these keys are often included as query parameters or headers in the HTTP requests. When working with OAuth tokens, the process generally involves obtaining a token through an authorization flow and then including this token in the headers of subsequent requests.

In ClojureScript, handling authentication can be managed through libraries such as `cljs-http` or `ajax.core`, which facilitate HTTP requests and responses. For API key-based authentication, you would generally set the `Authorization` header or include the key as a query parameter. For instance, when using `cljs-http`, setting headers is straightforward:

```clojure
(ns my-app.core
  (:require [cljs-http.client :as http]))

(defn fetch-data []
  (http/get "https://api.example.com/data"
       {:headers {"Authorization" "Bearer YOUR_API_KEY"}}))
```

In cases where OAuth is involved, managing token acquisition and renewal is essential. OAuth typically involves several steps, including redirecting users to an authorization server, obtaining an authorization code, and exchanging this code for an access token. Libraries like `cljs-oauth2` can assist with OAuth flows, but it's crucial to handle tokens securely and refresh them as needed to maintain continuous access to the API.

Once authentication is set up, managing API requests and responses becomes the focal point. Crafting robust and reliable API requests involves configuring the request method (GET, POST, PUT, DELETE), headers, and body as required by the API specification. For example, if you are making a POST request to create a resource, you need to include the appropriate headers and request body. Here's an example using `cljs-http` for a POST request:

```clojure
(defn create-resource [data]
  (http/post "https://api.example.com/resources"
       {:headers {"Authorization" "Bearer YOUR_API_KEY"
            "Content-Type" "application/json"}
        :body (js/JSON.stringify data)}))
```

Effective error handling is a crucial aspect of managing API interactions. APIs may return various HTTP status codes indicating different outcomes, such as success, client errors, or server errors. Implementing comprehensive error handling ensures that your application can gracefully manage unexpected issues. For instance, you might want to check for common status codes like 400 (Bad Request) or 500 (Internal Server Error) and handle them appropriately. Here's an example of how you might handle errors:

```clojure
(defn fetch-data []
 (http/get "https://api.example.com/data"
      {:headers {"Authorization" "Bearer YOUR_API_KEY"}}
      (fn [response]
       (if ( (:status response) 200)
         (process-response (:body response))
         (handle-error (:status response) (:body response))))))
```

Processing API responses effectively involves parsing the data returned by the API and incorporating it into your application. APIs often return data in JSON format, which must be parsed and transformed into ClojureScript data structures. Utilizing ClojureScript's JSON parsing capabilities can streamline this process. For example, you can use `js/JSON.parse` to convert JSON strings into JavaScript objects, which can then be processed further:

```clojure
(defn process-response [body]
 (let [data (js/JSON.parse body)]
  ;; Process and use the data
  ))
```

It is also essential to handle pagination and rate limits when working with APIs that provide large datasets or impose usage limits. Many APIs paginate their responses, requiring you to make multiple requests to retrieve all data. Handling pagination involves understanding the API's pagination mechanism (e.g., using `page` parameters or `next` links) and implementing logic to iterate through pages until all data is retrieved. For example:

```clojure
(defn fetch-all-data [url]
  (loop [current-url url
         all-data []]
    (let [response (http/get current-url)]
      (if ( (:status response) 200)
        (let [data (js/JSON.parse (:body response))]
          (recur (:next-url data) (concat all-data (:items data))))
        (handle-error (:status response) (:body response))))))
```

Rate limiting is another critical aspect to consider, as many APIs restrict the number of requests you can make within a given timeframe. Implementing rate-limiting logic, such as waiting for a specified duration before making additional requests, helps prevent exceeding these limits and avoids potential service interruptions.

In summary, integrating external APIs into ClojureScript applications involves a comprehensive approach to authentication, request management, and response processing. By understanding and implementing these practices, you ensure that your application can interact with third-party services securely and efficiently, providing a seamless user experience and robust functionality.

Integrating and managing external APIs requires a detailed understanding of how to structure your requests and manage responses to ensure both functionality and security. Once you have set up authentication and established the means to handle requests and responses, the next critical aspect involves error handling, security considerations, and optimizing interactions with external APIs.

Error handling in the context of API integration is crucial for creating resilient applications. APIs can fail for a variety of reasons, including network issues, server errors, or data format problems. To robustly handle errors, you need to anticipate and manage these scenarios effectively. Common practice involves checking the HTTP status codes returned by the API. For instance, status codes in the 200 range indicate successful requests, while codes in the 400 and 500 ranges signal client-side and server-side errors, respectively.

In ClojureScript, error handling can be managed using conditional logic to inspect the status code and response body. For example, a function might be structured to handle errors gracefully and provide informative feedback to users. Consider a scenario where a GET request fails due to a server error; your application should be designed to either retry the request, display a user-friendly error message, or log the error for further investigation:

```clojure
(defn handle-error [status body]
 (case status
   400 (js/console.error "Bad Request: " body)
   401 (js/console.error "Unauthorized: " body)
   500 (js/console.error "Server Error: " body)
   (js/console.error "Unknown Error: " status)))

(defn fetch-data []
 (http/get "https://api.example.com/data"
     {:headers {"Authorization" "Bearer YOUR_API_KEY"}}
     (fn [response]
       (if ( (:status response) 200)
```

```
      (process-response (:body response))
      (handle-error (:status response) (:body response))))))

(defn process-response [body]
  ;; Process the response body
  (let [data (js/JSON.parse body)]
    ;; Further processing
    ))
```

Beyond error handling, it is imperative to consider security implications when working with external APIs. API keys or tokens must be managed securely to prevent unauthorized access to your services. Avoid hardcoding sensitive information into your source code. Instead, consider using environment variables or secure vault services to store and retrieve these credentials safely. For instance, environment variables can be accessed within your application to manage API keys without exposing them directly in the code:

```clojure
(def api-key (js/process.env.API_KEY))

(defn fetch-data []
  (http/get "https://api.example.com/data"
       {:headers {"Authorization" (str "Bearer " api-key)}}))
```

Another security concern involves validating and sanitizing data received from external APIs. Even though APIs are generally designed to provide safe and accurate data, it is essential to validate and sanitize this data before using it within your application. This process helps protect against potential attacks such as cross-site scripting (XSS) or injection attacks. For example, if you receive user-generated content from an API, ensure that any HTML or JavaScript content is properly escaped or sanitized:

```clojure
(defn sanitize-content [content]
  ;; Implement sanitization logic
  (clojure.string/replace content "<script.?>.?</script>" ""))
```

Optimizing interactions with external APIs is another critical aspect. Many APIs have rate limits to prevent abuse and ensure fair usage among users. To avoid hitting these limits, implement strategies such as request throttling or batching. Request throttling involves pacing your requests to stay within the allowed rate, while batching consolidates multiple requests into a single call where possible. For instance, if an API allows batch processing, you can send a single request containing multiple queries rather than multiple separate requests:

```clojure
(defn batch-fetch [requests]
  (http/post "https://api.example.com/batch"
      {:headers {"Authorization" "Bearer YOUR_API_KEY"}
       :body (js/JSON.stringify {:requests requests})}))
```

Additionally, caching responses can significantly enhance performance and reduce the number of API calls. Implementing a caching mechanism allows you to store frequently accessed data locally, reducing the need for repeated requests to the external API. Caching strategies can vary from in-memory caching for short-term storage to more persistent solutions like local storage or databases:

```clojure
(def ^:dynamic cache (atom {}))

(defn cached-fetch [url]
  (if-let [cached-data (get @cache url)]
```

```
       (js/Promise.resolve cached-data)
    (let [response (http/get url {:headers {"Authorization" "Bearer YOUR_API_KEY"}})]
       (js/Promise.resolve (do
              (reset! cache (assoc @cache url (:body response)))
              (:body response))))))
```

In sum, integrating external APIs into your ClojureScript application involves a comprehensive approach to managing requests, handling errors, ensuring security, and optimizing performance. By implementing robust error handling, securing sensitive information, validating and sanitizing data, and optimizing interactions, you can create a resilient and efficient application that leverages external APIs effectively.

When integrating external APIs into a ClojureScript application, it's vital to consider how to handle complex data interactions and ensure the application's robustness under various conditions. As we delve deeper into this process, we need to focus on asynchronous operations, optimizing data handling, and ensuring consistency and reliability.

Asynchronous operations are central to working with external APIs, as most interactions involve network requests that do not complete immediately. In ClojureScript, you can leverage asynchronous constructs to manage these operations efficiently. The core of handling asynchronous operations lies in using promises or asynchronous functions. ClojureScript supports JavaScript's promise-based approach, which allows you to chain operations and handle results in a non-blocking manner. For instance, when making a request to an API, you typically initiate the request and then use `.then()` to process the response once it is received:

```clojure
(defn fetch-data [url]
    (-> (http/get url {:headers {"Authorization" "Bearer
```

YOUR_API_KEY"}})
    (.then (fn [response]
        (process-response (:body response))))
    (.catch (fn [error]
        (handle-error error)))))
```

Handling responses effectively involves parsing and processing the data returned by the API. Most APIs return data in JSON format, which needs to be parsed into a format that your application can work with. In ClojureScript, this typically involves using functions to convert JSON strings into ClojureScript data structures. After parsing, you can process the data according to your application's needs:

```clojure
(defn process-response [body]
  (let [data (js/JSON.parse body)]
    ;; Implement your logic to handle the data
    (handle-data data)))
```

In addition to parsing data, it's crucial to ensure that the data is used consistently across your application. Implementing data transformation functions can help standardize how data is represented and manipulated. For example, if the API returns dates in various formats, you might need a function to normalize these dates into a consistent format that your application expects:

```clojure
(defn normalize-date [date-string]
  (let [date (js/Date. date-string)]
    (js/Date.toISOString date)))
```

Consistency also involves managing state changes within your application. When working with APIs, it's common to update
```

the application's state based on the data received. This requires careful state management to ensure that the application remains responsive and accurate. In ClojureScript, you might use an atom to manage state, ensuring that updates are performed in a controlled manner:

```clojure
(def app-state (atom {}))

(defn update-state [new-data]
  (swap! app-state merge new-data))
```

Implementing caching strategies can further enhance the application's performance and reduce the load on external APIs. Caching involves storing frequently accessed data locally so that subsequent requests can be served from the cache rather than fetching from the API again. This can be particularly useful for data that doesn't change frequently. You can use local storage or in-memory caching mechanisms to store and retrieve cached data:

```clojure
(defn cache-data [key data]
  (js/localStorage.setItem key (js/JSON.stringify data)))

(defn retrieve-cached-data [key]
  (let [cached (js/localStorage.getItem key)]
    (when cached
      (js/JSON.parse cached))))
```

Additionally, handling rate limits and ensuring that your application adheres to API usage policies is essential. Most APIs impose rate limits to prevent abuse and ensure fair usage. To manage rate limits effectively, you can implement strategies such as exponential backoff, where you progressively increase the delay between retry attempts after each failure, or simply respect the rate limits specified by the API and design your application to avoid exceeding them:

```clojure
(defn retry-with-backoff [url retries delay]
  (http/get url
    {:headers {"Authorization" "Bearer YOUR_API_KEY"}}
    (fn [response]
      (if (< retries 1)
        (js/console.error "Max retries reached")
        (if ( (:status response) 429) ; Rate limit error
          (js/setTimeout (retry-with-backoff url (dec retries) ( 2 delay)) delay)
          (process-response (:body response)))))))
```

To summarize, integrating external APIs into a ClojureScript application requires managing asynchronous operations, processing and caching data, and ensuring compliance with rate limits and security practices. By implementing robust error handling, state management, and caching strategies, you can enhance your application's performance and reliability while effectively leveraging external API functionality. This approach not only ensures a seamless user experience but also maintains the application's efficiency and responsiveness in a dynamic environment.

CHAPTER 20: INTERNATIONALIZATION AND LOCALIZATION

When developing applications for a global audience, it is crucial to consider internationalization and localization to ensure that the application is accessible and usable across different languages and regional settings. Internationalization (i18n) refers to the design and development of an application so that it can be adapted to various languages and regions without requiring engineering changes. Localization (l10n), on the other hand, involves the actual adaptation of the application to specific locales, which includes translating text, adjusting formats, and complying with regional preferences.

The first step in implementing internationalization in a ClojureScript application involves designing the application to support multiple languages and regional formats from the outset. This process typically begins with separating text and locale-specific data from the application's core logic. By externalizing these elements, you make it easier to manage translations and adapt to different cultural norms without altering the underlying codebase. In ClojureScript, this often means using external resource files or data structures that can be dynamically loaded based on the user's locale.

To facilitate this, I use a combination of external JSON files or ClojureScript maps to store translations. Each file or map represents a different language or region and contains key-value pairs where the keys are identifiers for the text elements, and the values are the translated strings. For instance, you might have separate JSON files for English and French, with keys corresponding to different parts of the user interface:

```json
// en.json
{
 "greeting": "Hello",
 "farewell": "Goodbye"
}
```

```json
// fr.json
{
 "greeting": "Bonjour",
 "farewell": "Au revoir"
}
```

In the ClojureScript application, you can create a function to load the appropriate translation file based on the user's locale. This function can be called at runtime to dynamically switch languages:

```clojure
(defn load-translations [locale]
  (let [translations-url (str "/locales/" locale ".json")]
    (-> (js/fetch translations-url)
        (.then (fn [response] (.json response)))
              (.then (fn [data] (reset! translations (js->clj data :keywordize-keys true)))))))
```

Localization goes beyond just translating text; it involves adapting various aspects of the application to fit regional conventions. This includes formatting dates, times, numbers, and currencies according to local preferences. For instance, different regions use different date formats, such as MM/DD/YYYY in the United States versus DD/MM/YYYY in many European countries. Handling these variations requires using locale-aware formatting functions.

In ClojureScript, you can leverage JavaScript's `Intl` object, which provides robust support for internationalization, including formatting and parsing of dates, times, numbers, and currencies. For example, to format a date according to a specific locale, you might use the `Intl.DateTimeFormat` object:

```clojure
(defn format-date [date locale]
  (let [formatter (js/Intl.DateTimeFormat. locale)]
    (.format formatter date)))
```

Similarly, for currency formatting, you can use `Intl.NumberFormat` to ensure that monetary values are displayed correctly:

```clojure
(defn format-currency [amount currency locale]
  (let [formatter (js/Intl.NumberFormat. locale
                    (clj->js {:style "currency"
                              :currency currency}))]
    (.format formatter amount)))
```

Handling pluralization and gender-specific terms adds another layer of complexity. Many languages have different forms of words depending on the quantity or the gender of the subject. For instance, in some languages, the form of the word for "item" changes based on whether the number is singular, dual, or plural. To manage this in ClojureScript, you might need to implement pluralization rules that adjust the displayed text based on the context:

```clojure
(defn pluralize [count singular plural]
 (if ( count 1)
   singular
   plural))
```

Moreover, it's important to consider cultural differences in user interface design, such as text direction (left-to-right versus right-to-left) and iconography. For applications that support right-to-left languages like Arabic or Hebrew, you will need to ensure that the user interface adapts accordingly, including flipping the layout and aligning text properly.

To streamline the process, I use libraries and tools that facilitate internationalization and localization. For ClojureScript applications, libraries such as `clojure-i18n` can simplify the management of translations and locale-specific data. These libraries often provide abstractions and utilities for loading translations, formatting data, and handling pluralization.

In addition to code-based solutions, leveraging build tools and deployment processes to support multiple locales is beneficial. For instance, incorporating automated tests that verify the correct display of content in different languages and locales helps ensure the robustness of the internationalization and localization efforts.

Ultimately, integrating internationalization and localization into a ClojureScript application requires a thoughtful approach to design and implementation. By separating text from code, utilizing locale-aware formatting, and accommodating cultural differences, you can create an application that serves a global audience effectively.

Implementing internationalization and localization in ClojureScript applications requires not only translating text but also addressing a wide range of cultural and regional differences that affect user experience. This second part delves deeper into the intricacies of this process, focusing on handling user preferences, regional settings, and ensuring that your application behaves correctly across different locales.

To begin with, addressing user preferences is a crucial aspect of localization. Users often expect applications to adhere to their specific preferences for language and regional settings. This can include not only language but also date formats, time zones, and currency. Implementing a system that respects these preferences enhances the user experience and ensures that your application meets the needs of a diverse audience.

In a ClojureScript application, managing user preferences typically involves storing and retrieving locale settings from user profiles or browser settings. For web applications, you can often derive locale information from the `navigator` object available in the browser. This object provides details about the user's language preferences, which can be used to initialize the application with appropriate settings:

```clojure
(defn get-user-locale []
  (.-language js/navigator))
```

Once you have the user's preferred locale, it's essential to ensure that your application dynamically adjusts its content and behavior accordingly. This means that all date, time, number, and currency formats must be updated based on the locale. The `Intl` object in JavaScript is particularly useful here, as it allows for locale-specific formatting and parsing.

For instance, to handle date and time formats, you can create a function that uses `Intl.DateTimeFormat` to format dates according to the user's locale:

```clojure
(defn format-localized-date [date locale]
  (let [formatter (js/Intl.DateTimeFormat. locale)]
    (.format formatter date)))
```

Similarly, for numbers and currencies, `Intl.NumberFormat` provides a way to format values based on locale-specific conventions:

```clojure
(defn format-localized-number [number locale]
  (let [formatter (js/Intl.NumberFormat. locale)]
    (.format formatter number)))

(defn format-localized-currency [amount currency locale]
  (let [formatter (js/Intl.NumberFormat. locale
                    (clj->js {:style "currency"
                              :currency currency}))]
    (.format formatter amount)))
```

Addressing time zones is another critical component. Time zone differences can significantly impact the display and interpretation of time-related data. For applications that require displaying or processing dates and times in different time zones, using libraries such as `moment-timezone` can simplify these tasks. By converting dates and times to the user's local time zone, you ensure that time-based information is presented accurately:

```clojure
```

```
(defn convert-to-local-time [date-time timezone]
  (.format (js/moment-timezone date-time timezone) "YYYY-MM-DD HH:mm:ss"))
```

Handling pluralization is another challenge that often arises in internationalization. Different languages have varying rules for plural forms, which can complicate text translation. Many localization libraries and tools provide support for pluralization rules, but implementing these rules effectively requires a solid understanding of the specific pluralization rules for each language.

In ClojureScript, you might implement a pluralization function that adjusts the displayed text based on the quantity and language rules. For example, in English, you typically have singular and plural forms, but other languages might have additional forms:

```clojure
(defn pluralize [count singular plural]
  (if ( count 1)
    singular
    plural))
```

Cultural differences also play a significant role in localization. For example, the layout of a user interface might need to adapt based on text direction, such as right-to-left (RTL) languages like Arabic or Hebrew. Supporting RTL languages involves not only mirroring the layout but also adjusting text alignment and visual elements to match the reading direction.

To handle RTL support in ClojureScript, you might need to adjust the CSS dynamically based on the user's locale. For instance, you could include RTL-specific stylesheets or use CSS-in-JS solutions that allow for dynamic styling based on locale:

```clojure
(defn apply-rtl-styles [is-rtl?]
  (if is-rtl?
    (js/document.getElementById "app").classList.add "rtl")
    (js/document.getElementById "app").classList.remove "rtl"))
```

Testing your internationalized and localized application is vital to ensure that all aspects of the user interface function correctly across different locales. Automated tests should cover various scenarios, including switching languages, formatting dates and numbers, and verifying that UI elements are correctly aligned and displayed. Additionally, manual testing with native speakers and users from different regions can provide valuable feedback on the accuracy and appropriateness of translations and localized content.

Finally, continuous monitoring and updating of localization content are essential as your application evolves and expands to new regions. Regularly review and update translations, adjust locale-specific settings, and ensure that your application remains responsive to user needs and cultural nuances.

By addressing these considerations, you can create a ClojureScript application that is truly global in scope, offering a seamless and culturally appropriate experience for users around the world.

When implementing internationalization and localization in ClojureScript applications, handling text direction and UI layout considerations is crucial, particularly when dealing with right-to-left (RTL) languages. Proper support for RTL languages like Arabic and Hebrew involves more than just mirroring text; it requires a comprehensive approach to ensure that all UI components adapt appropriately to different reading directions. This can affect everything from text alignment to the positioning of icons and other elements.

To manage RTL support effectively in a ClojureScript application, a dynamic approach to CSS styling is often required. A practical strategy involves using conditional class names or inline styles to apply RTL-specific rules when necessary. For instance, you can dynamically add or remove RTL stylesheets based on the user's locale settings:

```clojure
(defn apply-rtl-styles [is-rtl?]
  (if is-rtl?
    (.add (.-classList (js/document.getElementById "app")) "rtl")
    (.remove (.-classList (js/document.getElementById "app")) "rtl")))
```

In this example, a CSS class named `rtl` would be defined in your stylesheet with rules for mirroring layouts and adjusting text alignment. This approach ensures that the UI correctly reflects the text direction, providing a seamless experience for RTL language users.

Handling user input in multiple languages also requires attention. For text inputs, it's important to support various character sets and encoding formats. ClojureScript, when combined with HTML5 and JavaScript, provides robust support for different input types and validation rules. However, additional measures may be needed to accommodate characters from languages with non-Latin scripts. Ensuring that your application can correctly handle input, display, and process such characters without data loss or corruption is essential for global usability.

Furthermore, internationalizing date and time inputs involves not only formatting but also parsing and validating dates according to different locale conventions. Leveraging libraries like `moment.js` or `date-fns` in combination with their internationalization extensions can simplify these tasks. By integrating these libraries, you can ensure that your application handles dates and times consistently and accurately across various locales:

```clojure
(defn parse-localized-date [date-string locale]
  (js/moment date-string locale))
```

Beyond text and input handling, internationalization affects various aspects of user interaction and functionality. For instance, localized error messages and notifications must be accurately translated and contextually relevant. This involves not only translating the text but also considering the appropriate tone and formality based on cultural norms.

Incorporating comprehensive testing practices is crucial for validating internationalization and localization implementations. Automated tests should be designed to check various locale-specific scenarios, including:

- Verifying that localized content is correctly displayed and formatted.
- Ensuring that the application can handle inputs in different languages and scripts.
- Confirming that RTL layouts are correctly applied where necessary.

Manual testing, involving native speakers or users from different regions, provides additional insights into the effectiveness of localization efforts. Feedback from these users can help identify issues that automated tests might overlook, such as subtleties in translation or cultural appropriateness.

As your application grows and evolves, maintaining up-to-date localization is an ongoing process. Regular updates to translations and locale-specific settings are essential to keep your application relevant and accurate. This might involve collaborating with translators and localization experts to address new features or changes in content.

Additionally, you should monitor user feedback and analytics to identify areas where localization might need improvement. For example, if users from specific regions report issues or express preferences, addressing these concerns promptly can enhance the user experience and broaden your application's appeal.

To summarize, implementing internationalization and localization in ClojureScript applications involves a multifaceted approach that addresses text translation, regional settings, RTL support, and user input handling. By carefully managing these aspects and incorporating comprehensive testing and feedback mechanisms, you can create a globally accessible application that meets the diverse needs of users worldwide.

CHAPTER 21: DEBUGGING AND ERROR HANDLING

Debugging and error handling are integral to developing resilient and reliable ClojureScript applications. Mastery of these aspects not only ensures that applications perform as expected but also enhances the development process by making it more efficient and manageable. This discussion will explore various techniques and tools for debugging ClojureScript code, along with strategies for effective error handling.

One of the fundamental steps in debugging ClojureScript applications involves understanding and utilizing the REPL (Read-Eval-Print Loop). The REPL serves as an interactive environment where developers can test code snippets, inspect data structures, and experiment with functions in real-time. This immediate feedback loop is invaluable for diagnosing issues and experimenting with potential solutions.

In ClojureScript, you can use the REPL to interactively debug code. By evaluating expressions and examining their results, you can isolate and identify problems. For instance, you can define and evaluate functions or variables directly within the REPL to check their behavior:

```clojure
;; Define a function
```

```
(defn add [a b]
  (+ a b))

;; Evaluate the function
(add 2 3) ;; Returns 5
```

If you encounter an issue with a function, you can modify it and re-evaluate it in the REPL to immediately see the effect of your changes. This iterative process helps in quickly isolating and fixing bugs.

Another essential tool for debugging in ClojureScript is the use of logging. Logging allows you to record information about the application's state and behavior at various points during execution. By strategically placing log statements in your code, you can trace the flow of execution and identify where things might be going wrong. ClojureScript provides functions like `println` for basic logging:

```clojure
(defn divide [a b]
  (println "Dividing" a "by" b)
  (/ a b))
```

For more advanced logging, you can integrate libraries such as `timbre` or `clojure.tools.logging`, which offer features like log levels, output to different targets, and structured logging.

When it comes to error handling, ClojureScript provides several mechanisms to manage exceptions and errors gracefully. One of the primary constructs for error handling in ClojureScript is the `try-catch` block. This allows you to catch and handle exceptions that occur during the execution of your code:

```clojure
(try
```

```
(println "Attempting division...")
(divide 10 0)
(catch js/Error e
  (println "An error occurred:" (.message e))))
```

In this example, the `divide` function will throw an exception due to division by zero. The `catch` block captures this exception and handles it by printing an error message. This approach ensures that the application can continue running even if an error occurs, rather than crashing abruptly.

Additionally, ClojureScript's error handling can be enhanced through the use of custom error types and defensive programming practices. Defining custom error types allows you to provide more specific and meaningful error messages, which can be particularly useful for debugging and user feedback. For instance:

```clojure
(defrecord DivisionError [message])

(throw (->DivisionError "Cannot divide by zero"))
```

Incorporating defensive programming practices such as input validation and precondition checks can also prevent many common errors. By ensuring that inputs are valid before processing them, you can reduce the likelihood of runtime exceptions and improve the overall robustness of your application:

```clojure
(defn safe-divide [a b]
  (when (zero? b)
    (throw (js/Error. "Division by zero is not allowed")))
  (/ a b))
```

By combining these techniques—leveraging the REPL for interactive debugging, using logging to monitor application behavior, and implementing robust error handling strategies—you can effectively manage and resolve issues within your ClojureScript applications. This comprehensive approach not only aids in troubleshooting but also contributes to building more reliable and maintainable software.

In tackling debugging within ClojureScript applications, one must delve beyond basic practices to incorporate sophisticated methods that enhance the development workflow. While the REPL and logging provide foundational support, there are additional techniques that offer deeper insights and more refined control over the debugging process.

One such technique involves leveraging source maps. Source maps are crucial when debugging ClojureScript applications because they map the compiled JavaScript code back to the original ClojureScript source. This mapping enables developers to set breakpoints and inspect variables directly within the original ClojureScript code in browser developer tools, making debugging much more intuitive. To effectively use source maps, ensure that your ClojureScript compiler is configured to generate them. This typically involves setting the `:source-map` option to `true` in your build configuration. Once enabled, you can use browser developer tools to inspect the original ClojureScript code, allowing for a more seamless debugging experience.

Another powerful debugging tool is the use of interactive debuggers, such as the `cljs.repl` and `cljs.test` libraries. The `cljs.repl` library provides an enhanced REPL environment that supports more advanced debugging features, such as stepping through code and evaluating expressions in context. By starting a REPL session with debugging capabilities, you can pause execution at specific points, inspect the call stack, and evaluate expressions in real-time, which can be particularly useful for diagnosing complex issues.

Testing plays a critical role in debugging and maintaining code quality. Automated tests, including unit tests and integration tests, can help identify issues early in the development process and ensure that code changes do not introduce new bugs. ClojureScript provides tools such as `cljs.test` for writing and running tests. This library integrates with various testing frameworks and can be used to create comprehensive test suites that verify the correctness of your code. By writing tests for your functions and modules, you create a safety net that helps catch regressions and ensures that your application behaves as expected.

Moreover, utilizing continuous integration (CI) systems enhances the robustness of your debugging and error-handling practices. CI tools automatically run your tests and build processes in isolated environments, providing early feedback on code changes. By integrating CI into your workflow, you can ensure that your application is continuously validated against a set of tests, reducing the likelihood of introducing errors into production.

Beyond these tools and techniques, effective error handling in ClojureScript requires a strategic approach to managing different types of errors. For instance, network errors and API failures are common in applications that interact with external services. To handle these gracefully, implement retry mechanisms and fallback strategies. For example, if an API request fails, you might retry the request a few times before showing an error message to the user. Using libraries such as `cljs-ajax` can simplify handling asynchronous requests and managing responses.

In addition to retries, providing meaningful error messages to users is essential for a good user experience. When an error occurs, instead of displaying generic messages, offer users clear and actionable information. This practice not only helps users understand what went wrong but also guides them on how to resolve the issue or contact support if needed. Error messages should be user-friendly and avoid exposing sensitive implementation details that could be exploited.

Custom error handling can further improve the robustness of your application. By defining specific error types and handling them in a controlled manner, you can create more granular and context-specific responses. For instance, you might define custom exceptions for different error scenarios and handle each type differently:

```clojure
(defrecord NetworkError [message])
(defrecord ApiError [message])
(defrecord ValidationError [message])
```

By catching these custom exceptions in your error-handling logic, you can tailor responses based on the type of error, improving the application's resilience and user experience.

To complement error handling, employing defensive programming practices can preemptively address potential issues before they escalate into errors. Implement input validation to ensure that data passed to functions and APIs is in the correct format and meets expected criteria. By validating inputs at both the client and server sides, you can prevent a range of errors from occurring and maintain the integrity of your application.

In conclusion, mastering debugging and error handling in ClojureScript involves a multifaceted approach that combines interactive debugging tools, automated testing, CI practices, robust error management, and defensive programming techniques. By integrating these practices into your development workflow, you enhance your ability to diagnose issues, handle errors gracefully, and maintain a high level of application quality and reliability.

An effective debugging strategy in ClojureScript must include the implementation of comprehensive logging. Logging provides visibility into application behavior, which is crucial for diagnosing issues and understanding application flow. I utilize various logging libraries to capture different levels of log messages, from informational logs to critical errors. Libraries such as `cljs-logging` can be configured to output logs in various formats, and integrating these logs into your application's error-handling strategy can significantly enhance your ability to trace and resolve issues.

In practice, I ensure that logging is implemented judiciously across the application. By placing strategic log statements throughout critical sections of code, such as in functions where errors are likely to occur, or around external API calls, I gain insights into the application's runtime behavior. It is essential to log not only errors but also warnings and informational messages to provide a comprehensive view of the application's state. This approach allows for early detection of potential issues before they escalate into significant problems.

In conjunction with logging, adopting a structured approach to error handling is vital. One effective strategy is to utilize try-catch blocks in ClojureScript to manage exceptions gracefully. By catching exceptions at appropriate levels in the application, I can handle errors in a way that prevents the application from crashing and provides useful feedback to users. For instance, when an unexpected condition occurs during a data fetch operation, I catch the exception, log the error details, and present a user-friendly error message without disrupting the overall application experience.

Furthermore, integrating error-handling middleware into your application's architecture can enhance your ability to manage errors. Middleware functions can intercept errors before they reach the user interface, allowing for centralized error handling and logging. This approach not only simplifies error management but also ensures consistency in how errors are handled and reported across different parts of the application.

Testing is another crucial aspect of a robust debugging strategy. Writing comprehensive test cases helps ensure that various parts of the application work as expected and that changes do not introduce new issues. I adopt a test-driven development (TDD) approach, where I write tests before implementing new features or making changes. This methodology encourages a focus on defining clear expectations for application behavior, which helps identify errors early in the development cycle.

Unit tests are particularly effective for testing individual functions and components in isolation. By writing unit tests that cover different scenarios, including edge cases and error conditions, I can ensure that each component behaves correctly under various conditions. In ClojureScript, I use testing frameworks such as `cljs.test` to create and run these tests. This library provides a rich set of features for writing and organizing tests, including assertions, fixtures, and test reporting.

Integration tests are equally important for verifying the interactions between different components of the application. These tests simulate real-world usage scenarios and check how components work together to achieve a specific outcome. For example, I might write an integration test to validate that data flows correctly from the user interface through to the backend services and back. Integration tests help uncover issues that may not be apparent in unit tests and provide a higher level of assurance that the application functions as intended.

Moreover, employing automated testing tools and continuous integration systems further supports a rigorous debugging process. Automated testing frameworks can execute tests automatically whenever changes are made, providing immediate feedback on the impact of code changes. Continuous integration systems integrate automated testing with the build process, ensuring that each code change is validated before it is deployed. This integration helps catch issues early and maintains a high level of code quality throughout the development lifecycle.

In addition to traditional debugging techniques, adopting advanced monitoring and observability practices can greatly enhance the ability to diagnose and resolve issues. Tools such as application performance monitoring (APM) systems and distributed tracing allow for real-time monitoring of application performance and behavior. By integrating these tools into your application, you gain insights into performance bottlenecks, resource usage, and overall application health. This information is invaluable for identifying issues that might not be apparent through debugging alone.

For instance, an APM tool can track response times, error rates, and resource utilization, providing a detailed view of how the application performs under different conditions. Distributed tracing helps track the flow of requests through various components of the application, allowing you to pinpoint where delays or failures occur. By analyzing this data, I can identify and address performance issues, optimize resource usage, and improve the overall reliability of the application.

Ultimately, effective debugging and error handling in ClojureScript involve a combination of strategic logging, robust error management, comprehensive testing, and advanced monitoring. By integrating these practices into your development workflow, you enhance your ability to diagnose and resolve issues, maintain high application quality, and provide a better experience for users.

CHAPTER 22: PERFORMANCE MONITORING AND OPTIMIZATION

Effective performance monitoring and optimization are crucial for ensuring that web applications run smoothly and efficiently. To achieve high performance, I first establish a robust monitoring framework that allows me to track various metrics and identify potential bottlenecks in the application. This process begins with selecting appropriate tools and techniques for capturing performance data.

The initial step in performance monitoring involves integrating monitoring tools into the application. I utilize tools such as New Relic, Datadog, or Prometheus, each of which provides comprehensive insights into different aspects of application performance. For instance, New Relic offers detailed transaction tracing and real-time analytics, while Datadog provides a unified view of application performance metrics, including response times, error rates, and resource utilization. Prometheus, on the other hand, excels in collecting and querying time-series data, making it suitable for monitoring metrics over time.

Once the monitoring tools are in place, I configure them to capture relevant performance metrics. These metrics typically include response times, throughput, error rates, and resource usage such as CPU and memory consumption. By setting up these metrics, I can track the performance of various components within the application, including the front-end, back-end, and external services. Additionally, I implement custom metrics to monitor specific application features or workflows that are critical to performance.

Real-time monitoring is essential for identifying performance issues as they occur. I use dashboards provided by monitoring tools to visualize performance metrics in real time. These dashboards allow me to observe trends, detect anomalies, and respond promptly to performance degradation. For example, if I notice an unexpected spike in response times, I can investigate further to determine the cause and take corrective action before it impacts users.

In addition to real-time monitoring, I also analyze historical performance data to identify trends and patterns. Historical analysis helps me understand how performance evolves over time and how changes to the application or infrastructure impact performance. For instance, I may analyze response time trends before and after deploying a new feature to assess its impact on overall application performance. This analysis enables me to make data-driven decisions about performance optimizations and capacity planning.

Identifying performance bottlenecks is a critical aspect of performance optimization. I approach this task by examining the collected performance data and using profiling tools to pinpoint areas of inefficiency. Profiling tools such as VisualVM or YourKit provide detailed information about the application's execution, including method execution times, memory usage, and thread activity. By profiling the application, I can identify slow-performing methods, memory leaks, and other issues that contribute to performance bottlenecks.

Once I have identified the bottlenecks, I focus on implementing optimizations to address them. Optimizations can be categorized into various types, including code-level optimizations, database optimizations, and infrastructure optimizations. At the code level, I look for opportunities to refactor inefficient code, optimize algorithms, and reduce complexity. For instance, I might optimize a slow database query by adding appropriate indexes or restructuring the query to improve performance.

Database optimization is another crucial area for enhancing application performance. I analyze database queries to identify slow or inefficient queries and use database profiling tools to gain insights into query execution plans. Based on this analysis, I implement optimizations such as query optimization, indexing, and caching to improve database performance. Additionally, I ensure that the database schema is properly designed to support efficient data access and retrieval.

Infrastructure optimizations involve improving the performance of the underlying hardware and network components. I assess the application's infrastructure to identify potential areas for improvement, such as upgrading server hardware, optimizing network configurations, and implementing load balancing. For example, I might use a content delivery network (CDN) to cache static assets and reduce the load on the application's servers, resulting in faster content delivery and improved performance.

Caching is a powerful optimization technique that I use to improve application performance. By caching frequently accessed data, I reduce the need for repetitive computations or database queries. I implement caching at various levels, including application-level caching, database caching, and HTTP caching. For example, I might use an in-memory cache such as Redis to store frequently accessed data, reducing the need to fetch it from the database repeatedly.

Monitoring and optimizing performance is an ongoing process that requires continuous attention and refinement. I regularly review performance metrics, analyze trends, and make adjustments as needed to maintain optimal performance. Additionally, I stay informed about new performance monitoring tools and optimization techniques to ensure that I am using the best practices for enhancing application performance.

By establishing a comprehensive performance monitoring framework, identifying and addressing performance bottlenecks, and implementing effective optimization techniques, I ensure that my web applications deliver high-quality performance and provide a seamless experience for users. Performance monitoring and optimization are integral to maintaining the overall health and efficiency of web applications, and a proactive approach to these practices helps me achieve and sustain excellent application performance.

Understanding how to effectively monitor and optimize web application performance involves not just the use of tools and techniques but also an in-depth grasp of the application's architecture and behavior. To dive deeper into performance optimization, I focus on several advanced strategies and methodologies that can yield significant improvements in both speed and responsiveness.

One of the crucial areas to address is the performance of asynchronous operations, which are prevalent in modern web applications. Asynchronous operations, such as API calls and background tasks, can often lead to performance issues if not managed properly. I begin by analyzing how these operations are handled and identifying any potential inefficiencies. For example, if multiple asynchronous tasks are executed simultaneously, it might result in excessive resource consumption or contention. To mitigate such issues, I implement proper concurrency management techniques, such as throttling or batching, to ensure that asynchronous tasks are executed in a controlled and efficient manner.

In addition to managing asynchronous operations, I also pay close attention to how data is loaded and rendered in the application. Performance issues often arise from inefficient data loading patterns, such as loading too much data at once or making redundant requests. I employ techniques like lazy loading and pagination to optimize data retrieval and rendering. Lazy loading involves loading data only when it is needed, reducing the initial load time and improving the perceived performance of the application. Pagination, on the other hand, allows me to divide large datasets into smaller, more manageable chunks, which improves both loading times and overall performance.

Another important aspect of performance optimization is the use of efficient algorithms and data structures. In many cases, the choice of algorithm or data structure can significantly impact the application's performance. I analyze the performance of various algorithms used within the application and make adjustments as necessary. For instance, if I identify that a particular sorting algorithm is causing performance issues, I might replace it with a more efficient one. Similarly, I review the data structures used for storing and retrieving information to ensure they are optimized for the specific use cases of the application.

Effective memory management is also critical for optimizing performance. I examine how memory is allocated and used by the application to identify any potential memory leaks or excessive memory consumption. Memory leaks occur when memory that is no longer needed is not released, leading to gradual degradation of performance over time. To address memory leaks, I use tools such as heap profilers and memory analyzers to track memory usage and identify areas where memory is not being properly managed. By addressing these issues, I can ensure that the application maintains optimal performance and stability.

Network performance is another key consideration in performance optimization. Network latency and bandwidth limitations can significantly impact the speed and responsiveness of web applications. I analyze network-related metrics, such as response times and throughput, to identify any potential bottlenecks. Techniques like compressing network requests, optimizing payload sizes, and minimizing the number of requests can help improve network performance. Additionally, I use content delivery networks (CDNs) to distribute content closer to users, reducing latency and improving overall performance.

Database performance is another critical area that requires attention. I evaluate the performance of database queries and identify any that are slow or inefficient. Indexing is a powerful technique for improving query performance by allowing the database to quickly locate the required data. I analyze query execution plans to determine which indexes are needed and ensure that they are used effectively. Additionally, I review database schema design and make adjustments to optimize data access patterns and reduce the need for complex queries.

Caching is a key technique for improving application performance by reducing the need for repeated computations or data retrieval. I implement caching strategies at various levels, including application-level caching, database caching, and HTTP caching. Application-level caching involves storing frequently accessed data in memory to reduce the need for repeated computations or database queries. Database caching involves caching query results to reduce the load on the database. HTTP caching involves storing responses from web requests to reduce the need for repeated network requests.

By implementing these caching strategies, I can significantly improve the application's performance and responsiveness.

Performance optimization is an iterative process that requires continuous monitoring and refinement. I regularly review performance metrics, analyze trends, and make adjustments as needed to maintain optimal performance. Additionally, I stay informed about new performance optimization techniques and best practices to ensure that I am using the most effective strategies for improving application performance.

By employing advanced techniques and strategies for monitoring and optimizing performance, I ensure that my web applications deliver a high-quality user experience. Addressing issues related to asynchronous operations, data loading, algorithms, memory management, network performance, database performance, and caching allows me to achieve and maintain excellent performance in web applications. Performance monitoring and optimization are ongoing processes that require vigilance and adaptability, but they are essential for delivering responsive and efficient web applications.

In the realm of performance monitoring and optimization, one must also address the nuances of concurrency and parallelism, particularly in the context of modern web applications where tasks often run concurrently. Concurrency issues can lead to various performance pitfalls, such as contention and resource starvation. To tackle these challenges, I focus on optimizing the concurrent execution of tasks and processes, ensuring that the application remains responsive and efficient even under heavy load.

Concurrency problems can arise when multiple tasks attempt to access shared resources simultaneously. These issues can be mitigated by employing synchronization mechanisms such as mutexes, semaphores, and locks, which help coordinate access to shared resources. For example, if multiple threads or processes need to read from or write to a shared data structure, employing a lock ensures that only one thread can modify the data at a time, preventing race conditions and data corruption. I carefully analyze the use of these synchronization mechanisms to balance between performance and correctness, avoiding overuse which could lead to bottlenecks.

Another crucial area is the optimization of I/O operations. Input/output operations, such as file access and network communication, often represent significant performance bottlenecks. I analyze and optimize these operations by minimizing synchronous I/O calls, which can block the application while waiting for operations to complete. Instead, I employ asynchronous I/O techniques to allow the application to continue executing other tasks while waiting for I/O operations to finish. This approach not only improves responsiveness but also enhances overall performance by making efficient use of system resources.

Caching strategies are essential for optimizing performance, and implementing them effectively requires a deep understanding of the application's data access patterns. I implement various types of caching, including in-memory caching, distributed caching, and cache invalidation strategies. In-memory caching, such as using Redis or Memcached, stores frequently accessed data in memory, reducing the need for repeated database queries or calculations. Distributed caching extends this approach to a distributed environment, where cached data is shared across multiple servers, ensuring consistency and availability. I also implement cache invalidation strategies to ensure that the cached data remains accurate and up-to-date, balancing between cache freshness and performance.

Load testing is an integral part of performance optimization.

By simulating high traffic conditions, I can identify potential bottlenecks and performance issues before they impact end users. I use load testing tools to generate simulated user traffic and analyze how the application performs under stress. This process helps me pinpoint areas of the application that need optimization, whether it be server configuration, application code, or database queries. The insights gained from load testing enable me to make data-driven decisions on where to focus optimization efforts.

Profiling is another critical technique for identifying performance issues. Profiling tools allow me to examine the execution of my application in detail, providing insights into which parts of the code are consuming the most resources. I use these tools to profile CPU usage, memory allocation, and function execution times. By identifying and addressing the parts of the code that are most resource-intensive, I can significantly improve the overall performance of the application. Profiling is an iterative process, and I frequently revisit it throughout the development lifecycle to ensure ongoing performance improvements.

Moreover, I address front-end performance optimizations, which can greatly impact user experience. Reducing the size and number of assets, such as JavaScript files, CSS stylesheets, and images, helps to decrease load times and improve responsiveness. I employ techniques such as minification and compression to reduce file sizes and use content delivery networks (CDNs) to deliver assets from locations closer to users. Additionally, I optimize rendering performance by minimizing layout reflows and repaints, using techniques such as requestAnimationFrame and CSS containment to manage how and when elements are updated on the page.

Lastly, I consider the impact of application architecture on performance. A well-designed architecture can greatly enhance performance by promoting efficient data flow and reducing unnecessary processing. I evaluate architectural patterns such as microservices, which can help distribute the workload across multiple services, improving scalability and resilience. I also assess the use of serverless architectures, which can automatically scale resources based on demand, reducing the need for manual intervention and optimizing resource utilization.

By addressing these advanced techniques and strategies, I ensure that performance monitoring and optimization are not just reactive measures but integral parts of the development process. Continuous performance assessment, combined with proactive optimization strategies, enables me to deliver web applications that not only meet but exceed user expectations for speed and responsiveness. This holistic approach to performance management is essential for maintaining the quality and efficiency of web applications in an increasingly demanding digital landscape.

CHAPTER 23: ADVANCED UI/ UX PATTERNS

Designing advanced user interfaces and experiences involves leveraging a range of sophisticated patterns and practices that enhance usability and engagement. In this section, I delve into these advanced UI/UX patterns, focusing on techniques and strategies that can elevate the quality of user interactions with applications built in ClojureScript.

A critical aspect of advanced UI/UX design is the application of context-aware design patterns. Context-aware interfaces adjust their behavior based on the user's context or environment, creating a more personalized experience. For instance, a mobile application might use location data to provide relevant content or features specific to the user's current location. In ClojureScript, this can be achieved by integrating geolocation APIs and leveraging libraries that facilitate dynamic content updates based on user context. The goal is to make interfaces more responsive to user needs and preferences, thereby improving the overall usability of the application.

Incorporating adaptive interfaces is another advanced pattern that involves adjusting the layout and functionality based on different factors such as screen size, device orientation, or user preferences. This approach ensures that the application maintains usability and visual appeal across various devices. In ClojureScript, I use responsive design principles along with media queries and dynamic styling to create adaptive interfaces. This includes implementing fluid grids, flexible images, and media queries that tailor the application's layout to different screen sizes and orientations, enhancing user experience on both mobile and desktop platforms.

Advanced animations and transitions play a significant role in creating engaging user experiences. Smooth and well-designed animations can provide visual feedback, guide user attention, and make interactions feel more intuitive. I use libraries and tools in ClojureScript that support animation and transitions, such as Reagent or cljs-react, to implement complex animations. These can include micro-interactions that respond to user actions, such as button presses or form submissions, as well as more elaborate transitions between different states of the application. The key is to ensure that animations enhance the user experience without detracting from the application's performance or usability.

One important technique is implementing Progressive Disclosure. This pattern involves revealing information gradually, based on user actions or interactions, to avoid overwhelming the user with too much information at once. For example, I design interfaces that start with minimal information and offer additional details or options as the user interacts with the application. This technique helps to simplify complex tasks and improve user focus. In ClojureScript, I manage this through dynamic component rendering and state management, using frameworks that allow me to control when and how additional information is presented to the user.

Another advanced pattern is the use of Contextual Help and Tooltips. Contextual help provides users with additional information or guidance relevant to their current task or location within the application. Tooltips can offer brief explanations or tips when users hover over or interact with certain elements. Implementing these features in ClojureScript involves creating interactive components that display context-sensitive information based on user actions or the current application state. By providing timely and relevant assistance, these patterns enhance usability and reduce the learning curve for users.

Designing for accessibility is a fundamental aspect of advanced UI/UX design. Accessibility ensures that applications are usable by people with various disabilities, such as visual impairments or motor difficulties. I integrate accessibility features into ClojureScript applications by adhering to web accessibility standards, such as the Web Content Accessibility Guidelines (WCAG). This includes implementing semantic HTML, ensuring proper contrast ratios, and providing keyboard navigation and screen reader support. By incorporating these accessibility features, I make sure that the application is inclusive and usable by a broader audience.

Personalization is another advanced pattern that involves tailoring the user experience based on individual user preferences, behaviors, or demographic information. Personalization can be achieved through user profiles, preferences settings, and adaptive content. In ClojureScript, I use state management and data-binding techniques to implement personalization features, such as customizing dashboards, content recommendations, and user-specific settings. The goal is to create a more relevant and engaging experience that resonates with individual users.

Integrating with third-party services and APIs can further enhance the user experience by incorporating additional functionalities and data. For example, integrating with social media platforms, payment gateways, or location-based services can provide users with more comprehensive and connected experiences. I utilize ClojureScript libraries and APIs to facilitate these integrations, ensuring that the application can seamlessly interact with external services and provide enriched features.

In summary, leveraging advanced UI/UX patterns requires a deep understanding of user needs and behavior, combined with the application of sophisticated design techniques. By implementing context-aware design, adaptive interfaces, advanced animations, progressive disclosure, contextual help, accessibility features, personalization, and third-party integrations, I create user interfaces that are not only functional but also engaging and intuitive. These patterns and practices are essential for developing applications that provide a seamless and enjoyable user experience, meeting the demands of modern users and enhancing overall satisfaction with the application.

Designing effective user interfaces goes beyond applying fundamental principles; it requires employing advanced patterns that cater to diverse user needs and scenarios. Among these, the principle of dynamic content loading stands out. This technique involves loading and displaying content dynamically as users interact with the application, rather than presenting all content at once. This approach can significantly enhance the performance and user experience by reducing initial load times and ensuring that only relevant information is processed. In ClojureScript, dynamic content loading is often managed through asynchronous data fetching mechanisms, such as AJAX calls or WebSockets, and rendered conditionally based on the current user interaction or state.

Building upon this, implementing infinite scrolling can be particularly effective for applications that handle large datasets or content streams, such as social media feeds or product catalogs. Infinite scrolling involves loading additional content automatically as the user scrolls down a page, eliminating the need for pagination and creating a more fluid and engaging browsing experience. In ClojureScript, infinite scrolling can be implemented by monitoring the user's scroll position and triggering data fetch requests when the user nears the bottom of the page. This pattern helps in maintaining a continuous flow of information without disrupting the user's experience with manual navigation.

Another crucial pattern to explore is responsive feedback. Responsive feedback encompasses various techniques used to inform users about the results of their actions, such as submitting a form or interacting with a UI element. Effective responsive feedback involves not only visual cues, such as loading spinners or success messages but also auditory and haptic feedback where applicable. In ClojureScript, responsive feedback can be implemented using a combination of visual components and state management, ensuring that users receive immediate and clear indications of the application's status or the results of their interactions.

Integrating predictive text and search suggestions can significantly improve the usability of applications that require user input, such as search functionalities or form fields. Predictive text offers users suggestions based on their input, enhancing their typing efficiency and reducing errors. This pattern is especially useful in applications where users frequently enter similar or repetitive data. In ClojureScript, predictive text can be implemented by analyzing user input and querying relevant datasets or APIs to provide real-time suggestions, thus streamlining the user experience and making data entry more intuitive.

The implementation of microinteractions is another advanced pattern that contributes to a refined user experience. Microinteractions refer to small, subtle animations or changes that occur in response to user actions, such as toggling a switch or completing a task. These interactions can provide immediate feedback, guide user behavior, and enhance the overall feel of the application. In ClojureScript, microinteractions are typically managed through CSS animations or JavaScript libraries that enable fine-tuned control over animations and transitions, ensuring that these elements enhance rather than detract from the user experience.

A sophisticated approach to user engagement involves gamification, where game-like elements are incorporated into non-game contexts to increase user motivation and interaction. Gamification can include features such as points, badges, leaderboards, and challenges. Implementing gamification in ClojureScript involves integrating these elements into the application's functionality, tracking user progress, and providing rewards or incentives based on user actions. This approach can drive higher levels of engagement and foster a more enjoyable user experience by incorporating elements of competition and achievement.

Customizable user interfaces are another advanced pattern that allows users to tailor the application's appearance and functionality to their preferences. This customization can include changing themes, layouts, or display options. By providing users with control over their interface, the application can cater to diverse preferences and improve overall satisfaction. In ClojureScript, customization features can be implemented by allowing users to save and apply their settings through persistent storage mechanisms, such as local storage or user profiles, ensuring that their preferences are retained across sessions.

The concept of context-aware interfaces extends beyond dynamic content loading to include adjusting the application's behavior based on contextual information, such as the user's location, time of day, or device type. For instance, a travel application might display different content based on the user's current location, or a shopping app might offer different promotions depending on the time of day. Implementing context-aware interfaces in ClojureScript involves utilizing context-specific data and integrating with APIs or services that provide relevant information, thereby personalizing the user experience and making it more relevant.

Finally, incorporating multimodal interactions can greatly enhance accessibility and user experience by allowing users to interact with the application through various modalities, such as voice, touch, or gestures. Multimodal interactions can cater to users with different preferences and needs, providing alternative ways to interact with the application's features. In ClojureScript, multimodal interactions are achieved by integrating with libraries or frameworks that support various input methods, ensuring that the application is versatile and inclusive.

By applying these advanced UI/UX patterns—dynamic content loading, infinite scrolling, responsive feedback, predictive text, microinteractions, gamification, customizable interfaces, context-aware design, and multimodal interactions —I enhance the usability and engagement of applications. Each pattern contributes to creating a more intuitive and enjoyable user experience, making the application not only functional but also compelling and user-centric. These patterns and techniques are essential for developing sophisticated and responsive user interfaces that meet the needs of modern users and elevate the overall quality of the application.

The application of advanced UI/UX patterns extends into the realm of contextual user interfaces, which dynamically adjust based on a user's current context or environment. This concept involves tailoring the interface elements to adapt to varying conditions such as the user's location, device, or even current activity. For instance, a location-based application might display different features or information depending on whether the user is at home, traveling, or at a specific venue. In ClojureScript, implementing contextual user interfaces involves integrating context-aware services or APIs that provide real-time data about the user's environment, allowing the application to present information and options that are most relevant at that moment.

Incorporating progressive disclosure as a design pattern ensures that users are not overwhelmed by too much information at once. This technique involves initially presenting only the most critical information and progressively revealing additional details as needed. By doing so, the interface remains uncluttered and manageable, enhancing the overall user experience. In ClojureScript, progressive disclosure can be achieved by employing conditional rendering techniques, where additional content or options are displayed based on user actions or inputs. This approach not only makes the interface more navigable but also helps users focus on the task at hand without distraction.

Another crucial pattern is adaptive layouts, which adjust the arrangement of UI components based on the user's device or screen size. This pattern ensures that the application provides an optimal viewing and interaction experience across various devices, from smartphones to large desktop monitors. In ClojureScript, adaptive layouts can be implemented using responsive design principles, employing flexible grid systems and media queries that adjust the layout dynamically based on the device's screen dimensions. This approach ensures that the application remains usable and visually appealing, regardless of the device used.

The implementation of behavior-driven design focuses on aligning the application's behavior with user expectations and preferences. This pattern involves designing interactions and features that respond to users' typical behaviors or anticipated needs. For example, if users frequently perform a particular action, the interface could be designed to streamline or simplify that action based on observed usage patterns. In ClojureScript, behavior-driven design can be achieved through data-driven analytics and user feedback, allowing for iterative refinements that align the application's functionality with user expectations.

Leveraging data visualization patterns can greatly enhance the clarity and effectiveness of presenting complex information. Data visualization involves using graphical representations, such as charts, graphs, and maps, to make data more accessible and interpretable. Advanced data visualization techniques include interactive charts that allow users to explore data dynamically, filter results, and view detailed information on demand. In ClojureScript, data visualization can be implemented using libraries such as Recharts or D3.js, which provide extensive capabilities for creating sophisticated and interactive visual representations of data.

The integration of seamless transitions between different states or views within the application is another advanced pattern that enhances user experience. Seamless transitions help maintain a sense of continuity and coherence, preventing disorienting jumps or abrupt changes in the interface. This can involve smooth animations when navigating between pages, loading new content, or updating information in real-time. In ClojureScript, seamless transitions are achieved using CSS transitions or JavaScript animation libraries, which provide control over the timing and effect of these changes, ensuring that users experience a fluid and polished interaction.

User-centric error handling is a critical aspect of advanced UI/UX design, focusing on how the application communicates errors and issues to users. Effective error handling involves not only displaying error messages but also providing actionable guidance to help users resolve problems. This can include offering suggestions for corrective actions, providing context-specific help, or allowing users to easily report issues. In ClojureScript, user-centric error handling can be implemented by designing error states and messages that are clear, concise, and tailored to the user's current task or context, enhancing the overall usability of the application.

Inclusive design is an essential pattern that ensures the application is accessible to all users, including those with disabilities. This involves designing UI elements and interactions that accommodate various accessibility needs, such as screen readers, keyboard navigation, and color contrast. In ClojureScript, inclusive design can be achieved by following accessibility guidelines and standards, ensuring that the application meets the needs of users with diverse abilities. This includes implementing semantic HTML, providing alternative text for images, and ensuring that all interactive elements are accessible via keyboard and assistive technologies.

Incorporating user feedback loops into the design process is vital for continuously improving the user experience. User feedback loops involve collecting and analyzing feedback from users to identify pain points, preferences, and areas for enhancement. This feedback can be gathered through surveys, user testing, and analytics, providing valuable insights into how users interact with the application and where improvements can be made. In ClojureScript, user feedback loops can be integrated by setting up mechanisms for collecting feedback, analyzing user behavior, and iteratively refining the application based on this input.

Advanced UI/UX patterns, such as contextual user interfaces, progressive disclosure, adaptive layouts, behavior-driven design, data visualization, seamless transitions, user-centric error handling, inclusive design, and user feedback loops, play a pivotal role in creating compelling and user-friendly applications. Each pattern contributes to enhancing the overall user experience, ensuring that the application is not only functional but also intuitive, engaging, and accessible. By implementing these patterns thoughtfully and effectively, I can build applications that resonate with users, meet their needs, and provide a seamless and enjoyable interaction.

CHAPTER 24: INTEGRATING WITH FRONTEND FRAMEWORKS

Integrating ClojureScript with popular frontend frameworks such as React and Vue requires a thoughtful approach to bridge the gap between ClojureScript's functional programming paradigm and the component-based architecture of these frameworks. This process involves setting up the necessary infrastructure, managing component lifecycles, and ensuring smooth interoperability. Let's begin by examining the foundational steps necessary to integrate ClojureScript with React.

To start integrating ClojureScript with React, the first task is to set up the ClojureScript environment to work with React. This typically involves including the necessary React libraries and ClojureScript interop libraries. The most common approach is to use the `cljs-react` library, which provides a ClojureScript wrapper around React, allowing you to use React components within a ClojureScript project. Begin by adding the React and Reagent libraries to your project's dependencies. Reagent, in particular, is a ClojureScript interface to React, offering a more idiomatic way to work with React components in ClojureScript.

Once the libraries are set up, the next step is to configure the build process to handle ClojureScript and React code. This typically involves setting up a build tool like Leiningen or shadow-cljs, which manages dependencies and compiles ClojureScript code into JavaScript. Ensure that the build configuration includes the necessary React and Reagent dependencies and that the output JavaScript is compatible with the React environment.

With the environment in place, you can start writing ClojureScript code that integrates with React components. React components in ClojureScript are typically written as functions that return React elements. These functions use the Reagent library's syntax to define components, manage state, and handle events. For example, a simple React component in ClojureScript might be defined as follows:

```clojure
(ns my-app.core
 (:require [reagent.core :as r]))

(defn my-component []
 [:div "Hello, world!"])
```

In this example, `my-component` is a function that returns a vector of React elements, which Reagent converts into the appropriate React component. This approach allows for a declarative style of UI development that leverages ClojureScript's functional programming capabilities.

Managing component lifecycles is another important aspect of integrating ClojureScript with React. React components have a well-defined lifecycle, which includes mounting, updating, and unmounting phases. In ClojureScript, you can manage these lifecycle events using Reagent's lifecycle hooks. For example, you can use the `reagent.core/with-let` macro to set up component-level state and clean up resources when a component is unmounted.

Interoperability between ClojureScript and React involves ensuring that data and state are shared seamlessly between ClojureScript components and React components. This often requires careful management of state and props to ensure that data flows correctly between components. In ClojureScript, you can use Reagent's reactive atoms to manage component state and pass data between components using props.

For instance, if you need to pass data from a parent component to a child component, you can define the child component to accept props and use these props within the component. Here's an example of how to pass data between components:

```clojure
(ns my-app.core
  (:require [reagent.core :as r]))

(defn child-component [props]
  [:div (str "Received data: " (:data props))])

(defn parent-component []
  (let [data (r/atom "Some data")]
    [:div
     [child-component {:data @data}]]))
```

In this example, `parent-component` passes a piece of data to `child-component` via props. This allows for a clear and structured way to manage data flow between components.

Integrating ClojureScript with Vue involves a similar approach, but with a focus on Vue's component-based architecture. The Vue ecosystem provides tools like `cljs-vue` to facilitate integration with ClojureScript. To start, you'll need to include Vue and `cljs-vue` in your project's dependencies and configure the build tool to handle these libraries.

Once the environment is set up, you can define Vue components using ClojureScript. Vue components in ClojureScript are typically written as ClojureScript maps that define the component's template, script, and style. For example, a basic Vue component might look like this:

```clojure
(ns my-app.core
  (:require [cljs-vue.core :refer [defcomponent]]))

(defcomponent my-component
  {:template "<div>Hello, world!</div>"})
```

In this example, `my-component` is a Vue component defined using ClojureScript syntax. The `defcomponent` macro allows you to define the component's template and other options.

Managing component lifecycles in Vue is handled through Vue's lifecycle hooks, which can be used to execute code at various stages of a component's life. In ClojureScript, you can use `cljs-vue` to interact with these hooks and manage component state and behavior effectively.

Ensuring interoperability between ClojureScript and Vue involves managing state and props in a way that aligns with Vue's reactivity system. Vue's reactivity system is built around reactive data properties and computed properties, which can be used to manage and display data in a reactive manner. In ClojureScript, you can leverage `cljs-vue` to work with Vue's reactivity system and ensure that your ClojureScript components integrate seamlessly with Vue components.

Integrating ClojureScript with frontend frameworks like React and Vue involves setting up the appropriate libraries and build tools, defining components in ClojureScript, and managing component lifecycles and state. By following these practices, you can leverage the power of ClojureScript while building intuitive and responsive user interfaces with popular frontend frameworks.

When integrating ClojureScript with frontend frameworks like React and Vue, the challenge extends beyond initial setup to effective management of interactions between ClojureScript and these frameworks. For a seamless integration, it's crucial to delve into specific practices and techniques that ensure ClojureScript components work harmoniously within the framework ecosystem. In this segment, we will focus on managing component lifecycles and handling state and props effectively to maintain consistency and performance.

Starting with React, one of the key aspects to master is the lifecycle of React components when working with ClojureScript. React components go through several phases: mounting, updating, and unmounting. Each of these phases provides opportunities for integrating ClojureScript-specific functionality. For instance, you may need to perform certain actions when a component is mounted or unmounted, such as fetching data from an API or cleaning up resources.

Reagent, a popular ClojureScript library that wraps React, provides mechanisms to manage these lifecycle events through its lifecycle hooks. For example, the `reagent.core/with-let` macro is an effective tool for managing local component state and side effects. By utilizing `with-let`, you can ensure that certain operations are executed when the component is first rendered and cleaned up when it is removed from the DOM.

Here is an example illustrating how to use `with-let` to manage a component's lifecycle:

```clojure
(ns my-app.core
```

```clojure
  (:require [reagent.core :as r]))

(defn my-component []
 (r/with-let [state (r/atom nil)]
  (r/create-class
   {:component-did-mount
    (fn []
     (reset! state (fetch-data)))
    :component-will-unmount
    (fn []
     (cleanup-resources))
    :reagent-render
    (fn []
     [:div "Data: " @state])})))
```

In this example, `component-did-mount` is used to fetch data when the component is first rendered, while `component-will-unmount` is used to clean up resources before the component is removed.

In addition to managing lifecycle events, handling state and props is essential for ensuring that data flows correctly between ClojureScript components and React components. Reagent facilitates this by allowing you to pass state and props between components using a declarative syntax. Props are used to pass data from parent components to child components, while state is used to manage local data within a component.

Consider a scenario where you need to pass user information from a parent component to a child component. You would define the parent component with a piece of state and pass this state as props to the child component:

```clojure
(ns my-app.core
 (:require [reagent.core :as r]))
```

```clojure
(defn child-component [props]
  [:div "User name: " (:name props)])

(defn parent-component []
  (let [user (r/atom {:name "Alice"})]
    [:div
     [child-component @user]]))
```

In this code snippet, `child-component` receives the `name` prop from the parent component, which holds the user data.

Transitioning to Vue integration, managing component lifecycles and state involves similar principles but tailored to Vue's reactivity system. Vue components are governed by a set of lifecycle hooks that allow you to run code at specific points during a component's existence. In ClojureScript, the `cljs-vue` library provides a way to interact with these hooks.

A key aspect of integrating ClojureScript with Vue is managing reactivity. Vue's reactivity system revolves around reactive data properties and computed properties. Reactive data properties are declared in a Vue component's `data` option and automatically track dependencies, ensuring that changes to data properties are reflected in the UI. Computed properties are used to derive new values based on reactive data properties.

Here is an example of defining a Vue component in ClojureScript with reactive data properties:

```clojure
(ns my-app.core
  (:require [cljs-vue.core :refer [defcomponent]]))

(defcomponent my-component
  {:data
   (fn []
     {:message "Hello, Vue!"})
```

```
  :template
  "<div>{{ message }}</div>"})
```

In this example, `data` is defined as a function returning a map with reactive data. Vue's reactivity system ensures that any changes to `message` are automatically updated in the UI.

Handling props and events in Vue components involves a similar approach to React but with Vue-specific patterns. Props are passed to components as attributes, and events are emitted using Vue's event system. In ClojureScript, you use the `:props` and `:methods` options to manage props and events.

For instance, to create a component that receives a prop and emits an event, you would define it as follows:

```clojure
(ns my-app.core
  (:require [cljs-vue.core :refer [defcomponent]]))

(defcomponent child-component
  {:props {:message :required}
   :methods {:notify (fn [] (this-as this (.emit this "notify")))}
   :template "<div>{{ message }} <button @click'notify'>Notify</button></div>"})
```

In this code, `child-component` accepts a `message` prop and emits a `notify` event when the button is clicked. This allows parent components to listen for events and react accordingly.

In conclusion, integrating ClojureScript with frontend frameworks like React and Vue involves setting up the appropriate libraries, managing component lifecycles, and handling state and props effectively. By leveraging tools like

Reagent for React and `cljs-vue` for Vue, you can ensure that your ClojureScript code works seamlessly within these frameworks, providing a robust foundation for building dynamic and responsive web applications.

Integrating ClojureScript with popular frontend frameworks like React and Vue not only involves setting up the frameworks but also requires fine-tuning the interactions between ClojureScript and these environments to ensure optimal performance and seamless user experiences. As we move forward, it is essential to delve into the more advanced aspects of this integration, including handling asynchronous operations, managing component updates, and maintaining consistency across different parts of the application.

When dealing with asynchronous operations in a ClojureScript application that integrates with frameworks such as React or Vue, managing data fetches and updates becomes critical. In ClojureScript, asynchronous operations can be handled using core.async, a library that provides facilities for managing asynchronous programming with channels and go blocks. Integrating core.async with React or Vue requires careful consideration to ensure that data is fetched and updated correctly without causing performance bottlenecks or race conditions.

For React, the integration involves managing side effects in components. React's lifecycle methods, such as `componentDidMount` and `componentDidUpdate`, are often used to initiate data fetching and update the state. When using ClojureScript with React, you might use core.async to fetch data and update the component state in a way that adheres to React's lifecycle. Here's an example of how you might handle asynchronous data fetching in a React component using Reagent and core.async:

```clojure
(ns my-app.core
```

```clojure
  (:require [reagent.core :as r]
    [clojure.core.async :refer [go <!]]
    [cljs-http.client :as http]))

(defn my-component []
 (let [data (r/atom nil)
    loading (r/atom true)]
  (r/create-class
   {:component-did-mount
    (fn []
     (go
       (let [response (<! (http/get "https://api.example.com/data"))]
      (reset! data (:body response))
      (reset! loading false))))
    :reagent-render
    (fn []
     (if @loading
      [:div "Loading..."]
      [:div "Data: " @data]))})))
```

In this example, data is fetched asynchronously using core.async and `cljs-http`, and the component's state is updated accordingly.

For Vue, handling asynchronous operations often involves using Vue's built-in `async` lifecycle hooks or methods. Vue's `mounted` hook is used for initiating data fetching when a component is first created. Integrating core.async with Vue follows a similar approach as with React but leverages Vue's reactive data system to ensure that updates are reflected in the UI. Here's how you might integrate core.async for data fetching in a Vue component:

```clojure
(ns my-app.core
```

```
(:require [cljs-vue.core :refer [defcomponent]]
         [clojure.core.async :refer [go <!]]
         [cljs-http.client :as http]))

(defcomponent my-component
 {:data
  (fn []
   {:data nil
    :loading true})
  :methods
  {:fetch-data
   (fn []
    (go
        (let [response (<! (http/get "https://api.example.com/data"))]
     (this-as this
      (reset! (.-data this) (:body response))
      (reset! (.-loading this) false))))}
  :mounted
  (fn []
   (this-as this
    (.fetch-data this)))
  :template
  "<div v-if'loading'>Loading...</div>
   <div v-else>Data: {{ data }}</div>"})
` ` `
```

In this Vue example, data fetching is managed within the `mounted` hook, and the reactive data properties ensure that the UI updates automatically when the data changes.

Another critical aspect of integrating ClojureScript with frontend frameworks is managing component updates and reactivity. React and Vue both utilize their respective state management systems to track and update component states. For React, the use of hooks like `useState` and `useEffect` simplifies managing state and side effects in functional components. For Vue, the reactivity system ensures that any changes to data properties are reflected in the UI.

When integrating with ClojureScript, ensuring that state updates are handled efficiently is crucial. For instance, in a React application using Reagent, you might leverage Reagent's reactive atoms to manage state changes. The `reagent.core/atom` function creates a reactive atom that updates components automatically when its value changes. This reactive nature allows for efficient state management without manually triggering re-renders.

Similarly, in Vue, utilizing computed properties and watchers can help manage reactivity efficiently. Computed properties are derived from reactive data and automatically update when their dependencies change, while watchers allow for executing custom logic when specific data properties change.

In addition to managing updates and reactivity, maintaining consistency across different parts of the application is essential for ensuring a smooth user experience. This involves coordinating data flow between components, handling user interactions consistently, and ensuring that the UI remains responsive and up-to-date.

In React, consistency can be achieved by leveraging context providers to manage global state and propagate data across components. React's Context API allows for creating global state providers that can be accessed by any component in the tree, ensuring that data remains consistent and synchronized.

In Vue, state management libraries like Vuex provide a centralized store for managing application state. Vuex allows for defining global state, mutations, and actions that ensure consistency and facilitate state management across different components.

By addressing these advanced aspects of integration, you

can build robust and responsive applications that leverage the strengths of both ClojureScript and popular frontend frameworks like React and Vue. Effective handling of asynchronous operations, state management, and consistency ensures that your application performs well and delivers a seamless user experience.

CHAPTER 25: IMPLEMENTING STATE MANAGEMENT

State management is essential for maintaining the consistency and responsiveness of web applications. In the context of ClojureScript, managing application state efficiently involves understanding various constructs and libraries designed to handle state in a functional and immutable way. As we explore this topic, we will delve into the principles of state management and the practices for leveraging ClojureScript's built-in tools, such as atoms and refs, as well as more advanced state management libraries.

To begin, ClojureScript provides several core constructs for managing state: atoms, refs, agents, and vars. Each of these constructs serves different purposes and is suited for specific use cases, allowing developers to choose the right tool based on the requirements of their application. At the heart of ClojureScript's state management are atoms, which offer a simple yet powerful mechanism for managing mutable state in a way that aligns with ClojureScript's immutable data principles.

Atoms provide a way to manage shared, synchronous, independent state. They are designed for scenarios where state changes are independent of each other and do not require coordination. Atoms are ideal for managing state in a single-threaded environment or where state changes are infrequent and do not involve complex interactions. The primary operations with atoms include reading, setting, and updating their state. Atoms offer atomic updates, meaning that state changes are guaranteed to be consistent and avoid race conditions, even in the presence of concurrent updates.

Here's an example of using atoms in ClojureScript to manage a simple counter:

```clojure
(ns my-app.core
  (:require [reagent.core :as r]))

(defonce counter (r/atom 0))

(defn increment []
  (swap! counter inc))

(defn decrement []
  (swap! counter dec))

(defn counter-component []
  [:div
   [:button {:on-click increment} "Increment"]
   [:span @counter]
   [:button {:on-click decrement} "Decrement"]])
```

In this example, the `counter` atom holds the current value of a counter. The `increment` and `decrement` functions update the atom's value, and the `counter-component` renders the current value and provides buttons to modify it.

Refs, on the other hand, are used for managing coordinated, synchronous state. They are designed for scenarios where multiple parts of an application need to read from and write to the same state in a coordinated fashion. Refs ensure consistency by providing a way to manage state changes within a transaction, where changes are applied atomically, preserving the integrity of the state.

Refs are typically used in situations where multiple pieces of state need to be updated together, ensuring that all changes are consistent. Transactions with refs are managed using the `dosync` macro, which groups state changes together, ensuring that they either all succeed or none do. Here's an example of using refs to manage a shared state in a ClojureScript application:

```clojure
(ns my-app.core
 (:require [clojure.core.async :refer [go <!]]
     [clojure.core.async :as async]))

(defonce shared-state (ref {:counter 0 :message "Hello"}))

(defn update-state [new-value]
 (dosync
  (alter shared-state assoc :message new-value)))

(defn fetch-data []
 (go
    (let [response (<! (http/get "https://api.example.com/message"))]
   (update-state (:body response)))))
```

In this example, the `shared-state` ref holds a map with multiple pieces of state. The `update-state` function updates the state within a transaction, ensuring that all changes are applied atomically.

Agents provide another approach to state management, designed for asynchronous updates. Unlike atoms and refs, agents allow for state changes to be managed independently of the threads that perform the updates. Agents are suitable for scenarios where state updates are infrequent or involve background processing. They offer a way to handle asynchronous updates without blocking the main thread.

Here's an example of using agents in ClojureScript:

```clojure
(ns my-app.core
 (:require [clojure.core.async :refer [go <!]]
    [clojure.core.async :as async]))

(defonce agent-state (agent 0))

(defn increment-agent []
 (send-off agent-state inc))

(defn fetch-data []
 (go
  (let [response (<! (http/get "https://api.example.com/data"))]
    (send-off agent-state (fn [state] (+ state (parse-int (:body response))))))))
```

In this example, the `agent-state` agent manages a counter that can be incremented asynchronously. The `increment-agent` function increments the counter, and `fetch-data` updates the counter with data fetched from an external API.

In addition to these core constructs, ClojureScript's ecosystem includes various state management libraries and tools that offer more advanced capabilities. Libraries like Re-frame and Reagent provide abstractions and patterns for managing application state in a way that integrates seamlessly with ClojureScript's functional paradigm. Re-frame, for example, builds on top of Reagent and provides a more structured approach to state management, leveraging an event-driven model and a centralized event handling system.

Understanding these tools and techniques allows developers to select the appropriate state management approach based on the specific needs of their application. By effectively utilizing atoms, refs, agents, and advanced libraries, developers can manage application state in a way that ensures consistency, responsiveness, and maintainability.

To manage state effectively in ClojureScript, it is important to understand not just the individual constructs like atoms, refs, and agents, but also how these tools interact with one another and integrate into broader application architectures. The nuanced handling of state within an application can greatly influence its performance, reliability, and maintainability.

When integrating state management constructs into a ClojureScript application, one of the critical aspects to consider is the application's architecture. In a well-designed system, state management is not a standalone concern but is interwoven with the architecture of the application. This includes how state is shared across components, how it is persisted and restored, and how different state management tools are utilized to address specific needs of the application.

Let us delve deeper into the use of atoms in more complex scenarios. Atoms are particularly useful in situations where state changes are relatively independent. For instance, in an application with a highly interactive user interface, multiple components might independently manage their own state. Here, atoms allow each component to manage its own state without the need for complex synchronization mechanisms. However, managing state in a distributed manner using atoms requires careful consideration to avoid inconsistencies and ensure that state changes are properly propagated.

Consider an example where an application has multiple independent counters, each represented by its own atom. Here's how you might manage these counters:

```clojure
(ns my-app.core
```

```
(:require [reagent.core :as r]))

(defonce counters (r/atom {:counter1 0 :counter2 0}))

(defn increment [counter-key]
  (swap! counters update counter-key inc))

(defn counter-component []
  [:div
     [:button {:on-click (increment :counter1)} "Increment Counter 1"]
     [:button {:on-click (increment :counter2)} "Increment Counter 2"]
    [:p "Counter 1: " (:counter1 @counters)]
    [:p "Counter 2: " (:counter2 @counters)]])
```

In this scenario, the `counters` atom holds a map with multiple counter values. Each button updates its respective counter, and the interface reflects these updates. This approach is effective when state changes are simple and do not need to be coordinated across different parts of the application.

When dealing with more complex state management needs, such as when state changes need to be coordinated or are dependent on multiple factors, refs become relevant. Refs provide a way to manage state changes that need to be synchronized across different parts of an application. They are particularly useful in scenarios where you need to ensure consistency and avoid race conditions. For example, if your application involves a form with multiple fields that must remain consistent, refs can help manage these fields as a cohesive unit.

Here's an example of using refs to manage the state of a form:

```clojure
(ns my-app.core
```

```clojure
  (:require [clojure.core.async :refer [go <!]]
      [clojure.core.async :as async]))

(defonce form-state (ref {:name "" :email ""}))

(defn update-form [field value]
 (dosync
   (alter form-state assoc field value)))

(defn form-component []
 [:div
  [:input {:type "text" :placeholder "Name" :on-change (update-form :name (-> % .-target .-value))}]
     [:input {:type "email" :placeholder "Email" :on-change (update-form :email (-> % .-target .-value))}]
  [:p "Name: " (:name @form-state)]
  [:p "Email: " (:email @form-state)]])
```

In this example, the `form-state` ref manages the state of a form with two fields, `name` and `email`. The `update-form` function uses a transaction to ensure that changes to the form fields are consistent.

Agents, with their focus on asynchronous state updates, offer another layer of complexity. Agents are well-suited for background processing tasks where state changes need to be handled separately from the main application flow. They allow for state updates that do not block the main thread, providing a mechanism to manage state in an asynchronous manner. This is particularly useful for operations such as fetching data from external sources or performing long-running computations.

Here's an example of using agents to handle asynchronous updates:

```clojure
(ns my-app.core
```

```clojure
(:require [clojure.core.async :refer [go <!]]
     [clojure.core.async :as async]))

(defonce async-state (agent 0))

(defn increment-async []
 (send-off async-state inc))

(defn fetch-data-async []
 (go
  (let [response (<! (http/get "https://api.example.com/data"))]
    (send-off async-state (fn [state] (+ state (parse-int (:body response)))))))))
```

In this example, `async-state` is an agent managing a counter that is updated asynchronously. The `increment-async` function increments the counter, while `fetch-data-async` demonstrates how to perform an asynchronous data fetch and update the state based on the fetched data.

Integrating these state management constructs into a cohesive architecture requires careful consideration of how state flows through the application. This includes designing components and functions that effectively manage and interact with state, ensuring that state changes are predictable and maintainable.

By leveraging atoms for independent state, refs for coordinated state, and agents for asynchronous updates, you can build robust ClojureScript applications that handle state management in a way that is both functional and efficient. Each construct offers unique advantages, and understanding their strengths and limitations allows you to apply them effectively within your application's architecture.

As we continue exploring the realm of state management within ClojureScript, it is essential to examine how these state management tools can be integrated into a larger application framework. The effective management of application state not only enhances the responsiveness and consistency of the application but also influences how components interact with one another. This integration often involves understanding how to transition between different state management constructs and ensuring that state remains synchronized across various components and layers of the application.

One of the significant challenges in state management is handling state transitions, especially in complex applications where state changes are frequent and interdependent. At this juncture, the choice of state management tool becomes crucial. While atoms, refs, and agents each offer distinct benefits, there are scenarios where a combination of these constructs may be necessary. For instance, a high-performance application might use atoms for simple, isolated states, refs for state that needs to be coordinated across components, and agents for background tasks.

In applications where a combination of state management strategies is used, it is vital to design the architecture in such a way that it prevents state conflicts and ensures smooth data flow. This often involves creating clear boundaries between different types of state and defining well-established protocols for how state transitions occur.

Consider an example of an application that needs to manage both user interactions and background data fetching. The application might use atoms to handle the state related to user inputs, refs to manage forms with interdependent fields, and agents to process and update data fetched from a server. Here's how you might approach this integration:

1. Managing User Interactions with Atoms: Atoms are well-suited for managing local, independent states. For instance, if you have a form where each field is managed independently, atoms provide a straightforward mechanism for tracking

changes.

2. Coordinating Form States with Refs: For a more complex form where fields depend on one another (e.g., a form with cascading dropdowns), refs are used to ensure consistency and to handle the interdependencies between different parts of the form.

3. Handling Background Data with Agents: Data that needs to be fetched asynchronously from a server can be managed using agents. For instance, an agent could handle updates to a list of items fetched from a remote API, while the application continues to function smoothly without waiting for the data fetch to complete.

An important aspect of integrating these state management strategies is understanding how to handle state transitions and synchronize state across components. For instance, when an agent updates its state, those updates must be reflected in the UI. This typically involves ensuring that the component re-renders appropriately to reflect the new state. In ClojureScript, tools such as Reagent make it easier to manage re-renders and ensure that state changes are properly reflected in the user interface.

Moreover, incorporating state management libraries into your ClojurcScript application can further enhance state handling. Libraries such as `re-frame` provide a framework for managing application state in a more structured manner, allowing for complex state transitions and interactions to be managed more effectively. Re-frame uses an event-based approach where state changes are triggered by events, and these events are handled by handlers that update the state. This approach provides a clear separation between the application's state and the logic that updates it, facilitating better maintainability and scalability.

For example, in a Re-frame application, you would define

events that represent user actions or other state changes, and then create event handlers that specify how the state should be updated in response to these events. Here's a simple example:

```clojure
(ns my-app.events
  (:require [re-frame.core :as re-frame]))

(re-frame/reg-event-db
 :update-name
 (fn [db [_ new-name]]
   (assoc db :name new-name)))
```

In this example, the `:update-name` event updates the application state with a new name. The event handler modifies the database (which represents the application state) and returns the updated state. The UI components then react to these state changes and re-render accordingly.

Implementing state management in a ClojureScript application also requires attention to best practices for managing state immutability and ensuring that state updates are predictable and manageable. Ensuring that state is immutable helps prevent unintended side effects and makes the application's behavior more predictable. This involves not only using immutable data structures but also ensuring that any state updates are performed in a functional manner, where new states are derived from existing states without modifying the original data.

In summary, integrating state management into a ClojureScript application involves a nuanced approach that balances the use of various state management constructs such as atoms, refs, and agents. By carefully considering the requirements of your application and choosing the appropriate state management strategies, you can build a robust and responsive application that handles state efficiently. Whether managing simple, independent states with atoms or complex, coordinated states with refs, or handling asynchronous updates with agents, the key is to design an architecture that ensures smooth and predictable state transitions, ultimately leading to a more maintainable and scalable application.

CHAPTER 26: FUNCTIONAL PROGRAMMING PATTERNS

Functional programming, a paradigm that emphasizes the evaluation of functions rather than the execution of commands, forms the bedrock of ClojureScript. To truly harness the power of ClojureScript, it is essential to grasp and apply advanced functional programming patterns. This discussion delves into the intricacies of higher-order functions, monads, and immutability, illustrating how these patterns can be leveraged to produce more maintainable and expressive code.

In functional programming, higher-order functions play a crucial role by operating on other functions or returning functions as their results. These functions embody the principle of treating functions as first-class citizens, which is central to functional programming. A quintessential example is the `map` function in ClojureScript, which applies a given function to each element of a collection, returning a new collection with the results. This operation exemplifies the power of higher-order functions by abstracting away the iteration process, allowing for a more declarative style of coding.

Consider a scenario where we need to transform a list of integers by squaring each element. Instead of manually iterating through the list with a loop, we can use the `map` function in ClojureScript to achieve this transformation concisely. By passing the squaring function and the list to `map`, we obtain a new list with squared values. This approach not only simplifies the code but also enhances its readability and maintainability.

Another powerful pattern within functional programming is the concept of monads. Monads provide a way to handle computations that involve side effects or require context, such as asynchronous operations or state management. The `Maybe` monad, for example, is used to encapsulate computations that may fail, allowing for graceful handling of errors without resorting to verbose error-checking code.

In ClojureScript, the `Maybe` monad can be implemented using a combination of functional constructs. The `maybe` function creates a monadic context that wraps a value, while the `bind` function allows for chaining computations within this context. This pattern ensures that computations are performed only when valid values are present, effectively managing potential errors and maintaining a clean flow of data.

For instance, imagine we have a function that retrieves a user's profile based on their ID. This function may return `nil` if the user is not found. By using the `Maybe` monad, we can chain subsequent computations, such as fetching the user's posts, only if the user profile is successfully retrieved. This approach prevents errors from propagating and maintains a more predictable control flow.

Immutability is another foundational principle of functional programming that is prominently featured in ClojureScript. Immutable data structures, which cannot be modified once created, offer several advantages, including ease of reasoning about code, safer concurrent operations, and simplified debugging. In ClojureScript, immutable data structures such as lists, vectors, and maps are integral to the language.

When working with immutable data, it is essential to understand that operations that appear to modify a data structure, such as `assoc` or `conj`, actually create new versions of the data structure with the modifications applied. This immutability ensures that previous versions of the data remain unchanged, preserving the integrity of the data across different parts of the program.

For example, consider a scenario where we need to update a user's profile information in a data structure. Using ClojureScript's immutable data structures, we can create a new version of the profile with the updated information without altering the original data. This approach guarantees that any previous references to the profile remain valid and unaffected by the update.

Moreover, immutability facilitates functional programming patterns like pure functions, which are functions that produce the same output given the same input and do not have side effects. Pure functions are essential for building reliable and predictable software, as they ensure that the behavior of a function is consistent and easy to reason about.

In practice, combining higher-order functions, monads, and immutability in ClojureScript enables developers to write code that is not only more concise and expressive but also more robust and maintainable. By embracing these advanced functional programming patterns, we can leverage the full potential of ClojureScript and create software that adheres to the principles of functional programming while addressing real-world challenges.

As we progress through the subsequent discussions, we

will continue to explore how these functional programming patterns can be applied in various scenarios, providing further insights into their practical benefits and applications in ClojureScript development.

Continuing our exploration of functional programming patterns, it is essential to delve deeper into the application of higher-order functions and monads, and how they interrelate with immutability to enhance code clarity and robustness. Understanding these concepts in greater detail provides a comprehensive view of their power and utility in ClojureScript programming.

A fundamental aspect of higher-order functions is their ability to compose other functions, allowing for the creation of more complex behaviors from simple building blocks. Function composition is a pattern where functions are combined to form a new function. In ClojureScript, this can be achieved using the `comp` function, which takes a sequence of functions and returns a new function that is the composition of these functions. The composed function processes its input through each of the constituent functions in sequence.

For instance, suppose we have two functions, `increment` and `double`, that respectively add one to a number and multiply it by two. By composing these functions, we create a new function that first increments a number and then doubles the result. This functional composition not only enhances modularity but also provides a clear and expressive way to construct complex data transformations.

Additionally, higher-order functions enable powerful patterns such as currying and partial application. Currying transforms a function that takes multiple arguments into a sequence of functions that each take a single argument. Partial application allows us to fix a number of arguments to a function, producing a new function with fewer parameters. These techniques are particularly useful in scenarios where functions need to be customized or specialized for specific tasks.

In ClojureScript, currying and partial application are facilitated by functions like `partial`, which allows for pre-filling some arguments of a function. By using `partial`, we can create a new function with some arguments preset, simplifying repetitive function calls and improving code reusability.

Moving on to monads, their utility in functional programming extends beyond simple error handling. Monads can also be employed for handling asynchronous computations, state management, and more complex data flows. One notable example is the `IO` monad, which encapsulates computations that involve input and output, thereby managing side effects in a controlled manner.

Implementing the `IO` monad in ClojureScript involves defining a monadic context for IO operations and providing functions to handle these operations in a pure functional style. By encapsulating IO operations within the `IO` monad, we ensure that these operations are sequenced correctly and that side effects are managed predictably. This approach contrasts with imperative programming, where side effects can lead to unpredictable behavior and harder-to-maintain code.

Furthermore, the concept of functors, which are a generalization of monads, also plays a significant role in functional programming. Functors provide a way to map functions over wrapped values, such as lists or options, while preserving the structure of the wrapper. In ClojureScript, the `map` function for collections is an example of a functor in action, demonstrating how functional programming patterns can be applied to various data types.

The interaction between monads and immutability is particularly noteworthy. Immutability ensures that data structures remain unchanged, which aligns well with the principles of monads that manage side effects and context without altering the underlying data. By combining immutability with monads, we achieve a functional programming paradigm where computations are performed in a predictable and controlled manner, with minimal risk of unintended side effects.

For example, consider a scenario where we need to perform a series of computations on a large dataset. Using immutable data structures alongside monadic patterns allows us to process the data efficiently while maintaining the integrity of the original dataset. This combination of immutability and monads facilitates the development of reliable and scalable applications.

Moreover, the use of persistent data structures in ClojureScript, such as those provided by the `clojure.core` library, exemplifies the power of immutability in practice. These data structures are designed to provide efficient operations while maintaining immutability, enabling developers to build applications that handle large volumes of data effectively without compromising performance.

In summary, the application of higher-order functions and monads, combined with the principles of immutability, provides a robust framework for developing expressive and maintainable ClojureScript code. By leveraging these advanced functional programming patterns, we can build software that is not only more modular and reusable but also more resilient and easier to reason about. As we continue to explore these concepts, it becomes increasingly clear how they contribute to the overall efficacy and elegance of functional programming in ClojureScript.

To further explore functional programming patterns, we need to delve into the concept of functional design patterns and their application within the ClojureScript environment. This includes understanding how to leverage these patterns to construct more robust and expressive software solutions.

One critical aspect of functional design is the use of pure functions. Pure functions are functions that always produce the same output given the same input and do not cause any side effects. They serve as the building blocks of functional programming, contributing to code that is predictable and easier to test. In ClojureScript, adhering to purity ensures that functions operate solely on their inputs and return values without altering any external state.

For instance, consider a function that calculates the factorial of a number. This function is pure because its result depends only on the input number and does not modify any external variables. Such purity makes the function highly predictable and facilitates straightforward testing, as the output can be determined solely based on the input.

In addition to pure functions, higher-order functions can be employed to implement more advanced patterns like function combinators. Combinators are higher-order functions that manipulate and combine other functions. An example is the `juxt` function in ClojureScript, which takes a collection of functions and returns a new function that applies each function to the same input, collecting the results into a vector. This pattern is particularly useful when you need to apply multiple transformations to data in parallel.

Function combinators also play a significant role in managing complexity and enhancing code reusability. By creating small, composable functions that each handle a specific aspect of a problem, developers can build more complex behaviors from these simpler components. This modular approach not only improves code clarity but also facilitates easier debugging and testing.

Another pattern worth exploring is the use of transducers,

which provide a powerful abstraction for processing sequences. Transducers are composable and reusable components that operate on sequences, transforming them in a way that is independent of the specific collection being used. This abstraction allows for more flexible and efficient data processing pipelines.

In ClojureScript, transducers are used with functions like `reduce`, `map`, and `filter`, allowing you to define data transformations in a manner that is both performant and elegant. For example, by combining transducers, you can create a data processing pipeline that efficiently performs multiple transformations on a sequence without creating intermediate collections.

In practice, transducers can be used to construct complex data processing workflows with minimal overhead. For instance, if you need to process a large dataset by filtering, mapping, and reducing the data, using transducers allows you to compose these operations into a single, efficient pipeline. This approach not only enhances performance but also simplifies the code, as the data transformations are defined declaratively rather than imperatively.

Incorporating functional patterns like immutability and higher-order functions with transducers exemplifies the power of functional programming in ClojureScript. By leveraging these patterns, developers can build applications that are both efficient and maintainable, addressing the challenges of modern software development with a functional programming mindset.

Furthermore, leveraging ClojureScript's built-in immutable data structures in conjunction with these patterns allows for creating highly reliable software systems. Immutable data structures ensure that data remains consistent and unchanged throughout its lifecycle, reducing the risk of unintended side effects and simplifying state management. This is particularly advantageous in concurrent programming scenarios, where immutability helps avoid common pitfalls associated with mutable state.

For instance, when building a real-time data processing application, using immutable data structures ensures that updates to the data are managed in a predictable manner. As the data flows through various stages of processing, the immutable structures preserve the integrity of the data, allowing for more reliable and consistent results.

Moreover, the functional programming patterns discussed also align well with the principles of declarative programming. Declarative programming focuses on expressing what should be done rather than how to do it, which complements the use of higher-order functions, monads, and immutability. By writing code in a declarative style, developers can specify the desired outcomes of computations without delving into the procedural details, leading to more concise and understandable code.

In summary, the application of advanced functional programming patterns in ClojureScript—such as higher-order functions, monads, and immutability—provides a robust foundation for creating expressive and maintainable software solutions. By understanding and applying these patterns effectively, developers can leverage the full potential of functional programming to build software that is both efficient and resilient. As we continue to explore these concepts, it becomes evident how they contribute to the overall effectiveness and elegance of functional programming in ClojureScript.

CHAPTER 27: TESTING AND TEST-DRIVEN DEVELOPMENT

Testing is a cornerstone of software development that ensures the reliability and functionality of applications. In the context of ClojureScript applications, employing a comprehensive testing strategy is crucial for maintaining code quality and fostering confidence in the software's behavior. This examination will delve into various testing strategies including unit testing, integration testing, and end-to-end testing, while also exploring the principles and practices of test-driven development (TDD) and their application in a ClojureScript environment.

Unit testing is the process of verifying individual components of a program to ensure that each part functions correctly in isolation. In ClojureScript, unit tests are typically written to test functions and modules in isolation from the rest of the application. The primary goal of unit testing is to validate that each function performs as expected for a given set of inputs and outputs. This involves creating test cases that cover various scenarios, including edge cases, to ensure robustness and correctness.

To implement unit testing in ClojureScript, one commonly

used library is `cljs.test`, which provides a framework for writing and running tests. This library offers a set of macros and functions that facilitate the creation of test suites and test cases. For instance, the `deftest` macro is used to define a test, while the `is` macro is employed to assert conditions. Writing unit tests with `cljs.test` involves specifying the expected outcomes for functions and using assertions to verify that the actual results match these expectations.

Integration testing, on the other hand, focuses on verifying the interactions between different components of the application. This type of testing is designed to ensure that the integrated components work together as expected, uncovering issues that may not be evident in unit tests. In ClojureScript applications, integration tests might involve testing how different modules or services interact with each other, including external dependencies such as APIs or databases.

When performing integration testing, it is essential to consider the setup and teardown of test environments to ensure that tests run consistently and do not interfere with each other. This may involve configuring mock services or using in-memory databases to simulate interactions without affecting the production environment. The goal is to create a controlled environment that accurately reflects the conditions under which the application will operate in production.

End-to-end testing, also known as functional testing, examines the application as a whole to validate that all components work together to achieve the desired functionality. This type of testing simulates real-world scenarios by interacting with the application through its user interface or API, verifying that the system performs as expected from start to finish. End-to-end tests are particularly valuable for ensuring that user workflows and business processes function correctly in the integrated application.

In ClojureScript, end-to-end testing can be implemented using tools such as `Cypress` or `Nightwatch`, which allow for automated testing of web applications. These tools enable developers to write tests that simulate user interactions, such as filling out forms, clicking buttons, and navigating through pages. By automating these interactions, end-to-end tests can help identify issues related to user experience and application behavior that might not be captured by unit or integration tests.

In addition to these testing strategies, adopting test-driven development (TDD) can further enhance the reliability and maintainability of ClojureScript applications. TDD is a development approach where tests are written before the actual code is implemented. The process involves writing a test case that defines the desired functionality, followed by writing the minimal code necessary to pass the test, and then refactoring the code while ensuring that all tests continue to pass.

Applying TDD in ClojureScript involves a cycle of writing failing tests, implementing the code to make the tests pass, and then refactoring the code to improve its design and maintainability. This approach encourages developers to think critically about the desired behavior of their code and ensures that tests are closely aligned with the requirements. TDD also promotes a test suite that serves as a safety net, providing confidence that changes to the code do not introduce regressions or break existing functionality.

One key benefit of TDD is that it helps to define clear and specific requirements for the code being developed. By writing tests first, developers clarify what the code is supposed to achieve, leading to more focused and purposeful implementation. Additionally, the practice of refactoring code after tests pass helps to maintain a clean and well-structured codebase, reducing technical debt and enhancing code quality.

Furthermore, TDD supports incremental development, allowing developers to build and test small pieces of functionality in isolation before integrating them into the larger system. This approach not only facilitates early detection of issues but also simplifies debugging and troubleshooting, as problems are more likely to be localized to specific areas of the code.

In summary, a robust testing strategy that includes unit testing, integration testing, and end-to-end testing is crucial for ensuring the reliability and functionality of ClojureScript applications. By adopting test-driven development practices, developers can further enhance the quality of their code and create a more maintainable and resilient software system. Through careful planning, execution, and adherence to testing principles, we can achieve greater confidence in the correctness and performance of our applications.

Building upon the foundational testing strategies, it's essential to delve into the specific practices and tools that can be employed to optimize testing for ClojureScript applications. This exploration involves examining techniques for writing effective test cases, leveraging mocking and stubbing for isolated testing, and utilizing advanced testing tools and frameworks that enhance testing capabilities.

When crafting test cases, the focus should be on achieving thorough coverage while maintaining clarity and relevance. Each test case should target a specific aspect of the functionality being tested, ensuring that it verifies the correct behavior of the component or function in question. To achieve this, it is crucial to define precise input values and expected outputs, capturing a range of scenarios including typical use cases, edge cases, and potential error conditions.

A robust approach to test case design involves the use of

property-based testing. Unlike traditional unit tests that rely on predefined inputs, property-based testing generates a wide range of test cases based on properties or characteristics of the data. In ClojureScript, the `clojure.test.check` library facilitates property-based testing by allowing developers to specify properties that should hold true for a given function or module. This approach can uncover subtle bugs and corner cases that might not be evident with manually written test cases.

Mocking and stubbing are critical techniques for isolating components during testing. Mocking involves creating mock objects that simulate the behavior of real dependencies, allowing for the isolation of the unit under test from external factors. Stubbing, on the other hand, involves replacing specific functions or methods with predefined responses to control the behavior of the test environment.

In ClojureScript, mocking can be achieved using libraries such as `mocking` or `clojure.mock`, which provide tools for creating mock objects and defining their interactions. These libraries enable developers to simulate the behavior of external services, APIs, or modules, ensuring that tests focus solely on the functionality of the component being tested. By isolating dependencies, mocking and stubbing contribute to more reliable and predictable test outcomes.

When dealing with integration tests, the emphasis shifts to verifying the interactions between different components and systems. This involves setting up test environments that accurately reflect the conditions of the production environment while isolating external factors that might affect the tests. Integration testing often requires creating test databases or services that mirror the production setup, ensuring that the interactions between components are tested in a realistic context.

Advanced integration testing techniques include the use of test containers or virtual environments. For example, tools like `TestContainers` allow developers to create and manage lightweight, disposable containers for testing purposes. This approach ensures that the test environment is consistent and isolated from other tests, reducing the risk of side effects and enabling more accurate verification of interactions between components.

In the realm of end-to-end testing, automation plays a pivotal role in simulating user interactions and verifying the application's overall functionality. Tools such as `Cypress` or `Nightwatch` offer robust frameworks for writing and executing end-to-end tests. These tools allow developers to define test scenarios that mimic real user behavior, interacting with the application through its user interface or API.

Automated end-to-end tests typically involve scripting user interactions, such as form submissions, navigation, and data input, to validate that the application performs as expected from the user's perspective. These tests provide valuable insights into the application's usability and ensure that integrated components work together seamlessly. By automating these tests, developers can achieve comprehensive coverage and detect issues that might arise during actual user interactions.

Incorporating continuous integration (CI) and continuous deployment (CD) practices further enhances the effectiveness of testing. CI systems automate the process of running tests and building applications with each code change, ensuring that issues are identified and addressed promptly. CD systems extend this automation to deploying applications to staging or production environments, facilitating a streamlined and reliable release process.

Integrating testing with CI/CD pipelines involves configuring automated workflows that include steps for running unit tests, integration tests, and end-to-end tests. Tools such as Jenkins, CircleCI, or GitHub Actions can be used to set up these workflows, providing feedback on code quality and ensuring that the application meets the required standards before deployment.

Furthermore, the adoption of test coverage tools can provide insights into the effectiveness of the testing strategy. Tools like `Istanbul` or `Clover` analyze the test suite to identify areas of code that are not covered by tests, allowing developers to address gaps and improve overall coverage. Monitoring test coverage helps ensure that critical components are thoroughly tested and that the application remains reliable and robust.

By employing these practices and tools, developers can create a comprehensive and effective testing strategy for ClojureScript applications. This strategy not only ensures the correctness and functionality of the code but also contributes to a more maintainable and resilient software system. As testing continues to evolve, staying abreast of new techniques and tools will further enhance the ability to deliver high-quality applications.

A key aspect of adopting test-driven development (TDD) principles involves integrating these practices into a cohesive workflow that enhances code quality and development efficiency. Test-driven development is characterized by its iterative approach, where tests are written before the actual implementation code. This practice emphasizes the creation of automated tests that drive the design and functionality of the code, leading to more robust and reliable software.

The TDD cycle is often described using the "Red-Green-Refactor" mantra. Initially, one writes a test that fails, representing a new piece of functionality or a fix for a defect. This failing test, referred to as the "Red" phase, highlights what needs to be implemented. Following this, the focus shifts to writing the minimal amount of code necessary to pass the test, which is the "Green" phase. This ensures that the new code meets the requirements specified by the test. Finally, during the "Refactor" phase, the newly written code is optimized and cleaned up, ensuring that it adheres to coding standards without altering its functionality.

Applying TDD in ClojureScript begins with selecting an appropriate testing framework. ClojureScript developers frequently utilize `cljs.test`, a testing library built into ClojureScript that offers a comprehensive set of functions for writing and running tests. This library supports assertions, test grouping, and fixtures, making it a suitable choice for implementing TDD practices.

When starting with TDD, it is crucial to define clear, precise test cases that capture the intended behavior of the code. Each test should represent a specific scenario or requirement and should be structured to cover various aspects of the functionality being developed. For instance, if you are implementing a function to compute the total price of items in a shopping cart, your tests should cover normal scenarios, such as adding items and applying discounts, as well as edge cases, such as handling empty carts or invalid inputs.

To ensure that the tests are comprehensive, it's essential to consider both positive and negative test cases. Positive tests verify that the function behaves as expected under normal conditions, while negative tests ensure that the function handles invalid or unexpected inputs gracefully. This balanced approach helps in identifying potential issues early in the development process and provides a solid foundation for creating reliable code.

One of the key advantages of TDD is its emphasis on simplicity and incremental development. By writing tests before implementing the functionality, developers are encouraged to create only the necessary code required to pass the tests. This approach helps prevent over-engineering and promotes a focus on delivering incremental improvements. Each small step in the development process is verified by automated tests, reducing the risk of introducing defects and ensuring that the codebase remains stable.

Refactoring, an integral part of the TDD process, involves revisiting and improving the code after it has successfully passed the tests. This step is crucial for maintaining code quality and ensuring that it adheres to best practices. During the refactoring phase, developers can enhance the design, improve readability, and optimize performance without changing the existing functionality. This iterative process contributes to a cleaner and more maintainable codebase.

Additionally, integrating TDD into the development workflow often requires configuring continuous integration (CI) systems to run tests automatically. CI tools, such as Jenkins, CircleCI, or GitHub Actions, can be set up to execute tests whenever code changes are committed. This automation provides immediate feedback on the quality of the code and ensures that tests are consistently run, facilitating early detection of issues and fostering a culture of continuous improvement.

Incorporating TDD principles also involves aligning testing practices with code reviews and other quality assurance measures. Code reviews should focus on evaluating the effectiveness of the tests, ensuring that they accurately represent the requirements and cover a broad range of scenarios. Collaboration between team members during code reviews can provide valuable insights and feedback, contributing to a more thorough testing process.

Furthermore, documenting the testing process and maintaining comprehensive test suites are essential practices for ensuring long-term success with TDD. Well-documented tests provide a valuable reference for understanding the expected behavior of the code and serve as a form of living documentation that can be consulted during future development or maintenance tasks. Comprehensive test suites contribute to higher confidence in the codebase, making it easier to identify and address issues as the application evolves.

In conclusion, adopting test-driven development principles in ClojureScript involves a systematic approach to writing and running tests that drive code design and ensure functionality. By following the TDD cycle of writing failing tests, implementing minimal code to pass the tests, and refactoring the code, developers can create robust and reliable software. Integrating TDD with continuous integration, code reviews, and comprehensive documentation further enhances the effectiveness of the testing process, leading to higher code quality and improved development efficiency. Embracing these practices fosters a disciplined approach to development and contributes to the creation of maintainable and resilient applications.

CHAPTER 28: BUILDING COMMAND-LINE TOOLS

Building command-line tools in ClojureScript offers a powerful way to automate tasks and enhance your development workflow. These tools can range from simple scripts to complex applications that interact with the system, process data, or perform various administrative functions. To create effective command-line tools, it's crucial to understand how to handle user input, manage commands, and ensure robust and reliable application behavior.

To start, one of the fundamental aspects of building command-line tools is handling user input. ClojureScript provides several libraries and approaches for managing input and output operations. One of the primary libraries for this purpose is `clojure.tools.cli`, which offers a simple and flexible way to parse command-line arguments. This library allows you to define expected options and arguments, validate user input, and generate helpful usage messages.

When designing command-line tools, it's essential to define a clear and intuitive interface for users. The interface typically consists of commands and options that control the tool's behavior. Commands represent distinct operations or functionalities, while options modify or provide additional parameters for those commands. For instance, a command-line tool for file processing might include commands such as `process` and `clean`, with options to specify file paths, output formats, and other parameters.

To effectively manage commands and options, you should structure your tool's logic to handle different scenarios based on user input. This involves creating a command dispatcher that interprets the user's input and invokes the appropriate functionality. The `clojure.tools.cli` library can be used to parse arguments and options, providing a map of parsed values that can be used to control the tool's behavior. This approach ensures that your tool can handle various commands and options gracefully.

A key consideration when building command-line tools is error handling. Command-line tools should be resilient and provide meaningful feedback to users when something goes wrong. This involves validating user input to ensure it meets the expected format and constraints, as well as handling exceptions and errors that may occur during execution. Providing clear error messages and usage instructions helps users understand and correct any issues they encounter.

Another important aspect of building robust command-line tools is implementing logging and debugging capabilities. Logging allows you to track the tool's behavior and diagnose issues, while debugging features can help you test and troubleshoot the tool during development. In ClojureScript, you can use libraries such as `clojure.tools.logging` to manage logging and configure different log levels, such as info, warning, and error. This helps ensure that you can monitor and debug the tool effectively, both during development and in production environments.

In addition to handling user input and managing commands,

creating command-line tools involves designing a user-friendly interface. This includes providing helpful usage information, such as descriptions of available commands and options, as well as examples of how to use the tool. The `clojure.tools.cli` library supports generating usage messages, which can be customized to provide clear and concise instructions to users.

Moreover, testing command-line tools is crucial to ensure their reliability and functionality. Testing involves verifying that the tool behaves as expected under various scenarios and handles edge cases appropriately. You can use testing frameworks such as `cljs.test` to write unit tests for individual components of the tool and integration tests to ensure that different parts of the tool work together correctly. Additionally, writing end-to-end tests that simulate user interactions with the command-line tool can help you identify and address any issues in the tool's overall behavior.

Building command-line tools also requires considering performance and efficiency. Depending on the complexity and functionality of your tool, performance optimizations may be necessary to ensure that it operates efficiently and handles large volumes of data or complex operations without significant delays. Profiling tools and performance monitoring can help identify and address performance bottlenecks.

In summary, creating command-line tools with ClojureScript involves handling user input, managing commands, and ensuring robust functionality. By leveraging libraries such as `clojure.tools.cli`, implementing error handling, logging, and debugging, and designing a user-friendly interface, you can build effective and reliable command-line tools. Testing and performance considerations further contribute to the tool's overall quality and effectiveness, ensuring that it meets user needs and performs well in various scenarios.

To effectively develop command-line tools with ClojureScript, we must delve into the practical aspects of building these applications. The focus shifts from theoretical design to practical implementation, including how to efficiently handle user input, manage command parsing, and ensure the tool operates smoothly under various conditions.

Handling user input is central to the functionality of any command-line tool. To accomplish this, ClojureScript provides several libraries and techniques for capturing and processing command-line arguments. Among these, `clojure.tools.cli` stands out as a versatile library for parsing command-line options and arguments. By defining a specification for expected arguments and options, you can guide the tool in correctly interpreting user inputs. This specification typically includes defining required and optional arguments, setting default values, and specifying constraints.

When implementing argument parsing, it's essential to ensure that your tool can handle a variety of input scenarios. This involves validating user input to prevent errors and providing meaningful feedback when the input does not meet the expected criteria. For instance, if your tool requires a file path as an argument, the validation logic should confirm that the provided path exists and is accessible. This validation helps in avoiding runtime errors and improving the overall user experience.

Managing commands is another crucial aspect of building command-line tools. Commands represent distinct functionalities within the tool, and their proper management ensures that the tool responds appropriately to user instructions. A well-designed command parser should be capable of recognizing and executing different commands based on user input. The logic for command dispatching often involves mapping commands to specific functions or actions, allowing the tool to execute the correct functionality in response to user requests.

In addition to managing commands, it is important to implement robust error handling. Command-line tools must be able to gracefully handle errors and provide clear and informative messages to users. This includes handling cases where the user provides invalid arguments, encounters unexpected conditions, or when there are issues during execution. Clear error messages not only help users understand what went wrong but also guide them on how to correct the issues.

For effective command-line tool development, incorporating logging and debugging features is vital. Logging allows you to record important events, track the tool's behavior, and diagnose issues. In ClojureScript, you can use libraries like `clojure.tools.logging` to implement logging with various log levels, such as info, warning, and error. This functionality is crucial for identifying problems during development and for monitoring the tool's performance in production environments.

Debugging command-line tools involves testing and refining the tool to ensure it operates as intended. Writing unit tests for individual components and integration tests for overall functionality helps ensure that the tool behaves correctly under different scenarios. Tools such as `cljs.test` can be used for writing and running tests, allowing you to verify that each component of the tool performs as expected.

Another important consideration is designing a user-friendly interface. A well-designed interface includes clear and concise usage instructions, descriptions of available commands and options, and examples of how to use the tool effectively. Providing users with helpful information not only enhances their experience but also reduces the likelihood of errors and misunderstandings.

Performance and efficiency are also critical aspects of building command-line tools. Depending on the tool's complexity and the tasks it performs, optimizing performance may be necessary to ensure that it operates efficiently and handles large amounts of data or complex operations effectively. Performance profiling tools can help identify bottlenecks and optimize the tool's performance.

Integrating command-line tools with other systems or processes can further enhance their functionality. For example, you might want to integrate your tool with external APIs, databases, or other command-line utilities. This integration can extend the tool's capabilities and make it more versatile and powerful.

As we explore the nuances of command-line tool development, it's essential to focus on the specific needs of your tool and the requirements of its intended use cases. Tailoring the tool's design and functionality to meet these needs ensures that it provides maximum value and performs reliably in various scenarios.

In summary, building command-line tools with ClojureScript involves a thorough understanding of user input handling, command management, error handling, logging, debugging, and performance optimization. By applying these principles and techniques, you can create robust and effective command-line tools that enhance your development workflow and automate tasks efficiently.

To build robust command-line tools with ClojureScript, it is crucial to address several advanced aspects that contribute to the tool's effectiveness and user experience. As we move deeper into the development process, we need to explore sophisticated techniques for command execution, resource management, and user feedback, ensuring that the tool is not only functional but also intuitive and reliable.

One of the essential aspects of building a command-line

tool is managing dependencies and integrating with external resources. Often, command-line tools need to interact with various system resources or external services, such as APIs, databases, or file systems. For instance, if your tool performs data processing or integrates with a web service, you must handle these interactions efficiently. In ClojureScript, this involves making use of asynchronous operations and ensuring that your tool handles network latency, errors, and potential timeouts gracefully. Libraries like `cljs-http` can assist with making HTTP requests, while ClojureScript's core.async library provides tools for managing asynchronous operations and concurrency.

Effective resource management also entails dealing with file input and output operations. When a tool reads from or writes to files, it is crucial to handle file access permissions, file existence checks, and proper resource cleanup. Implementing these features ensures that the tool operates reliably in different environments and avoids common pitfalls such as file locks or missing files. For example, using `clojure.java.io` for file operations allows you to handle files in a platform-independent manner, ensuring that file paths and operations are managed correctly across different operating systems.

Another important consideration is the design of a flexible and extensible architecture for your command-line tool. As your tool evolves, you may need to add new features or modify existing ones. Designing your tool with modularity in mind allows you to extend its functionality without introducing significant changes to the existing codebase. This approach involves creating well-defined modules or components that handle specific aspects of the tool's functionality, such as command parsing, data processing, or output formatting. By keeping these components separate, you can modify or replace them independently, making the tool easier to maintain and extend.

In addition to modular design, implementing a comprehensive configuration system can greatly enhance the flexibility of your command-line tool. A configuration system allows users to specify settings and options through configuration files or environment variables, enabling them to customize the tool's behavior without modifying the code. ClojureScript provides several ways to handle configuration, including reading configuration files in formats like JSON or EDN and accessing environment variables. This approach not only makes the tool more adaptable but also facilitates integration into different environments and workflows.

To further enhance user experience, consider implementing features that provide feedback and guidance throughout the tool's usage. Providing meaningful messages and prompts can help users understand how to use the tool effectively and troubleshoot any issues they encounter. This includes offering detailed help messages for commands, explaining the purpose of each option, and providing examples of usage. A well-designed help system not only improves the usability of the tool but also reduces the learning curve for new users.

When building command-line tools, security is an often overlooked but crucial aspect. Ensuring that your tool handles sensitive information securely and operates safely in various environments is essential. This includes validating and sanitizing user input to prevent injection attacks, securing any credentials or tokens used in interactions with external services, and implementing proper error handling to avoid exposing sensitive information through error messages or logs. By addressing these security concerns, you can protect both your tool and its users from potential threats.

Testing your command-line tool thoroughly is an integral part of the development process. Beyond basic unit testing, you should also consider writing integration tests to verify that the tool works correctly when interacting with external systems or handling complex scenarios. This includes testing how the tool behaves with various types of input, how it manages different system states, and how it integrates with other components or services. Comprehensive testing helps identify and address issues before the tool is deployed, ensuring that it performs reliably in real-world situations.

As you finalize the development of your command-line tool, it is also important to document the tool's features, usage instructions, and any known limitations. Providing clear and comprehensive documentation not only helps users understand how to use the tool but also aids in troubleshooting and support. Well-documented tools are easier to maintain and support, and they contribute to a better overall user experience.

By focusing on these advanced aspects of command-line tool development, you can create tools that are not only functional but also user-friendly, secure, and adaptable. From managing dependencies and resources to designing a flexible architecture and ensuring thorough testing, each step contributes to building a tool that meets the needs of its users and enhances the development workflow.

CHAPTER 29: INTEGRATING WITH BACKEND SERVICES

Integrating with backend services is a crucial aspect of modern application development, especially when using ClojureScript. As applications grow in complexity, the need for efficient and reliable communication between the frontend and backend becomes increasingly important. This segment delves into various techniques and best practices for integrating with backend services, including RESTful APIs, GraphQL endpoints, and messaging systems.

To begin, integrating with RESTful APIs is a common requirement. REST (Representational State Transfer) is a widely adopted architectural style for designing networked applications. It relies on stateless, client-server communication and uses standard HTTP methods such as GET, POST, PUT, and DELETE. ClojureScript provides several libraries and tools to facilitate interaction with RESTful APIs. One of the primary libraries used for making HTTP requests is `cljs-http`. This library offers a straightforward API for performing asynchronous HTTP operations, handling responses, and managing errors.

When working with `cljs-http`, you should handle responses and potential errors with care. Successful API calls return data in formats such as JSON or XML, which you need to parse and process. ClojureScript's built-in libraries, such as `clojure.data.json`, can assist with JSON parsing. Error handling is equally important; ensure your application gracefully handles scenarios like network failures, server errors, or unexpected response formats. Implementing retry logic and user notifications can improve the resilience of your application in the face of transient issues.

Another approach to integrating with backend services involves GraphQL, a query language for APIs that provides a more flexible alternative to REST. GraphQL allows clients to request specific data, reducing the amount of data transferred over the network and potentially simplifying the data retrieval process. For ClojureScript applications, interacting with GraphQL endpoints involves constructing and sending GraphQL queries, handling responses, and integrating the results into the application's state.

Libraries such as `cljs-graphql` or `apollo-client` (if using JavaScript interop) can facilitate communication with GraphQL endpoints. When working with GraphQL, you need to manage the complexity of constructing queries and mutations. GraphQL's ability to request exactly the data needed can reduce over-fetching and under-fetching issues that are common with RESTful APIs. Additionally, implementing caching strategies and managing the state of your application efficiently are crucial for optimizing the performance and user experience.

Beyond REST and GraphQL, integrating with messaging systems is another critical aspect of backend communication. Messaging systems, such as RabbitMQ, Kafka, or even WebSocket-based systems, provide mechanisms for real-time communication and message queuing. These systems are often used for handling events, distributing tasks, or enabling real-time updates in applications.

When integrating with messaging systems, you need to handle asynchronous communication effectively. In ClojureScript, libraries like `cljs-websockets` can help manage WebSocket connections, allowing your application to send and receive real-time data. For message queuing systems, you may need to use JavaScript interop or external libraries to interface with the messaging system's API. Ensuring reliable message delivery, handling connection interruptions, and processing messages in a timely manner are essential considerations for maintaining the robustness of your application.

Effective integration with backend services also involves managing authentication and authorization. Many backend services require authentication tokens or credentials to access their endpoints. ClojureScript applications must securely handle these credentials, manage token expiration, and refresh tokens as needed. Additionally, implementing secure communication channels, such as HTTPS, is critical for protecting sensitive data during transmission.

State management in your application is another aspect closely tied to backend integration. As data is fetched from or sent to backend services, it needs to be incorporated into the application's state. Using state management libraries, such as `re-frame`, can help organize and manage state changes in a predictable manner. This approach ensures that data flows smoothly between the frontend and backend while maintaining consistency and coherence in your application's state.

Testing is an integral part of integrating with backend services. Ensure that your integration points are thoroughly tested, including both unit tests for individual components and integration tests for end-to-end scenarios. Mocking backend services during testing can help simulate various conditions and verify that your application handles them correctly without relying on real backend services.

As you develop and refine your application, continually review and optimize your integration strategies. Pay attention to performance metrics, such as response times and data transfer rates, and make adjustments to improve efficiency. Regularly updating libraries and dependencies used for backend integration can also help address security vulnerabilities and enhance functionality.

In conclusion, integrating with backend services in ClojureScript involves a range of techniques and best practices tailored to various types of services, including RESTful APIs, GraphQL endpoints, and messaging systems. By employing robust libraries, managing authentication and state effectively, and ensuring comprehensive testing, you can build applications that communicate seamlessly with backend services while providing a reliable and efficient user experience.

In the context of integrating ClojureScript with backend services, ensuring that the communication is both efficient and reliable is paramount. The techniques for achieving this involve a deep understanding of how various backend systems operate and how best to interface with them from a ClojureScript application.

When interacting with RESTful APIs, one of the most fundamental aspects is to construct requests that align with the API's expectations. REST APIs typically use HTTP methods to perform actions on resources identified by URLs. For instance, a GET request might be used to retrieve data, while a POST request would create a new resource. In ClojureScript, handling these requests effectively means utilizing libraries that can manage the intricacies of HTTP communication. The `cljs-http` library is a prominent choice, offering a straightforward API for making requests and processing responses. It supports both synchronous and asynchronous operations, though asynchronous communication is generally preferred for non-blocking interactions.

When sending a request, it is essential to construct the request payload accurately. For JSON data, this involves serializing ClojureScript data structures into JSON format before sending them. Conversely, when receiving data, you must deserialize the JSON responses into ClojureScript data structures. Handling these transformations properly ensures that the data is correctly interpreted and utilized within your application. Moreover, error handling during API interactions cannot be overstated. Implementing robust error handling mechanisms helps manage various potential issues such as network errors, invalid responses, or server-side problems. This involves checking HTTP status codes, parsing error messages, and implementing retry logic if necessary. Such practices ensure that the application can gracefully handle unexpected situations and provide a better user experience.

In contrast, GraphQL presents a more flexible alternative to RESTful APIs by allowing clients to request exactly the data they need. This query language facilitates more precise data retrieval and can reduce the over-fetching or under-fetching of data. To integrate with GraphQL in a ClojureScript application, constructing GraphQL queries and mutations becomes a core task. These queries define the structure of the data required from the server, and mutations specify data changes. Libraries such as `cljs-graphql` can be utilized for handling GraphQL requests in ClojureScript. This library provides tools for building queries and processing responses efficiently.

Handling GraphQL responses involves parsing the JSON data returned by the server. Unlike REST, where each endpoint corresponds to a specific resource, GraphQL queries are more dynamic, requiring a flexible approach to handle varying data structures. It is crucial to design your queries to be as efficient as possible to avoid unnecessary data transfer. Additionally, managing query complexity and ensuring that queries do not adversely impact server performance is vital for maintaining a performant application.

When dealing with messaging systems, such as WebSocket-based systems or message queues like RabbitMQ or Kafka, the focus shifts to managing asynchronous communication. WebSockets provide a persistent connection between the client and server, enabling real-time data exchange. ClojureScript's `cljs-websockets` library facilitates WebSocket interactions by providing a means to establish connections, send messages, and receive data.

For message queues, integrating with a messaging system often requires interfacing with external libraries or services that support the queue's protocol. This integration involves managing message production and consumption, ensuring that messages are correctly formatted and processed. Handling asynchronous messages requires careful consideration of the application's state and ensuring that messages are processed in the correct order. This often involves implementing message acknowledgment and retry mechanisms to handle potential delivery issues.

An important consideration across all these integration techniques is managing authentication and authorization. Many backend services require authentication tokens or credentials to validate requests. In ClojureScript, securely managing these credentials is crucial to avoid exposing sensitive information. Techniques such as token storage, secure transmission (using HTTPS), and token refresh mechanisms are essential for maintaining security. Additionally, implementing proper authorization checks ensures that users can only access resources they are permitted to.

State management is another critical aspect when integrating with backend services. Asynchronous operations, such as fetching data from APIs or processing messages, often result in changes to the application state. Using state management libraries like `re-frame` helps manage these state changes predictably. This approach ensures that the application's state remains consistent and coherent, even as data is fetched from or sent to backend services.

Testing plays a significant role in ensuring that integrations with backend services are robust and reliable. Implementing unit tests for individual components and integration tests for end-to-end scenarios helps verify that your application interacts correctly with backend services. Mocking backend responses during testing can simulate various conditions and validate that your application handles them appropriately.

As the development process progresses, regularly reviewing and optimizing integration strategies is necessary. Performance monitoring tools can provide insights into how well the backend interactions are functioning and highlight areas for improvement. Keeping libraries and dependencies up to date also helps address security vulnerabilities and maintain compatibility with evolving backend services.

Effective integration with backend services requires a comprehensive approach, involving accurate request construction, robust error handling, flexible data handling, and secure communication. By employing these strategies, you can build applications that not only interact seamlessly with backend systems but also deliver a reliable and efficient user experience.

When working with backend services, another vital aspect to address is managing the data lifecycle effectively. This involves not only fetching and displaying data but also handling data updates and synchronization between the frontend and backend. Efficiently managing the data lifecycle ensures that your application remains responsive and up-to-date with the latest information.

One common approach to handling data synchronization is to implement polling mechanisms. Polling involves periodically sending requests to the backend to check for updates. Although straightforward, polling can be inefficient, particularly if updates are infrequent or if the polling interval is too short, leading to unnecessary network traffic and server load. To mitigate these issues, consider optimizing the polling frequency based on the specific needs of your application. Additionally, implementing exponential backoff strategies—where the time between successive polls increases progressively—can help balance the trade-off between update freshness and resource consumption.

In contrast to polling, real-time data synchronization can be achieved through techniques such as WebSockets or server-sent events (SSE). WebSockets, as previously discussed, establish a persistent connection between the client and server, enabling the server to push updates to the client as soon as they occur. This approach is particularly useful for applications requiring real-time interactions, such as chat applications or live data feeds. Implementing WebSockets in ClojureScript involves setting up listeners for incoming messages and updating the application state accordingly.

Server-sent events (SSE) offer another real-time communication mechanism where the server sends updates to the client over a single, long-lived HTTP connection. Unlike WebSockets, SSE is a unidirectional communication channel, meaning that the server can push updates to the client, but the client cannot send messages back over the same connection. SSE is well-suited for scenarios where real-time updates are needed, but bidirectional communication is not required.

Error handling remains a crucial consideration when dealing with real-time data synchronization. Whether using polling, WebSockets, or SSE, it is essential to implement mechanisms to detect and respond to connectivity issues or message failures. For instance, in the case of WebSockets, handling scenarios where the connection is unexpectedly closed or encounters errors involves implementing reconnection strategies. This might include automatically attempting to reconnect after a delay and notifying users of connectivity issues when appropriate.

Beyond managing real-time updates, ensuring the robustness of your backend integrations requires attention to data consistency and conflict resolution. When multiple instances of your application are interacting with the backend concurrently, conflicts can arise if different instances attempt to modify the same data. Implementing optimistic concurrency control mechanisms—where changes are made based on the assumption that conflicts are rare, with subsequent checks to resolve any discrepancies—can help manage such scenarios. This approach involves including versioning information or timestamps with data updates to detect and resolve conflicts.

Another critical aspect is the security of your data interactions. Ensuring that data transmitted between your application and backend services is secure involves employing encryption both in transit and at rest. HTTPS should be used to encrypt data transmitted over the network, preventing unauthorized access and eavesdropping. Additionally, implementing proper authentication and authorization mechanisms helps secure access to sensitive data and functionality. Token-based authentication, such as using JSON Web Tokens (JWTs), provides a means to verify the identity of users and ensure they have the appropriate permissions.

Integrating with backend services also requires managing various types of data and interactions, such as file uploads and downloads. Handling file uploads involves constructing multipart form-data requests, managing file size limitations, and ensuring proper server-side processing. For file downloads, implementing mechanisms to handle large files, such as streaming, can enhance the user experience and avoid performance issues.

Caching is another technique that can significantly impact the efficiency of your backend integrations. Implementing caching strategies helps reduce the need for repeated requests to the backend, thus minimizing network traffic and improving response times. In ClojureScript, caching can be managed through various means, including in-memory caches or integrating with caching services. Ensuring that cached data is kept up-to-date and invalidated appropriately when changes occur is crucial for maintaining data accuracy.

As you develop and refine your integration strategies, continuously testing and monitoring the performance of your interactions with backend services is essential. Performance testing helps identify bottlenecks and areas for optimization, ensuring that your application can handle the expected load and provide a smooth user experience. Monitoring tools can provide insights into various metrics, such as response times, error rates, and throughput, allowing you to make informed decisions about scaling and improving your backend interactions.

By addressing these considerations—data synchronization, error handling, consistency, security, file management, and caching—you can build robust and efficient integrations between your ClojureScript application and backend services. This comprehensive approach ensures that your application remains responsive, secure, and capable of handling complex interactions with various backend systems, ultimately contributing to a more reliable and user-friendly application.

CHAPTER 30: WORKING WITH WEBASSEMBLY

WebAssembly (Wasm) represents a significant advancement in web technology, allowing for the execution of code at near-native speeds within the browser. As a binary instruction format designed for efficient compilation and execution, WebAssembly enables developers to run high-performance applications directly in the web environment. Integrating WebAssembly with ClojureScript opens up opportunities to leverage this performance enhancement in your projects, particularly for compute-intensive tasks. This discussion delves into how to utilize WebAssembly within ClojureScript applications, covering the process of compiling code to WebAssembly and the subsequent integration into your projects.

To begin with, understanding the fundamentals of WebAssembly is crucial. WebAssembly is a low-level bytecode format that can be executed by modern web browsers. It provides a compilation target for languages like C, C++, and Rust, enabling developers to write code in these languages and compile it into WebAssembly modules. These modules can then be imported into web applications and executed with high efficiency. WebAssembly operates alongside JavaScript, allowing for interoperability between the two, which is particularly relevant when integrating with ClojureScript.

In ClojureScript, the integration of WebAssembly involves a few key steps: compiling source code into WebAssembly, loading the WebAssembly module, and interfacing with it through ClojureScript. Let's explore each of these steps in detail.

The first step is compiling code to WebAssembly. To illustrate this process, let's consider a scenario where we want to use Rust to write performance-critical code. Rust is a language well-suited for this purpose due to its safety guarantees and efficient compilation. Writing the performance-critical component in Rust, we then compile it into WebAssembly using tools such as `wasm-pack`. This tool simplifies the process of building and packaging Rust code as WebAssembly modules.

Once the code is compiled into a `.wasm` file, the next step is to load this module into your ClojureScript application. ClojureScript provides interoperability with JavaScript through its JavaScript interop capabilities, allowing us to interact with WebAssembly modules seamlessly. Using the `js/` namespace, you can invoke JavaScript functions that load and instantiate WebAssembly modules. This involves using the `WebAssembly.instantiateStreaming` function, which loads a `.wasm` file from a URL and instantiates it. The instantiation process converts the bytecode into executable code and provides access to its exports.

Here's an example of how you might load and instantiate a WebAssembly module in a ClojureScript application. First, define a JavaScript function to handle the WebAssembly instantiation:

```javascript
async function loadWasmModule(url) {
  const response  await fetch(url);
  const wasmArrayBuffer  await response.arrayBuffer();
```

```
  const { instance } = await
WebAssembly.instantiate(wasmArrayBuffer);
  return instance.exports;
}
```

In your ClojureScript code, you can call this JavaScript function using the `js/` interop syntax. For instance:

```clojure
(ns my-app.core
  (:require [cljs.core :as cljs]))

(defn init []
  (let [wasm-url "/path/to/your/module.wasm"]
    (js/loadWasmModule wasm-url
      (fn [exports]
        ;; Access WebAssembly exports here
        (let [my-function (.-my_function exports)]
          ;; Call the function and handle results
          (println "Result:" (my-function 42)))))))
```

Once the WebAssembly module is loaded, you can access its exported functions and integrate them into your ClojureScript application. This allows you to offload performance-critical tasks to WebAssembly, leveraging its efficiency while maintaining the flexibility of ClojureScript for higher-level application logic.

Another important consideration is how to handle data exchange between ClojureScript and WebAssembly. WebAssembly supports passing data through function parameters and global memory. For more complex interactions, such as working with large data structures or arrays, you might need to use `SharedArrayBuffer` or similar constructs to efficiently manage memory and data transfers between ClojureScript and WebAssembly.

Furthermore, debugging and optimizing WebAssembly code is a crucial aspect of ensuring performance and correctness. Tools like WebAssembly's built-in support for source maps can help in debugging by mapping the WebAssembly instructions back to the original source code. Additionally, performance profiling tools available in modern browsers can assist in identifying bottlenecks and optimizing the WebAssembly module.

Finally, it is important to consider the security implications of using WebAssembly. Since WebAssembly code runs with near-native speed, it has the potential to perform intensive operations that could impact the security and stability of your application if not properly managed. Always ensure that your WebAssembly modules are from trusted sources, and consider implementing additional security measures such as content security policies (CSP) and sandboxing to mitigate potential risks.

Integrating WebAssembly into ClojureScript applications enables you to harness the power of high-performance code execution in the browser. By carefully managing the compilation process, interfacing with WebAssembly modules, and considering data handling, debugging, and security aspects, you can effectively leverage WebAssembly to enhance the performance and capabilities of your web applications.

To maximize the benefits of WebAssembly in your ClojureScript applications, it is essential to delve deeper into the nuances of its integration and usage. The seamless interaction between ClojureScript and WebAssembly hinges on understanding the intricacies of WebAssembly's execution environment and optimizing the interoperation between these technologies.

WebAssembly modules are designed to be platform-independent, executing code at near-native speed by directly interacting with the browser's underlying hardware. However, achieving this efficiency involves careful management of how WebAssembly interfaces with JavaScript and, by extension, with ClojureScript. One of the primary considerations is managing the lifecycle of WebAssembly modules. Efficient loading and unloading of these modules are crucial for maintaining application performance and memory usage.

When integrating WebAssembly into a ClojureScript project, it is beneficial to use asynchronous JavaScript functions to handle the instantiation of WebAssembly modules. This approach allows the browser to continue performing other tasks while the WebAssembly module is being loaded, thus improving the user experience. The use of JavaScript promises, as demonstrated earlier, is instrumental in this process. Once the module is loaded, it becomes accessible through the JavaScript `exports` object, which exposes the functions and memory that can be utilized in your ClojureScript code.

For more complex use cases, such as when dealing with larger data sets or requiring significant computation, leveraging WebAssembly's linear memory model is advantageous. WebAssembly's memory is represented as a contiguous block of bytes, and it supports operations such as memory allocation and deallocation directly. This memory model allows you to interact with large data structures more efficiently compared to traditional JavaScript methods. In ClojureScript, you can interface with this memory by using JavaScript interop functions to read from and write to the WebAssembly memory buffer.

An important aspect of integrating WebAssembly with ClojureScript is managing data exchange between the two environments. This involves converting data formats between WebAssembly and JavaScript. For instance, if your WebAssembly module processes numerical data or arrays, you need to convert these data structures between JavaScript arrays and WebAssembly's linear memory. Utilizing typed arrays in JavaScript, such as `Uint8Array` or `Float64Array`, facilitates this conversion. These typed arrays provide a view of the WebAssembly memory, allowing you to manipulate data directly.

Moreover, debugging WebAssembly code can be challenging due to its low-level nature. Although WebAssembly does provide source maps, making debugging more manageable, the complexity of the bytecode can still be a hurdle. To alleviate this, you should ensure that you have a robust debugging workflow. Modern browser developer tools support WebAssembly debugging, offering features like stepping through code and inspecting variables. Additionally, profiling tools can help identify performance bottlenecks in both the WebAssembly code and the surrounding JavaScript/ClojureScript code.

Performance optimization is another critical area when working with WebAssembly. While WebAssembly is inherently faster than JavaScript for certain tasks, inefficient use of WebAssembly can still lead to performance issues. Profiling tools, such as those built into browsers, can assist in pinpointing performance issues by showing how much time is spent in WebAssembly compared to JavaScript. Techniques such as minimizing the size of WebAssembly modules and optimizing the algorithms used can further enhance performance.

When considering the deployment of WebAssembly modules, it is essential to ensure they are served efficiently. This includes using appropriate caching strategies and content delivery networks (CDNs) to minimize load times and improve accessibility. Properly configuring HTTP headers for caching and compression can also contribute to a more responsive user experience.

Security considerations are paramount when incorporating WebAssembly into your applications. Although WebAssembly runs in a sandboxed environment, it is still crucial to follow best practices for web security. Ensure that your WebAssembly modules are sourced from trusted origins and consider implementing content security policies (CSP) to prevent unauthorized access. Additionally, scrutinize the WebAssembly code for vulnerabilities, especially when incorporating third-party modules.

Integrating WebAssembly into a ClojureScript project requires a thoughtful approach to leverage its performance benefits while managing the complexities of its integration. By carefully handling module loading, optimizing data exchange, utilizing debugging tools, and addressing security concerns, you can effectively enhance the performance and functionality of your web applications. The synergy between ClojureScript and WebAssembly opens up opportunities for creating more efficient and capable web applications, provided that these considerations are diligently addressed.

When leveraging WebAssembly within ClojureScript applications, a crucial aspect is the interoperability between the ClojureScript code and WebAssembly modules. To facilitate this interaction, one needs to focus on how ClojureScript can effectively call WebAssembly functions and handle data between the two environments. Understanding the mechanisms of this interoperation will help in optimizing both performance and usability.

The WebAssembly module exposes its functions and memory through an interface that JavaScript can interact with. In ClojureScript, this typically involves using the JavaScript interop features to interact with the WebAssembly module. For instance, if you have a WebAssembly function that performs a computation, you will need to invoke this function from ClojureScript and handle the returned results.

Consider a scenario where you have a WebAssembly module compiled from C code that provides a function to perform matrix multiplication. The first step is to ensure that the WebAssembly module is correctly loaded and instantiated. This involves using JavaScript to handle the module loading, which can be achieved through asynchronous functions. Once the module is loaded, you will use JavaScript interop in ClojureScript to call the WebAssembly function.

Here's how you might approach it:

1. Loading the WebAssembly Module: Use JavaScript's `WebAssembly.instantiateStreaming` or `WebAssembly.instantiate` to compile and instantiate the module. This operation returns a promise that resolves with an instance of the module and its exports. From ClojureScript, you can interact with this using JavaScript interop features.

2. Calling WebAssembly Functions: After loading, the functions exposed by the WebAssembly module are accessible through the `exports` object. In ClojureScript, you use JavaScript interop to call these functions. For example, if the WebAssembly module exports a function named `multiply_matrices`, you can call this function using ClojureScript's `js/` namespace to access the JavaScript function.

3. Handling Data: Data exchange between WebAssembly and ClojureScript requires careful handling, especially when dealing with complex data types. WebAssembly modules typically use raw memory buffers to exchange data. If the WebAssembly module expects a buffer or array, you can utilize JavaScript's typed arrays to manage this data. In ClojureScript, you'll use `js/Uint8Array` or similar constructs to interact with this memory.

For instance, to pass a matrix to the WebAssembly module,

you would:

- Allocate Memory: Use JavaScript to allocate a memory buffer for the matrix.
- Write Data: Populate the buffer with matrix data in a format that the WebAssembly module can understand.
- Invoke Function: Call the WebAssembly function with the memory buffer as an argument.
- Read Results: After execution, read the results back from the WebAssembly memory buffer.

One important consideration is managing the memory and performance implications of this data exchange. WebAssembly operates with a linear memory model, which means you must be meticulous about memory allocation and deallocation. This involves not only ensuring that the memory used is correctly managed but also understanding the performance characteristics of different data types and operations.

In addition, WebAssembly's synchronous nature requires that you handle potential blocking issues. While WebAssembly executes code rapidly, integrating it with asynchronous JavaScript code demands careful attention to ensure that the application remains responsive. This often involves using asynchronous patterns in ClojureScript, such as promises or asynchronous functions, to manage interactions with WebAssembly efficiently.

Another aspect to consider is the compilation process. WebAssembly modules are typically compiled from languages like C or Rust. Ensuring that the code is optimized for performance and that it interacts seamlessly with ClojureScript involves understanding the compilation options and ensuring that the WebAssembly module is built with the appropriate settings. This includes optimizations for size and speed that can significantly impact the overall performance of your application.

Testing and debugging WebAssembly modules integrated with ClojureScript can also pose challenges. Although WebAssembly has support for source maps, debugging can be intricate due to the low-level nature of the code. It is advisable to use modern browser developer tools to step through both the WebAssembly and ClojureScript code. Tools such as Chrome DevTools provide insights into performance bottlenecks and help in diagnosing issues within the WebAssembly module.

Furthermore, as WebAssembly is still evolving, staying informed about the latest updates and best practices is crucial. The WebAssembly ecosystem is continuously improving, with new features and optimizations being introduced regularly. Keeping abreast of these developments will enable you to leverage the latest advancements and maintain an edge in utilizing WebAssembly effectively in your ClojureScript applications.

Integrating WebAssembly with ClojureScript offers significant performance enhancements for compute-intensive tasks. By managing the interplay between WebAssembly and ClojureScript with attention to detail—particularly in loading, data handling, and performance optimization—you can harness the full potential of WebAssembly. This integration allows for creating robust and high-performance applications, pushing the boundaries of what is achievable within the browser environment.

CHAPTER 31: HANDLING ASYNCHRONOUS OPERATIONS

Asynchronous operations play a pivotal role in the development of modern web applications, allowing developers to manage tasks that do not need to be completed immediately, such as data fetching, file processing, or network requests. In ClojureScript, handling these operations efficiently is crucial for creating responsive and high-performance applications. This section will explore the various techniques for managing asynchronous tasks in ClojureScript, focusing on promises, the `async`/`await` syntax, and best practices for asynchronous data fetching.

To begin, promises are a foundational concept in asynchronous programming. A promise represents a value that may be available now, or in the future, or never. This abstraction allows for handling asynchronous results in a more manageable way compared to traditional callback-based approaches. In ClojureScript, promises can be created and manipulated using JavaScript interop. The `js/Promise` constructor is used to create a new promise, while methods like `then`, `catch`, and `finally` are employed to handle the resolved value, errors, and completion events respectively.

When dealing with promises in ClojureScript, it's common to use the `js/Promise` constructor to initiate a new promise. The promise constructor takes a function with two parameters: `resolve` and `reject`. These parameters are functions that are called to resolve or reject the promise. For example, if you're making an HTTP request, you would create a promise to handle the asynchronous response. Inside the promise, you would perform the request and call `resolve` with the response data if the request is successful, or `reject` with an error if it fails.

One of the key benefits of promises is the ability to chain multiple asynchronous operations. This is achieved using the `then` method, which returns a new promise, allowing for subsequent `then` calls. This chaining mechanism helps in handling sequences of asynchronous tasks in a clean and readable manner. For instance, if you need to make multiple HTTP requests in sequence, you would use `then` to wait for the first request to complete before starting the next one.

However, promises can become cumbersome when dealing with complex chains of asynchronous operations. This is where the `async`/`await` syntax comes into play. Introduced in ECMAScript 2017, `async`/`await` provides a more synchronous-like approach to asynchronous programming, making the code easier to read and maintain. An `async` function automatically returns a promise, and within this function, the `await` keyword can be used to pause the execution until the promise is resolved. This allows you to write asynchronous code in a style that closely resembles synchronous code.

In ClojureScript, using `async`/`await` involves defining an `async` function and using `await` to handle promises. For example, if you're fetching data from an API, you would define an `async` function that makes the request and `await` the promise returned by the HTTP call. This way, you can work with the result of the HTTP call directly, without the need for chaining multiple `then` calls.

An important consideration when working with `async`/`await` is error handling. Since `await` expressions can throw errors if the promise is rejected, it is crucial to use `try`/`catch` blocks to handle exceptions gracefully. This approach ensures that errors are caught and handled properly, preventing unhandled promise rejections from disrupting the application.

In addition to promises and `async`/`await`, effective management of asynchronous data fetching is essential for modern web applications. Asynchronous data fetching typically involves making HTTP requests to retrieve data from a server or API. In ClojureScript, this is often done using JavaScript interop functions like `js/fetch` or libraries such as Axios.

The `js/fetch` API is a modern interface for making HTTP requests and returns a promise that resolves with the `Response` object representing the response to the request. This API supports a wide range of options, including request methods, headers, and body content. To handle the response, you use `then` to process the response data or `catch` to handle errors.

Libraries like Axios provide additional features and convenience methods for handling HTTP requests. Axios, for example, simplifies the process of setting up requests and provides an intuitive API for managing request and response data. Using such libraries can enhance productivity and reduce boilerplate code, especially in complex applications with multiple data sources and request configurations.

When working with asynchronous operations, managing state effectively is also crucial. In web applications, especially those with user interfaces, state management libraries or patterns can be employed to handle the results of asynchronous operations and update the UI accordingly. Libraries like Reagent or frameworks like Re-frame in ClojureScript provide mechanisms to manage state and trigger UI updates based on asynchronous data.

Effective state management involves understanding how to synchronize the application state with the results of asynchronous operations. For example, when fetching data from an API, you would typically update the application state once the data is successfully retrieved, which in turn updates the UI to reflect the new data. This process should be seamless and responsive to ensure a smooth user experience.

In conclusion, handling asynchronous operations in ClojureScript requires a thorough understanding of promises, the `async`/`await` syntax, and best practices for asynchronous data fetching. By leveraging these techniques effectively, you can build responsive and efficient web applications that handle asynchronous tasks with ease. Whether using promises for straightforward tasks or `async`/`await` for more complex scenarios, the goal is to create code that is both functional and maintainable, ensuring a robust user experience and efficient performance.

When dealing with asynchronous operations in ClojureScript, ensuring that your application remains responsive and efficient requires a deep understanding of how to manage these operations effectively. Building on the foundation laid by promises and `async`/`await`, it's crucial to explore advanced patterns and techniques that enhance the robustness of your asynchronous workflows.

One significant aspect of managing asynchronous operations is the coordination of multiple asynchronous tasks. In scenarios where you need to perform several asynchronous operations concurrently, understanding how to synchronize their results is essential. This is commonly addressed using mechanisms such as `Promise.all` or `Promise.race`, which are available in JavaScript and, by extension, in ClojureScript via interop.

The `Promise.all` method allows you to execute multiple promises concurrently and wait for all of them to complete. This is particularly useful when you have several independent asynchronous tasks that need to be completed before proceeding. For example, if your application needs to fetch data from multiple API endpoints simultaneously, you can use `Promise.all` to initiate all the requests at once and handle the results collectively. This approach not only improves efficiency but also simplifies the code by handling multiple promises as a single entity.

On the other hand, `Promise.race` can be used when you only need to wait for the first promise to complete out of several concurrent tasks. This method is valuable in scenarios where you are interested in the result of the fastest operation, such as when you want to implement a timeout mechanism or select the fastest response from multiple sources. The result of the first promise to settle, whether resolved or rejected, will be returned, allowing your application to handle the result accordingly.

In addition to these methods, managing the lifecycle of asynchronous tasks can also be complex. In scenarios where tasks may need to be canceled or cleaned up, it's important to incorporate strategies for handling such cases. For instance, when dealing with long-running operations, such as fetching large amounts of data or processing intensive computations, the ability to cancel or abort these tasks can enhance user experience and prevent unnecessary resource usage. In JavaScript, this is often achieved using the `AbortController` interface, which can be utilized in ClojureScript through JavaScript interop.

By creating an `AbortController` instance, you can signal an ongoing request to be aborted. This can be integrated into your asynchronous operations by attaching the controller's signal to the request options. If the operation needs to be canceled, calling the `abort` method on the controller will reject the associated promise, allowing you to handle the cancellation gracefully.

Furthermore, managing asynchronous state is crucial, especially in applications with complex UIs. Asynchronous operations often involve updating the user interface based on the results of data fetching or processing tasks. To ensure that these updates are handled efficiently and do not lead to inconsistent or outdated states, it's important to use state management techniques that integrate well with asynchronous operations.

In ClojureScript, leveraging state management libraries or frameworks can streamline the process of handling asynchronous data and updating the UI. Libraries like Re-frame, which provide a structured approach to state management, can be particularly effective. By defining events and subscriptions that react to asynchronous state changes, you can maintain a consistent and responsive user experience.

Another advanced pattern in asynchronous programming involves handling error scenarios effectively. While using `try`/`catch` blocks with `async`/`await` is a common approach, there are additional techniques to consider for robust error handling. Implementing retry logic, fallback mechanisms, and error boundaries can improve the resilience of your application.

Retry logic allows you to automatically retry an asynchronous operation if it fails due to transient issues, such as network instability. This can be achieved by wrapping the operation in a retry function that attempts the task a specified number of times before giving up. Fallback mechanisms can provide alternative actions or default responses in case of failures, ensuring that the application remains functional even when some operations encounter issues.

Error boundaries, particularly in the context of modern frameworks, are designed to catch and handle errors in the rendering process of a component. This can be extended to asynchronous operations by ensuring that errors from these operations are properly caught and managed, preventing them from causing application crashes or rendering issues.

Lastly, performance considerations are integral when handling asynchronous operations. Inefficient handling of asynchronous tasks can lead to performance bottlenecks, especially in high-load scenarios. Profiling and optimizing your asynchronous code can help identify and address performance issues. Techniques such as debouncing, throttling, and optimizing network requests can enhance the overall efficiency of your application.

Debouncing and throttling are techniques used to limit the rate at which asynchronous functions are executed. Debouncing ensures that a function is only executed after a specified delay since the last invocation, which is useful for handling events like user input or resizing. Throttling, on the other hand, restricts the function execution rate to a maximum frequency, which can be beneficial for tasks like API polling or scrolling events.

In conclusion, handling asynchronous operations in ClojureScript involves a combination of techniques and best practices to ensure efficiency, responsiveness, and robustness. By mastering the use of promises, `async`/`await`, and advanced patterns for managing and coordinating tasks, you can build high-performance applications that handle asynchronous operations seamlessly. Incorporating strategies for error handling, state management, and performance optimization further enhances the reliability and user experience of your applications.

When managing asynchronous operations in ClojureScript, it's vital to consider how these tasks interact with other parts of your application and how they affect the overall user experience. One aspect that warrants careful attention is how to handle the synchronization and sequencing of asynchronous tasks. This becomes particularly relevant when your application relies on the outcome of multiple asynchronous operations that need to occur in a specific order.

A common approach to managing such scenarios involves the use of chaining promises. This technique ensures that one asynchronous task starts only after the previous one has completed. By chaining promises, you can maintain a sequential flow of operations, which is crucial for scenarios where the results of previous tasks are required for subsequent ones. In ClojureScript, this can be elegantly handled using the `then` method provided by the promise API. Each `then` callback returns a new promise, allowing for the chaining of subsequent operations. This pattern ensures that tasks are executed in the desired sequence, avoiding issues related to race conditions or out-of-order execution.

In addition to chaining, managing concurrent asynchronous tasks often requires coordination to handle dependencies and shared resources efficiently. One effective strategy is to use a combination of promise-based concurrency control techniques, such as using `Promise.all` for parallel execution and `Promise.allSettled` for handling a mix of fulfilled and rejected promises. For instance, when dealing with a group of independent tasks that need to be completed before proceeding, `Promise.all` can be used to ensure all tasks are completed successfully. Conversely, if you need to handle tasks that might succeed or fail individually, `Promise.allSettled` provides a way to collect results from all promises, regardless of their outcome, allowing for more granular error handling and recovery strategies.

Error handling in asynchronous operations requires a nuanced approach, particularly when dealing with multiple concurrent tasks. Ensuring that your application can gracefully manage and recover from errors without disrupting the user experience is crucial. Implementing robust error handling mechanisms involves not only catching errors but also providing feedback and recovery options. For instance, when using `Promise.all`, if any of the promises reject, the entire operation fails. To mitigate this, it's important to incorporate error handling logic within each promise chain, allowing for individual promise errors to be managed without affecting the overall process. Using `try`/`catch` blocks within `async` functions can help capture and manage errors more effectively, providing an opportunity to offer meaningful error messages or fallback options to users.

Another important consideration is managing asynchronous operations in the context of component lifecycles in a ClojureScript application, particularly when using frameworks like Reagent or Re-frame. Asynchronous tasks that interact with component state or rely on data fetching need to be handled in a way that aligns with the component lifecycle to prevent issues such as memory leaks or state inconsistencies. Leveraging the lifecycle hooks provided by these frameworks allows for proper initialization and cleanup of asynchronous operations. For example, in Reagent, you can use `reagent/ratom` to create reactive atoms that can be updated in response to asynchronous data changes, ensuring that components react appropriately to data updates.

Handling user interactions and asynchronous operations in a responsive manner is another key aspect. User-driven actions, such as form submissions or search queries, often trigger asynchronous operations that need to be managed efficiently to maintain a smooth user experience. Implementing features like debouncing or throttling can help manage frequent user actions that initiate asynchronous tasks. Debouncing delays the execution of a function until a specified period of inactivity, which is useful for scenarios like search input where you want to limit the frequency of API calls. Throttling, on the other hand, ensures that a function is executed at a controlled rate, which can prevent excessive requests or processing during high-frequency events like scrolling.

Performance considerations also play a significant role in managing asynchronous operations. Monitoring and optimizing the performance of asynchronous tasks can help ensure that your application remains responsive and efficient. Techniques such as lazy loading, code splitting, and caching can be employed to enhance performance. Lazy loading allows for the deferred loading of resources until they are needed, reducing initial load times. Code splitting divides your application into smaller chunks that are loaded on demand, improving the responsiveness of your application. Caching frequently accessed data or results of asynchronous operations can also reduce redundant network requests and improve overall performance.

Moreover, managing state and effects in asynchronous contexts requires careful consideration. State management solutions, such as Re-frame, provide a structured approach to handling state updates and effects that result from asynchronous operations. By defining events and handlers that respond to asynchronous results, you can maintain a consistent state and manage side effects effectively. This structured approach ensures that your application remains maintainable and that asynchronous operations are handled in a predictable manner.

In summary, managing asynchronous operations in

ClojureScript involves a comprehensive approach that includes handling sequencing, concurrency, error management, component lifecycles, user interactions, and performance considerations. By leveraging advanced techniques for promise chaining, concurrency control, and error handling, you can build robust and responsive applications. Incorporating best practices for managing state, effects, and performance further enhances the efficiency and user experience of your application.

CHAPTER 32: EXPLORING CLOJURESCRIPT ECOSYSTEM TOOLS

The ClojureScript ecosystem provides a rich array of tools and libraries that can significantly enhance the development process, facilitating everything from project setup to advanced functionality integration. The efficient use of these tools can streamline workflows, improve productivity, and ensure that projects are built with the highest quality. This exploration will delve into key components of the ecosystem, focusing on build tools, development environments, and libraries that cater to common tasks, and will provide a comprehensive understanding of how to integrate and utilize these tools effectively.

Build tools are foundational to any development process, as they automate and manage various aspects of the project lifecycle, including compilation, testing, and deployment. In the ClojureScript ecosystem, Leiningen stands out as a prominent build tool. Leiningen simplifies project management by providing a straightforward configuration syntax and a wide array of plugins. By specifying dependencies, build instructions, and project settings in a `project.clj` file, developers can automate tasks such as compiling ClojureScript code, running tests, and creating deployable artifacts. Leiningen's integration with ClojureScript is facilitated through the `lein-cljsbuild` plugin, which handles the compilation of ClojureScript source code into JavaScript. This tool supports various compilation optimizations, including code minification and source maps, which are essential for production-ready builds.

Another significant build tool in the ClojureScript ecosystem is shadow-cljs. This tool offers a modern approach to managing ClojureScript projects, with a focus on fast compilation and seamless integration with JavaScript tooling. Shadow-cljs supports advanced features such as hot reloading, which enhances the development experience by providing instant feedback during code changes. It also integrates well with popular JavaScript bundlers like Webpack, allowing for a cohesive workflow when dealing with mixed JavaScript and ClojureScript projects. The configuration for shadow-cljs is managed in a `shadow-cljs.edn` file, where developers can specify build configurations, dependencies, and source directories. This tool's support for multiple build targets and environments makes it a versatile choice for projects with complex requirements.

In addition to build tools, development environments play a crucial role in enhancing productivity and ensuring an efficient coding experience. Cursive, a Clojure and ClojureScript plugin for IntelliJ IDEA, is a powerful integrated development environment (IDE) that provides extensive support for ClojureScript development. Cursive offers features such as intelligent code completion, refactoring tools, and integrated REPL support, which can significantly accelerate development workflows. The IDE's ability to understand ClojureScript's syntax and provide context-aware suggestions makes it a valuable tool for both new and experienced developers.

For those who prefer a lighter development environment, VS Code combined with Calva provides an excellent alternative. Calva is a VS Code extension that adds support for Clojure and ClojureScript, offering features such as inline evaluation, code navigation, and a REPL interface. This setup provides a streamlined and efficient environment for ClojureScript development, with the added benefit of VS Code's extensibility and customization options.

Libraries are another vital aspect of the ClojureScript ecosystem, as they provide pre-built functionalities that can be integrated into projects to address common tasks and challenges. Reagent is a prominent library that simplifies the development of user interfaces in ClojureScript. Built on top of React, Reagent provides a reactive programming model that aligns with ClojureScript's functional paradigm. By using Reagent's components and reactive atoms, developers can build dynamic and efficient user interfaces with ease. Reagent's seamless integration with React's ecosystem also allows for the use of existing React components and libraries, broadening the scope of available UI solutions.

Another important library is cljs-http, which facilitates HTTP requests in ClojureScript applications. This library provides a simple and idiomatic way to perform asynchronous HTTP operations, including GET and POST requests, and supports various response formats. By using cljs-http, developers can handle network communication efficiently, with built-in support for promise-based asynchronous operations and error handling.

For managing state in ClojureScript applications, Re-frame is a widely adopted library that provides a framework for managing application state and side effects in a predictable manner. Re-frame uses an event-driven architecture, where application state is managed through a centralized event handling system. This approach allows for clear separation of concerns, making it easier to reason about state changes and side effects. The library's integration with ClojureScript's immutable data structures and functional programming principles ensures that state management remains robust and maintainable.

Finally, Garden is a library that allows developers to write CSS stylesheets in ClojureScript. By leveraging ClojureScript's data structures and macros, Garden enables the creation of dynamic and reusable stylesheets in a declarative manner. This library supports various CSS features, including media queries and nested rules, and integrates well with other ClojureScript tools and libraries.

In summary, the ClojureScript ecosystem offers a diverse set of tools and libraries that can significantly enhance the development process. Build tools like Leiningen and shadow-cljs streamline project management and compilation, while development environments such as Cursive and Calva provide powerful support for coding and debugging. Libraries like Reagent, cljs-http, Re-frame, and Garden address common tasks and challenges, enabling developers to build robust and feature-rich applications efficiently. Understanding and integrating these tools into your projects can lead to more productive development experiences and higher-quality outcomes.

Understanding the intricacies of the ClojureScript ecosystem tools requires a deep dive into several essential components, each designed to enhance different facets of the development process. As we continue our exploration, we delve further into the range of tools and libraries available, examining their integration and utilization within ClojureScript projects.

One particularly noteworthy tool in the ecosystem is figwheel-main, which is a development server that facilitates live reloading of ClojureScript code. Figwheel-main is designed to improve the development workflow by automatically recompiling code and refreshing the browser when changes are detected. This tool is built to work seamlessly with ClojureScript and can be configured to handle various build environments. The use of figwheel-main greatly enhances productivity by reducing the need for manual reloads and allowing developers to see changes in real-time. Its configuration is managed through a `figwheel-main.edn` file, where developers specify build settings, source directories, and other parameters. By integrating figwheel-main into your development setup, you can streamline the coding process and maintain a more dynamic and responsive development environment.

Another tool that complements figwheel-main is ClojureScript's own REPL (Read-Eval-Print Loop). The REPL is a powerful interactive environment that allows for incremental development and testing of ClojureScript code. Using the REPL, developers can evaluate expressions, test functions, and inspect results on the fly. This interactive approach is invaluable for experimenting with code and debugging. The REPL integrates with various development environments and can be accessed through tools like Leiningen, shadow-cljs, or even from within IDEs like Cursive and VS Code. Leveraging the REPL effectively requires familiarity with its commands and the ability to manage its state, but it provides a flexible and iterative way to develop ClojureScript applications.

Beyond the immediate development tools, the ClojureScript ecosystem also includes libraries that provide extensive support for various application needs. One such library is cljs.spec, which provides a powerful framework for specifying and validating data structures in ClojureScript. The cljs.spec library allows developers to define specifications for their data using a declarative approach, which can then be used to validate data at runtime. This is particularly useful for ensuring data integrity and preventing errors caused by invalid or unexpected input. By integrating cljs.spec into your project, you can enhance data validation processes and build more reliable and robust applications.

For managing complex state and handling side effects, re-frame is a library that offers a comprehensive framework for application state management. Re-frame introduces a reactive data flow model that relies on events and subscriptions to manage state changes. This event-driven architecture is based on a centralized event handling system that processes user actions and application events. Re-frame integrates well with ClojureScript's immutable data structures, making it a natural fit for functional programming paradigms. By using re-frame, you can achieve a clear separation of concerns within your application, making it easier to manage and reason about state changes and side effects.

In addition to state management, reagent is another influential library that provides a reactive interface for building user interfaces. Built on React, reagent allows developers to leverage React's component-based architecture while using ClojureScript's functional programming features. Reagent's reactive atoms provide a way to manage and update application state efficiently. The library supports features such as component lifecycle management, event handling, and integration with other JavaScript libraries. By utilizing reagent, developers can build dynamic and performant user interfaces while maintaining a consistent and idiomatic ClojureScript codebase.

cljs-http is a library designed to facilitate HTTP requests and communication within ClojureScript applications. This library simplifies the process of making asynchronous HTTP requests, handling responses, and managing error conditions. With cljs-http, developers can perform operations such as GET and POST requests, parse JSON responses, and handle various response statuses. The library's design promotes a functional approach to handling HTTP interactions, integrating seamlessly with ClojureScript's promise-based concurrency model. By incorporating cljs-http into your project, you can manage network communication more effectively and build applications that interact with external services and APIs.

For styling and theming in ClojureScript applications, garden is a library that allows developers to write CSS in a programmatic and declarative manner. Garden provides a way to generate CSS stylesheets using ClojureScript's data structures and macros. This approach offers advantages such as dynamic styling, reusable style definitions, and integration with ClojureScript's functional programming capabilities. By using garden, you can manage your application's styles in a more modular and maintainable way, leveraging the full power of ClojureScript's syntax and features.

Each of these tools and libraries plays a crucial role in enhancing the development experience and expanding the capabilities of ClojureScript applications. By understanding how to effectively integrate and utilize these tools, you can streamline your development workflows, improve application performance, and build robust and feature-rich applications. The ClojureScript ecosystem provides a versatile and powerful set of tools that, when combined thoughtfully, can greatly enhance your development process and help you achieve your project goals with greater efficiency and effectiveness.

In exploring the ClojureScript ecosystem, it is essential to also consider tools that facilitate project management and build processes, alongside development tools and libraries. Among these, Leiningen and shadow-cljs are pivotal in managing ClojureScript projects. Both tools cater to different aspects of the development workflow, and understanding their unique capabilities can significantly impact project efficiency and organization.

Leiningen is a build automation tool that has long been a cornerstone of the Clojure ecosystem. It simplifies project setup, dependency management, and build processes through a declarative configuration file known as `project.clj`. Leiningen allows developers to define project dependencies, build configurations, and plugin requirements in a centralized manner. One of its strengths is its ability to manage ClojureScript projects alongside Clojure code within the same ecosystem, making it a versatile choice for projects that incorporate both languages. By using Leiningen, you can streamline your build processes, handle project dependencies efficiently, and integrate various tools and libraries into your development environment.

On the other hand, shadow-cljs provides a more modern approach to building ClojureScript projects, focusing specifically on improving the development experience with advanced features and integrations. Unlike Leiningen, shadow-cljs integrates tightly with modern JavaScript tooling and workflows, including support for npm packages and module systems. Its configuration is managed through a `shadow-cljs.edn` file, which offers a flexible and powerful way to define builds, targets, and dependencies. Shadow-cljs excels in providing a seamless experience when working with JavaScript libraries and frameworks, making it an excellent choice for projects that need to interact closely with the broader JavaScript ecosystem. By leveraging shadow-cljs, you can benefit from features like incremental builds, advanced source mapping, and a robust development server that supports live reloading.

Another aspect of the ClojureScript ecosystem worth exploring is the range of testing tools available for ensuring code quality and reliability. cljs-test is a library that provides a framework for writing and running tests for ClojureScript code. It integrates with various testing libraries and tools, allowing you to write unit tests, integration tests, and other types of tests in a consistent and structured manner. By incorporating cljs-test into your project, you can establish a comprehensive testing strategy that helps catch bugs and validate functionality throughout the development process.

For projects that require more advanced testing capabilities, doo is a testing framework that offers a powerful solution for running ClojureScript tests across different browsers and environments. Doo supports various testing libraries, including cljs.test and Midje, and can be configured to run tests in multiple browser contexts, including headless browsers for automated testing. This tool is particularly useful for ensuring cross-browser compatibility and conducting thorough testing of ClojureScript applications in diverse environments.

As you work with ClojureScript, you will also encounter code formatting and linting tools that help maintain code quality and adhere to best practices. clj-kondo is a static analysis tool that provides linting and code quality checks for both Clojure and ClojureScript code. It offers real-time feedback on code style issues, potential errors, and code smells, helping you enforce consistent coding standards across your project. By integrating clj-kondo into your development workflow, you can catch potential issues early and ensure that your codebase remains clean and maintainable.

cljsfmt is another tool designed for formatting ClojureScript code automatically. It ensures that your code adheres to a consistent style and formatting conventions, reducing the need for manual formatting and improving overall code readability. Integrating cljsfmt into your build process or development environment can streamline code reviews and enhance collaboration among team members by enforcing a standardized code style.

To support documentation generation, codox is a tool

that generates documentation for ClojureScript codebases. It extracts docstrings and other metadata from your code and produces comprehensive API documentation that can be published and shared with your team or the wider community. By using codox, you can maintain up-to-date documentation that reflects the structure and functionality of your code, facilitating better understanding and usage of your project's components.

In addition to these tools, the ClojureScript ecosystem is rich with libraries and utilities that cater to specific needs and preferences. Exploring these resources allows you to tailor your development environment to fit your project requirements and personal workflow preferences. By integrating and utilizing the right combination of tools, you can optimize your development process, enhance code quality, and build robust and efficient ClojureScript applications.

The ClojureScript ecosystem continues to evolve, with new tools and libraries emerging to address various development challenges and needs. Staying informed about these developments and understanding how to leverage the available tools effectively will enable you to stay ahead in your development efforts and make the most of the rich set of resources that ClojureScript offers.

CHAPTER 33: BEST PRACTICES FOR CLOJURESCRIPT DEVELOPMENT

In approaching ClojureScript development with an eye toward high-quality and maintainable projects, it is vital to establish and adhere to best practices that govern coding standards, project structure, and documentation. These practices are not mere suggestions but essential components that contribute to the overall effectiveness and sustainability of your codebase.

When it comes to coding standards, consistency is paramount. ClojureScript, much like its parent language Clojure, thrives on immutability and functional programming principles. It is crucial to adhere to these principles throughout your code. This involves using immutable data structures whenever possible and embracing functions as first-class citizens. Ensuring that functions are pure, meaning they have no side effects and return the same result given the same inputs, is a cornerstone of functional programming. This practice not only makes the code more predictable and easier to test but also enhances its reusability and composability.

Another critical aspect of coding standards involves naming conventions. Consistent and descriptive naming of functions, variables, and namespaces helps in understanding the purpose and behavior of code at a glance. In ClojureScript, it is common to use kebab-case for naming functions and variables and PascalCase for naming namespaces. For instance, `calculate-total` is a descriptive function name that immediately indicates its purpose, whereas `calculateTotal` might be used for naming a JavaScript function in a mixed environment. Adhering to these naming conventions fosters readability and reduces cognitive load for developers.

When structuring a ClojureScript project, the organization of files and directories plays a significant role in maintaining clarity and manageability. A well-structured project not only facilitates ease of navigation but also supports scalability as the project grows. Typically, a ClojureScript project is organized with a `src` directory housing the source code and a `test` directory for test cases. Within the `src` directory, code is often segmented into logical namespaces that reflect the project's functionality. This modular approach allows developers to isolate and manage different aspects of the application effectively.

Documentation is another critical aspect of best practices in ClojureScript development. Comprehensive and clear documentation enhances the maintainability of the codebase by providing context and explanations for complex logic and usage. In ClojureScript, documentation is typically embedded within the code using docstrings. A docstring is a string literal placed immediately after a function definition or a namespace declaration that explains its purpose, parameters, and return values. Utilizing docstrings ensures that the documentation is kept close to the code it describes, which helps in keeping it relevant and up-to-date.

Moreover, employing tools such as `cljdoc` or `codox` can automate the generation of API documentation from docstrings. This approach not only maintains consistency but also provides a structured format for presenting documentation. Clear and thorough documentation is invaluable for onboarding new developers and for maintaining the codebase over time.

Testing is an integral part of the best practices for ClojureScript development. Ensuring that your code is well-tested contributes to its reliability and robustness. ClojureScript provides a range of testing frameworks, including `cljs.test` and `midje`, which support writing unit tests, integration tests, and other forms of testing. A good testing strategy involves writing tests for critical paths and edge cases, using test fixtures to set up and tear down test environments, and employing assertions to verify expected outcomes. Automated testing should be incorporated into the development workflow to catch regressions and verify that new changes do not introduce unexpected issues.

In addition to writing tests, it is also important to use continuous integration (CI) tools to automate the testing process. CI tools can be configured to run tests on every code commit or pull request, ensuring that changes are validated before they are merged into the main codebase. This practice helps maintain code quality and prevents the introduction of defects.

Code reviews are another best practice that complements the efforts of coding standards and testing. Conducting code reviews involves having peers examine code changes to ensure that they meet quality standards and adhere to project conventions. Code reviews provide an opportunity for knowledge sharing, catching potential issues early, and maintaining consistency across the codebase. A structured review process, including checklists and guidelines, can further enhance the effectiveness of code reviews.

Maintaining an up-to-date dependency management strategy is also crucial in ClojureScript development. Dependencies should be regularly reviewed and updated to benefit from the latest features, bug fixes, and security patches. Tools like Leiningen and shadow-cljs provide mechanisms for managing dependencies and can help in keeping the project's dependencies current.

In conclusion, adhering to best practices in ClojureScript development is essential for producing high-quality, maintainable, and scalable projects. By focusing on coding standards, project structure, documentation, testing, and code reviews, you can ensure that your ClojureScript codebase remains clean, effective, and resilient to change. These practices not only enhance the immediate quality of the code but also contribute to the long-term sustainability and success of your development efforts.

When discussing best practices for ClojureScript development, one must delve deeply into aspects such as code quality, efficient use of libraries, and project management. These areas are integral to achieving clean, effective, and maintainable code. As we continue, a focus on optimizing code performance and integrating with external tools and libraries will be pivotal in shaping a robust development workflow.

A crucial aspect of writing high-quality ClojureScript code is optimizing performance. In ClojureScript, performance considerations often involve efficient data handling and minimizing unnecessary computations. Leveraging immutable data structures provided by ClojureScript can lead to significant performance benefits. Immutability ensures that data is not modified in place, which helps prevent unexpected side effects and promotes safer concurrent programming. When dealing with large datasets or performance-critical applications, using data structures like vectors, maps, and sets effectively is important. ClojureScript's persistent data structures offer performance optimizations that are crucial for handling large-scale data processing efficiently.

When optimizing performance, it is also essential to understand how to leverage ClojureScript's ability to interoperate with JavaScript. ClojureScript compiles to JavaScript, so understanding the underlying JavaScript engine's performance characteristics can guide better decisions in your code. For instance, optimizing how you interact with JavaScript libraries or APIs can reduce the overhead and improve the responsiveness of your application. Minifying and bundling your JavaScript output through tools like advanced optimizations in the ClojureScript compiler or integrating with build tools like Webpack can also enhance performance and reduce load times.

Managing dependencies efficiently is another crucial practice for maintaining a high-quality ClojureScript project. Dependencies should be carefully selected to avoid bloating the project with unnecessary libraries. When integrating third-party libraries, it is essential to evaluate their stability, compatibility, and the support provided by the community. Tools like Leiningen or shadow-cljs can assist in managing dependencies and ensuring that your project remains up-to-date with the latest versions. Additionally, it is beneficial to periodically review and clean up unused dependencies to keep the project lightweight and manageable.

Effective integration with external tools and libraries can significantly enhance the development process. For instance, integrating with build tools like Figwheel or Shadow-CLJS can streamline the development workflow by providing features such as live reloading and efficient compilation. Figwheel provides a live-reloading development environment, which is invaluable for rapid prototyping and testing. On the other hand, Shadow-CLJS offers a powerful build system with support for modern JavaScript features and optimized integration with NPM packages. Both tools contribute to a more efficient and responsive development experience.

Documentation extends beyond just writing docstrings within the code. Creating comprehensive documentation for your ClojureScript projects involves maintaining README files, creating usage examples, and providing clear API documentation. A well-maintained README file should provide an overview of the project, instructions for setting up the development environment, and guidelines for contributing to the project. This level of documentation ensures that new developers can quickly understand the project and begin contributing without extensive onboarding.

In addition to README files, using tools like Codox or Cljdoc to generate API documentation directly from docstrings is highly beneficial. These tools provide a structured format for documenting your functions and namespaces, making it easier for other developers to understand and use your code. Generating API documentation as part of the build process ensures that documentation remains up-to-date with the latest code changes.

Maintaining a consistent coding style is another key aspect of best practices. Adopting a style guide that defines conventions for indentation, naming, and code organization helps maintain consistency across the codebase. In ClojureScript, adhering to the Clojure style guide is recommended, as it provides a standardized approach to writing code that aligns with community practices. Tools like `cljfmt` can automate code formatting according to predefined style rules, further ensuring consistency and reducing the burden of manual formatting.

Adhering to best practices also involves actively managing and addressing technical debt. Technical debt refers to the cost of maintaining code that was written quickly or without proper consideration for long-term quality. Regularly reviewing and refactoring code to address technical debt ensures that the codebase remains maintainable and adaptable. Techniques such as code reviews, automated testing, and continuous integration play a crucial role in identifying and addressing technical debt.

Lastly, fostering a collaborative development environment enhances the overall quality and maintainability of the codebase. Encouraging practices such as pair programming, knowledge sharing, and regular team meetings can help ensure that best practices are followed consistently across the project. Collaboration also facilitates the exchange of ideas and solutions, leading to better decision-making and more robust code.

In summary, adhering to best practices in ClojureScript development involves a comprehensive approach that encompasses performance optimization, effective dependency management, seamless integration with tools and libraries, thorough documentation, consistent coding style, and active management of technical debt. By embracing these practices, developers can ensure that their ClojureScript projects are not only functional and efficient but also maintainable and scalable over time.

When considering best practices for ClojureScript development, one must not overlook the significance of robust testing strategies. Testing ensures that code behaves as expected and helps catch potential issues before they affect the end-users. A comprehensive testing approach encompasses unit testing, integration testing, and end-to-end testing. Each of these testing layers plays a distinct role in validating different aspects of the application.

Unit testing is fundamental in verifying the functionality of individual components or functions. In ClojureScript, testing frameworks like `cljs.test` offer a way to write and execute unit tests. By writing tests that cover various edge cases and potential failure modes, developers can ensure that their code operates correctly under a wide range of conditions. Tests should be designed to be isolated, meaning that they do not depend on the state or behavior of other tests. This isolation allows for more reliable test outcomes and easier debugging.

Integration testing goes beyond individual components to validate how different parts of the application work together. For ClojureScript applications, this often involves testing how components interact with each other and how data flows through the system. Integration tests can help identify issues related to data management, state synchronization, and component interactions. By simulating real-world usage scenarios, integration tests provide insights into how the application performs in a more holistic context.

End-to-end testing is crucial for verifying the complete functionality of the application from the user's perspective. Tools such as Selenium or Puppeteer can be employed to automate browser interactions and simulate user behavior. These tests are essential for ensuring that the application meets user requirements and delivers a seamless user experience. End-to-end tests can help identify issues related to user interface elements, navigation, and overall application flow.

In addition to traditional testing methods, adopting a test-driven development (TDD) approach can enhance code quality and maintainability. TDD involves writing tests before the actual implementation code, which encourages developers to think about the desired behavior and edge cases before coding. This approach leads to more focused and reliable tests and can result in a more thoughtful and deliberate design process.

Another key aspect of maintaining high-quality ClojureScript code is effective version control. Using a version control system like Git allows for tracking changes, collaborating with team members, and managing different versions of the codebase. Best practices in version control include writing clear commit messages, using meaningful branch names, and regularly merging changes to keep the codebase up-to-date. Effective version control practices help in managing project history, coordinating team efforts, and rolling back changes if necessary.

Project structure also plays a vital role in the maintainability of ClojureScript applications. Adopting a clear and organized project structure facilitates navigation and understanding of the codebase. In ClojureScript projects, a common practice is to organize code into directories based on functionality or modules. This organization helps in separating concerns, making it easier to locate and modify specific parts of the application. Additionally, following conventions for naming files and directories can enhance clarity and consistency across the project.

Moreover, integrating continuous integration (CI) and continuous deployment (CD) practices into the development workflow ensures that code changes are automatically tested and deployed. CI/CD pipelines automate the process of building, testing, and deploying applications, which helps in catching issues early and maintaining a reliable and consistent deployment process. Tools like Jenkins, Travis CI, or GitHub Actions can be configured to run tests and deploy code changes to different environments, providing a streamlined approach to managing code quality and deployment.

Documentation remains a critical aspect of best practices in ClojureScript development. Beyond generating API documentation, it is important to maintain clear and comprehensive guides for the project. This includes writing user guides, developer guides, and onboarding documentation for new team members. Good documentation improves the accessibility of the project and reduces the learning curve for new contributors. It also serves as a valuable reference for maintaining and extending the application over time.

Lastly, embracing community standards and staying updated with best practices from the broader ClojureScript community can greatly enhance the quality of your code. Participating in community forums, attending conferences, and following relevant blogs and publications can provide insights into emerging trends and best practices. Engaging with the community helps in keeping abreast of new tools, techniques, and methodologies that can improve your development process.

In conclusion, maintaining high-quality ClojureScript code involves a multifaceted approach that includes robust testing strategies, effective version control, organized project structure, and comprehensive documentation. By integrating these practices into your development workflow, you can ensure that your ClojureScript projects are reliable, maintainable, and aligned with industry standards. This commitment to best practices not only enhances the quality of the code but also contributes to a more efficient and effective development process.

CHAPTER 34: FUTURE TRENDS AND NEXT STEPS

Looking ahead, the future of ClojureScript presents a landscape rich with potential and innovation. As web development continues to evolve, ClojureScript, with its unique functional programming paradigm and rich ecosystem, is poised to adapt and grow. This discussion will explore the emerging trends and advancements that are likely to shape the future of ClojureScript, and provide guidance on how developers can continue to grow and learn in this dynamic field.

One of the most prominent trends on the horizon is the increasing integration of ClojureScript with modern frontend frameworks and libraries. While ClojureScript has traditionally been used in conjunction with its own set of tools and libraries, there is a growing movement towards leveraging popular JavaScript libraries and frameworks, such as React and Vue.js, within the ClojureScript ecosystem. This integration allows ClojureScript developers to tap into the vast array of resources, components, and community support available in the JavaScript ecosystem, while still benefiting from the advantages of functional programming and immutable data structures.

The React ecosystem, in particular, has seen a significant

rise in interest from the ClojureScript community. Tools like Reagent, which provide a ClojureScript wrapper around React, are becoming increasingly popular. Reagent offers a way to build reactive user interfaces using ClojureScript's data-driven approach, making it easier to create complex and interactive web applications. As React continues to evolve, with updates and new features being regularly introduced, keeping abreast of these changes and integrating them into ClojureScript projects will be crucial for developers looking to stay at the forefront of web development.

Another area of growth is the expansion of ClojureScript's support for new and emerging web standards. The web development landscape is constantly evolving, with new technologies and standards being introduced at a rapid pace. Staying informed about these changes and understanding how they can be leveraged in ClojureScript is essential for maintaining a competitive edge. For instance, advancements in WebAssembly (Wasm) and its integration with JavaScript provide new opportunities for performance optimization and interoperability. Exploring how ClojureScript can interact with WebAssembly and other modern web standards will be a key area of interest for developers looking to push the boundaries of what's possible in web applications.

In addition to technological advancements, there is also a growing emphasis on improving the developer experience within the ClojureScript ecosystem. Efforts to enhance tooling, debugging capabilities, and development workflows are ongoing. The introduction of new tools and enhancements to existing ones can significantly impact productivity and the overall development process. For example, improvements in build tools, such as shadow-cljs and Figwheel Main, are making it easier to develop and debug ClojureScript applications. These tools offer features like hot-reloading, improved integration with modern JavaScript tools, and better support for complex project structures.

Furthermore, the ClojureScript community itself is a vital aspect of its future. Community-driven initiatives, open-source contributions, and collaboration are essential for the continued growth and evolution of the ecosystem. Engaging with the community through forums, conferences, and collaborative projects provides valuable opportunities for learning and contributing to the advancement of ClojureScript. Staying connected with community developments and participating in discussions about future directions can provide insights into emerging trends and opportunities for professional growth.

As the ClojureScript ecosystem evolves, developers should also consider exploring adjacent technologies and methodologies that complement ClojureScript development. For example, gaining proficiency in related languages and tools, such as Clojure for server-side development or various DevOps practices, can enhance a developer's skill set and broaden their understanding of the full software development lifecycle. This holistic approach to learning can provide a more comprehensive perspective and enable developers to tackle a wider range of challenges.

Looking ahead, it is also important for developers to focus on continuous learning and professional development. The field of web development is dynamic and ever-changing, with new technologies, methodologies, and best practices emerging regularly. Engaging in ongoing education through courses, workshops, and reading relevant literature can help developers stay current and adapt to new developments. Online resources, including documentation, tutorials, and community forums, provide valuable learning opportunities and can assist in keeping up with the latest advancements in ClojureScript and web development.

In summary, the future of ClojureScript is marked by exciting trends and opportunities for growth. The integration with modern frontend frameworks, support for new web standards, improvements in developer tooling, and active community engagement all contribute to a vibrant and evolving ecosystem. By staying informed about emerging trends, exploring complementary technologies, and committing to continuous learning, developers can position themselves for success in the ever-changing landscape of web development. The journey of mastering ClojureScript is ongoing, and embracing these future trends will pave the way for continued innovation and advancement in the field.

As we delve deeper into the future landscape of ClojureScript, it's important to consider how emerging tools and libraries are shaping its evolution. One significant area of development is the growing ecosystem of libraries that enhance the capabilities of ClojureScript. For instance, libraries that facilitate state management, like Re-frame, are continuously evolving to offer more robust and scalable solutions for handling complex application states. The ongoing improvements in these libraries reflect the community's commitment to addressing the challenges of modern web applications and adapting to new patterns and practices.

Re-frame, in particular, has established itself as a powerful tool for managing application state in a declarative manner. Its emphasis on using event handling and subscriptions to manage state aligns well with ClojureScript's functional paradigm. As the library progresses, new features and enhancements are likely to further streamline state management and improve developer productivity. Staying updated with these advancements will be crucial for leveraging the full potential of Re-frame and other similar libraries.

Another noteworthy development is the integration of

ClojureScript with advanced web development frameworks and tools. For example, the rise of server-side rendering (SSR) and static site generation (SSG) in the JavaScript ecosystem has prompted the creation of ClojureScript solutions that cater to these needs. Tools like Shadow CLJS offer seamless integration with modern JavaScript tooling, enabling developers to build applications that can benefit from features such as faster load times and improved SEO.

The evolution of SSR and SSG is indicative of a broader trend towards enhancing performance and user experience in web applications. By embracing these technologies and understanding how they can be applied within the ClojureScript ecosystem, developers can create more efficient and scalable applications. This involves not only integrating existing tools but also exploring how ClojureScript can contribute to or improve upon these emerging practices.

In parallel, the advancements in WebAssembly (Wasm) present new opportunities for ClojureScript developers. WebAssembly allows for high-performance execution of code on the web, enabling languages other than JavaScript to run in the browser with near-native speed. The potential for integrating ClojureScript with Wasm opens up possibilities for performance-critical applications, such as those involving complex computations or real-time processing. Understanding how to leverage Wasm alongside ClojureScript could become a significant advantage as the demand for high-performance web applications grows.

Additionally, the adoption of new JavaScript standards and APIs will continue to influence ClojureScript development. The ECMAScript specification is regularly updated with new features and improvements that impact the JavaScript ecosystem. As these standards evolve, ClojureScript's ability to interoperate with modern JavaScript features will be crucial. Keeping abreast of changes in JavaScript and understanding how to integrate them into ClojureScript projects will ensure that applications remain compatible with current best practices and technologies.

Furthermore, the ClojureScript community plays a vital role in shaping the future of the language. The collaborative nature of open-source development fosters innovation and ensures that new ideas and improvements are continuously introduced. Engaging with community-driven projects, contributing to open-source initiatives, and participating in discussions can provide valuable insights and influence the direction of ClojureScript's development. The dynamic nature of the community ensures that the language evolves in response to real-world needs and emerging trends.

For developers seeking to stay at the cutting edge of ClojureScript development, investing in ongoing education and skill enhancement is essential. This includes not only staying updated with the latest tools and libraries but also engaging in professional development opportunities such as workshops, conferences, and advanced courses. By actively participating in the ClojureScript ecosystem and expanding their skill set, developers can remain competitive and effectively contribute to the evolution of the language.

Moreover, exploring complementary technologies and methodologies can further enhance a developer's proficiency. For instance, understanding the principles of functional programming in other languages, or gaining experience with adjacent technologies like Clojure for backend development, can provide a broader perspective and improve overall development practices. This holistic approach to learning supports the development of more robust and adaptable solutions.

As we anticipate future advancements, it is clear that the ClojureScript ecosystem will continue to evolve in response to new challenges and opportunities. By embracing emerging trends, exploring innovative tools and libraries, and committing to continuous learning, developers can position themselves to effectively navigate the changing landscape of web development. The journey of mastering ClojureScript is one of ongoing exploration and adaptation, and staying engaged with the latest developments will be key to achieving continued success in this dynamic field.

As we advance into the future of ClojureScript, it is essential to recognize the broader context of web development trends that will likely influence its trajectory. One significant trend is the increased emphasis on microservices and distributed architectures. Microservices offer a way to decompose large, monolithic applications into smaller, more manageable services that can be developed, deployed, and scaled independently. This architectural shift can benefit ClojureScript developers by promoting modularity and enhancing the ability to integrate with various services and APIs. Leveraging tools like ClojureScript's interop capabilities with JavaScript can facilitate seamless communication between services, making it possible to build complex applications with a clean and maintainable codebase.

The rise of edge computing is another trend that will likely impact ClojureScript development. Edge computing involves processing data closer to where it is generated, rather than relying solely on centralized cloud servers. This approach can reduce latency and improve performance, particularly for applications that require real-time data processing. In the context of ClojureScript, this might mean integrating with edge computing platforms or optimizing applications to make the most of local data processing capabilities. Understanding how to develop applications that can effectively operate in a distributed environment will be crucial for staying relevant in this evolving landscape.

Another notable advancement is the growing importance of artificial intelligence (AI) and machine learning (ML) in web development. As AI and ML become more integrated into web applications, ClojureScript developers will need to consider how to incorporate these technologies into their projects. While ClojureScript itself is not typically used for heavy computational tasks, it can interact with AI and ML services through APIs. Understanding how to integrate with these services, as well as how to manage and present AI-driven insights in a ClojureScript application, will be essential skills. This involves leveraging existing libraries and tools to connect with machine learning models and processing frameworks, ensuring that applications can harness the power of AI without compromising on performance.

The expansion of Progressive Web Apps (PWAs) is another trend that is shaping the future of web development. PWAs offer a more app-like experience by combining the best features of web and mobile applications. They provide offline functionality, push notifications, and faster load times, which are increasingly becoming standard expectations for modern web applications. ClojureScript developers can benefit from understanding how to build PWAs using the language's capabilities and existing tools. This includes working with service workers, caching strategies, and integrating with web manifests to create seamless and engaging user experiences.

Additionally, the evolving landscape of frontend development frameworks and libraries will continue to influence ClojureScript. While libraries like React and Vue.js have dominated the frontend space, new frameworks and paradigms are emerging. Keeping an eye on these developments and understanding how they align with ClojureScript's principles can provide insights into new ways to approach frontend development. For instance, the increasing popularity of component-based architectures and declarative programming can be harnessed within the ClojureScript ecosystem to build more efficient and modular user interfaces.

Furthermore, as web security concerns grow, the importance of integrating robust security practices into ClojureScript applications will become increasingly apparent. Security best practices, such as implementing proper authentication and authorization mechanisms, protecting against common vulnerabilities, and ensuring data privacy, will be critical. Developers will need to stay informed about the latest security threats and how they can mitigate risks within their ClojureScript projects. This includes understanding how to securely handle user data, protect against cross-site scripting (XSS) and cross-site request forgery (CSRF), and implement secure communication protocols.

Lastly, continued engagement with the ClojureScript community will be crucial for staying informed about the latest advancements and best practices. The community plays a pivotal role in driving innovation and providing support through forums, conferences, and open-source projects. Actively participating in discussions, contributing to projects, and collaborating with other developers can provide valuable insights and help in staying ahead of emerging trends. Additionally, keeping abreast of academic research and industry reports related to ClojureScript and web development will further enhance one's understanding and ability to adapt to new developments.

In summary, as ClojureScript moves forward, it will intersect with a variety of evolving trends and technologies. Embracing microservices, edge computing, AI and ML, PWAs, and frontend framework advancements will be key to leveraging the language's potential. By integrating these trends and maintaining an active presence in the community, developers can continue to build innovative and high-quality applications, positioning themselves effectively for future growth and success in the ever-evolving landscape of web development.

www.ingramcontent.com/pod-product-compliance
Lightning Source LLC
Chambersburg PA
CBHW052139220526
45471CB00004B/1444